Library of
Davidson College

JEWISH SURVIVAL

BOOKS BY TRUDE WEISS-ROSMARIN

*Aribi und Arabien in den Babylonisch-Assyrischen Quellen*
*Religion of Reason: The Philosophy of Hermann Cohen*
*The Hebrew Moses*
*Highlights of Jewish History*
*New Light on the Bible*
*Jewish Women Through the Ages*
*The Oneg Shabbat Book*
*Judaism and Christianity: The Differences*

TRUDE WEISS-ROSMARIN

# JEWISH SURVIVAL

## ESSAYS AND STUDIES

KTAV PUBLISHING HOUSE, INC.
NEW YORK, N. Y.

NEW MATTER
© COPYRIGHT 1977
TRUDE WEISS ROSMARIN

**Library of Congress Cataloging in Publication Data**

Weiss-Rosmarin, Trude, 1908-
  Jewish survival.

  Reprint of the 1950 ed. published by Philosophical Library, New York.
  Includes index.
  1. Judaism—Essence, genius, nature—Addresses, essays, lectures. I. Title.
BM565.R62   1976     296     76-56117
ISBN 0-87068-426-4

MANUFACTURED IN THE UNITED STATES OF AMERICA

למשה

בן יקיר שלי

# BIBLIOGRAPHICAL ACKNOWLEDGMENTS

The English versions of quoted Hebrew texts are by the author, with the exception of the following:

BIBLICAL QUOTATIONS: *The Holy Scriptures*, The Jewish Publication Society of America, 1917.

RASHI (excerpt quoted on page 353f.): *The Jew in the Medieval World*. A Source Book. By Jacob R. Marcus. Union of American Hebrew Congregations, 1938.

SOLOMON IBN GABIROL: *Selected Religious Poems of Solomon Ibn Gabirol*. Translated into English Verse by Israel Zangwill. Jewish Publication Society of America, 1923.

YEHUDAH HALEVI: *Selected Poems of Yehudah Halevi*. Translated into English by Nina Salaman. Jewish Publication Society of America, 1928.

MEDIEVAL ETHICAL WILLS AND TESTAMENTS: *Hebrew Ethical Wills*. Selected and edited by Israel Abrahams, 2 Vols. Jewish Publication Society of America, 1926.

LEV TOV (Isaac Ben Eliakim) quoted on p. 357): *The Jew in the Medieval World*. A Source Book. By Jacob R. Marcus. Union of American Hebrew Congregations, 1938.

# Contents

1. Israel and the Atomic Challenge — 5
2. The Long Vigil — 27
3. The Partial Consummation — 56
4. Toward A Definition of the Jewish Genius — 103
5. Jewish Survival — Why and How? — 153
6. A Manifesto of Diaspora Survivalism — 182
7. Zest for Life — 202
8. Distinctiveness — 214
9. The Chosen People Idea — 222
10. Study of the Torah — 245
11. The Joyful Burden of the Law — 276
12. God — 293
13. Fellow Man — 319
14. The Family — 342
15. The Paths of Piety — 361
16. The Future to Come — 372
    Index — 399

*Preface to the Paperback Edition*

The reissue of a book that was originally published twenty-seven years ago is justified only if the work has not become obsolete.

The problems and issues to which *Jewish Survival* addresses itself are still with us (unfortunately!); and the solutions suggested remain suggestions and—hopes.

The subject of the opening chapter, "The Atomic Challenge," confronts us now even more menacingly than after Hiroshima. And the need to tame technology and its potential destructiveness with the *Jewish* variety of ethical wisdom is more urgent now than it was in 1949.

The chapters on the events that culminated in the rise of the State of Israel, "The Long Vigil" and "The Partial Consummation," anticipated, on the morrow of the rebirth of Jewish statehood, the ongoing controversies over the relationship of Israel and the Diaspora, and the role of Zionism after the implementation of the Basle Program.

The *interdependence* of Israel and the Diaspora, together with a qualified and limited "Negation of the Diaspora," which I suggested, continues as the agenda of "Israel-Diaspora Dialogues" under various auspices.

Some reviewers of *Jewish Survival* took issue with my thesis that the unique distinctiveness of the Jewish culture is its concentration upon *the word* and its indifference to art and the arts, amounting at times to their total negation.

The late Professor Ralph Marcus, a classicist and scholar of Hellenism, held that this "iconoclastic author" was "under the sway of Orthodox Judaism when she wrote 'we need not apologize for nor explain the paucity of Jewish art' " (*Commentary*, August 1950). But George Steiner, who is not under the sway of Orthodox Judaism, now raises the same questions of why art and the arts "prove so fragile a barrier against political bestiality" (see *In Bluebeard's Castle*, 1971). Steiner and other intellectuals *now* speak of Western "post-culture," and all that Steiner offers as a consolation for the failure of art to civilize Western man is: "To be able to envisage possibilities of self-destruction, yet to press home the debate with the unknown is no mean thing."

Jewish Survival does not "envisage possibilities of self-destruction." On the contrary, it celebrates "Zest for Life," *Jewish* zest for life, sustained now as always by the Jewish ideas and ideals to which I devote the chapters "Distinctiveness," "The Chosen People Idea," "The Joyful Burden of the Law," "God," "Fellow Man," "The Family," "The Paths of Piety," and "The Future to Come."

Orthodox reviewers of *Jewish Survival* welcomed it as an apologia for Orthodoxy, (Chief Rabbi Louis L. Rabinowitz in *Jewish Affairs* and the late Professor Moses Jung in *In Jewish Bookland*). Professor Marcus, however, expressed doubts "that the kind of Orthodoxy she so ardently champions will survive in the Western World."

*Jewish Survival* does not "champion" Orthodoxy. It "champions" the wisdom and ethics of the Hebrew Bible and the "Great Jewish Books" (some of them are veritable encyclopedias, like the Talmud) which were reared, and are reared, on the biblical foundation.

In 1950 it was logical to doubt the survival of Orthodoxy in the Western world. However, over the past twenty-five

years the Orthodoxy which I could not espouse in 1949—
and cannot espouse today—although I know it is the ground
of Jewish eternity, has not only "survived" but has exploded
into a dynamic movement in this country and the world
over, even in Soviet Russia and its satellites.

In 1949 my son Moshe, to whom this book is dedicated,
was about to enter the kindergarten class of Ramaz School.
Today he is a *Rosh Yeshiva* in Israel, and his commentary
on the Talmudic tractate *Sanhedrin* was recently published.
It is the kind of *sefer* a *Rosh Yeshiva* of two centuries ago
would have been proud, according to what I hear in the
*lomdishe* world.

About a year ago Moshe said he has one great *zechus*
(pious merit): he has set the clock of our family back to
where it ticked four or five generations ago. "And so we
can hope for another *Jewish Survival* in another hundred
and fifty years," he added with a tease in his voice. And
maybe there won't be a need for another *Jewish Survival*,
considering that my nine-year-old grandson, David, on his
own decision wears long *peyot* (sidelocks), lets his *tzitziyot*
hang down almost to his feet, and critically examines the
*kashrut* of a certain brand of cookies baked in Meah
Shearim—none of which his father does.

My certainty that Jewish survival is safe has grown since
*Jewish Survival* was published in 1949.

TRUDE WEISS-ROSMARIN

New York
September, 1976

CHAPTER 1

## *Israel and the Atomic Challenge*

I

WHEN THE first atomic bomb exploded on August 6, 1945, leaving in its wake death and havoc in shattered Hiroshima, the holocaust unnerved not only the Japanese but mankind as a whole. The only ones who kept their composure in the fear epidemic induced by "The Bomb" were the thinkers and analysts, who had foretold what was coming more than a quarter of a century before "The Bomb" made its terrifying debut.

Since 1918, when Oswald Splengler bemoaned "The Decline of the West," virtually all thinkers and critics worth their salt of philosophical, sociological and theological renown have been grappling with the predicament of modern man: the rapid advance of technique and the stagnant arrest of spiritual unfolding. The recognition is widespread that the 20th century debacle is not so much of the making of "the machine" as of its makers, for the modern crisis is not due to the advance of science and technique but to the lopsided emphasis on material and technical expansion. Modern man is intoxicated with his mastery over nature and thus he is blind to the truth that brute force and unrestrained power must lead to disaster.

Far from being a curse and a scourge of mankind, "the machine," properly controlled, could be our greatest blessing. "The machine" relieves us from arduous, time-consuming work; it provides leisure and makes life more enjoyable and comfortable with a multitude of gadgets placed at our disposal by technical ingenuity. It is not "the machine" which is at fault. The guilt for the havoc created by "the machine" is man's who has sold himself *body and soul* to "the machine," which only demanded his physical strength and technical ingenuity, but not the sacrifice of his soul-self and spirit.

"The Decline of the West" is a spiritual-ethical eclipse. Drunk with the power "the machine" has given him, modern man no longer sees that the human personality must be acknowledged as the measure of all things if civilization is to endure. He has sold himself to "the machine" and thus, inevitably, he placed himself in the bondage of his technical ingenuity and its fruits. In the pursuit of bigger and better "machines" he lost sight of the ends they are to serve. He achieved power for power's sake, efficiency for efficiency's sake, and speed for speed's sake.

Our generation is avowedly committed to realistic pragmatism. We exalt the "practical" things. Practicality has become our aim and purpose. Our houses are more spacious and comfortable than the dwellings of any previous generation of men; science and technique serve us with a bewildering variety of things which make life more interesting, agreeable and enjoyable. Yet there is more unhappiness abroad today than ever before. Why? Modern man is unhappy because in the pursuit of the improvement of the mechanical side of life he has lost sight of its meaning. We have cut to a tenth or less the time required for travelling a distance of 1,000 miles, but we have not learned to put the time saved to constructive and purposive use.

The crux of the predicament is that our material and technical advance has been far ahead of our spiritual and ethical progress. Our technical ingenuity has produced machines which our moral and spiritual acumen cannot control. We intended the machine to be a Golem and serve us with its superior strength. But our ethical control mechanism has proved impotent to infuse the automaton with a spark of goodness—and so the Golem is leading us to destruction.

Modern culture has become sensate to an extent that the spiritual and ethical areas have been all but crowded out. Modern man has lost his zest for ideas and ideals. Instead he strives mechanically to perfect tools and things. As a result there has ensued a barrenness in the spiritual realm which will doom mankind, unless the overemphasis placed on technique is recognized as the danger it presents to mankind's survival.

Instead of permitting technique to displace the spiritual areas, we must synthesize and harmonize matter and spirit. Technique, the body, as it were, must be quickened with the spirit of ethical purpose, or catastrophe will ensue. Already the virtual deification of technique has led us to regard the machine as more precious and valuable even than its maker. This does not militate against the machine but against those who made it and who, in the quest for bigger and more powerful machines, have lost sight of the purpose of technical progress: social and ethical advance.

*Per se* the machine is neutral. It can be employed for constructive or destructive purposes. Factories can produce automobiles for the recreation of the masses or tanks for their destruction. The airplane can peacefully link continents and countries, or it can shower ruin and death upon flourishing cities. Iron, as Isaiah already knew, can be cast either into swords or plowshares. The machine is neutral—it is its maker who turns it into a blight.

Modern man has enthroned the machine (the term "machine" is used rather loosely) as his idol and so he has lost the sense of appreciation for the *dignity of man* which is firmly anchored in the dignity of God. Speed, mass production and mechanical perfection have become the ideals of our society, which worships the machine rather than the God of ethics Whose teachings point to man as the measure of all things and to goodness and humaneness as the only values of supreme import. Practicality has become the watchword of our civilization—practicality for practicality's sake and efficiency for efficiency's sake. Instead of employing the machine as a *means* toward the *end* of the betterment and spiritualization of life, we have enthroned the machine as an end in itself while deprecating the eternal things of the spirit to which alone belongs the dignity associated with ultimate, purposive goals.

## II

Is there any hope for averting the calamity threatening modern man who, precisely upon attaining to the pinnacle of technical progress, has perverted its potential blessings into instruments for his own destruction?

The consensus of the many scholars, historians and critics who have tackled this problem in recent years is that, first and above all, the machine must be relegated to its proper place. It must be evaluated as a mere means to ethical, spiritual and humane ends, and not as an independent value. In the words of Dr. W. M. Horton, "modern machinery, however massive and costly, is a mere means to human ends, valueless in itself, which must be removed from its present ridiculous prominence and pushed into the background."

The challenge with which we are confronted is "whether Western man, the main protagonist of a supposedly progressive civilization, has the moral and intellectual forces to master and subdue the mechanisms which he created, but which he cannot keep safely in their place and in their subservient role."

The nineteenth century enthroned the scientific fact supreme, with the result that religion, ethics and the humanities were reduced to handmaidens of technique. In the flush of the elation that came to him with his machine-made mastery over matter, time and space, man forgot that there is a realm of values beyond the scientific fact. Now, however, a sorely chastened generation is beginning to recognize its error.

Only "ethical man," as postulated by religion, and not "man the scientific fact" can lead the way out of the present confusion. The emancipation of "ethical man," however, requires, first of all, a vigorous affirmation of man's innate dignity, which is priceless and cannot be delimited in contradistinction to the finite, circumscribed and delimited value of the machine. Respect for the human personality has therefore become the watchword of the many would-be architects of a better world who hold with Archibald MacLeish, that "if the man can be taught to believe in the worth of man, in the dignity of man, in the 'characteristic perfection' of man, he can be taught not only to survive but to live. If the world can be governed in belief in the worth of man, in the dignity of man, it can be governed in peace."

Affirmation of the dignity and infinite value of man, of human equality, respect for the intrinsic value of the ethical personality, neighborly love for all "children of God," humaneness and the cultivation of the arts of peace—these are some of the remedies which thoughtful social engineers recommend for extricating our civilization from the tentacles of the crisis which threatens to become its doom, unless there will be effected a complete revision and a total re-evaluation of hitherto accepted standards and values.

But how can "the return to humaneness," predicated on the recognition of the limited value of the machine as a mere means, become a potent reality? The secularist answer is that we must effect a complete revision of our educational system and place more emphasis on the humanities and non-technical studies. History, however, disproves this thesis. In ancient Greece and Rome the humanities, art and philosophy celebrated singular triumphs—yet Plato's and Aristotle's ideas and ideals did not give rise to general, universal regard for human dignity and to the avowal of the infinite value of *every* man. Was it not Aristotle who defined the slave as "an animated machine?" And did not the outstanding thinkers and artists of Greece and Rome accept in matter of fact fashion the many assaults upon the dignity of man which are implicit in slavery? The records of Greece and Rome, as well as of the European Renaissance, prove conclusively that the "humanities" never yet engendered respect for human dignity and equality.

The humaneness which is needed for the reconstruction of our shattered world requires a stronger basis than philosophy. It calls for the religious conviction that all men are brothers in God. There are many voices clamoring, as Ralph T. Flewelling does, for a civilization which "is not dominion, wealth, material luxury; nay, not even a great literature and education widespread, good though these may be. Civilization is not a veneer; it must penetrate to the very heart and core of the societies of men. Its true signs are thought for the poor and suffering, chivalrous regard and respect for women, the frank recognition of human brotherhood irrespective of race or color or nation or religion, the narrowing of the domain of mere force as a governing factor in the world, abhorrence of what is mean and cruel and vile, ceaseless devotion to the claims of justice."

It is here where Judaism must *again* come to the rescue of man, as it attempted once—but not very successfully—when it shared a rich endowment of teachings on human equality and brotherhood with its daughter religion, Christianity. Western civilization, the amalgam of the legacies of Athens, Rome and Jerusalem, is termed "Christian Civilization." But, as it has often been noted by thoughtful students, Western man has not been very effectively Christianized. Although "Christian love" has been extolled for almost two millennia, the world of today is more engulfed in hate than it was at the time when the *Jewish* commandment "and thou shalt love thy neighbor as thyself" was broadcast among the heathen nations as a Christian ideal. Many thoughtful Christian theologians now own up to Christianity's failure to "humanize" its confessors. "By their fruits you shall know them," is Professor Leroy Waterman's challenge to Christianity. In his judgment, "the Christianity that has failed to produce enduring peace and good will even among its own adherents through the generations can offer no assurances that the fruits of religious rivalries and violence will not reproduce themselves in whatever existence they are permitted to act."

This failure is largely due to Christianity's quest for wider spheres of influence. Transformed by Paul into a missionary religion of world-wide ambitions and universal claims, Christianity had to sacrifice substance and agree to compromise in order to become the dominant faith. In the quest for power and influence, Christianity—as all movements aspiring to power—had to sacrifice principles. Like Paul who, for the sake of the propagation of the faith, became "everything to all men," being a Greek among the Greeks and a Hebrew among the Hebrews, Christianity had to yield on principles. The Church managed to achieve a *modus vivendi* with all types of governments and economic systems, invariably casting its lot with the mighty. This is the true reason why Christianity has failed to infuse its followers with Christian ethics.

In contradistinction to the makers of Judaism, who vigorously opposed existing conditions, refusing to acquiesce in injustice and oppression, Christianity consoled its followers with the better Hereafter while admonishing them to endure on earth everyone in the station he was born and not to strive for improvement of his temporal lot.

Christianity is essentially other-worldly. The kingdom which Jesus preached was not of this world. As a result, Christianity could not but fail in its attempts to improve *this* world. Its gaze has always wandered to the hills that lie beyond.

### III

Judaism was first to preach and demand the practice of ethics in all realms of *this* life. The Jewish teachers never made concessions or compromises where basic principles of goodness were at stake. Perhaps this is why Judaism has remained "unsuccessful," if success is measured in numbers and political influence, while Christianity has become the ruling faith of the Western world.

If, in the words of John Adams, "the Hebrews have done

more to civilize men than any other nation," it was because they discovered the idea of "fellow man." The Hebrew genius saw early that all men are created equal, and that, through their Creator, all are brothers, irrespective of secondary racial, national, religious and economic differences. A pithy talmudic homily stresses that God created only *one* man in the beginning, so that no one should be able to claim nobler descent than his fellow. The same motive inspired the talmudic tale which has is that when God created Adam He formed him from dust collected from all the four ends of the world, so that no single country or continent should be able to lay claim to having supplied the stuff of which the ancestor of the human race was made.

Judaism demands recognition of the dignity of man on the strength of the exalted dignity of the Creator. Every man is infused with a spark of the Spirit in whose image man was created. To degrade man thus becomes tantamount to degrading God. Thanks to this identification of the dignity of man with the honor of God, the religious-ethical spirit gained early ascendancy in Israel. It became the mainspring of Jewish social ethics and the legislation informed by it. Over and over again, biblical, talmudic and rabbinic literature emphasise that every human being has infinite value by dint of his endowment with a spark of the Divine in whose image all men are created. Wrong inflicted upon *any* man thus becomes a transgression against God, and "he who sheds blood diminishes something from the Likeness in which man is made." Lest one assume that God sorrows, as it were, only for the hurt inflicted upon the righteous, the Sages stressed that he mourns also for the blood of the sinners for they, too, are "His children."

Man *as such* is the highest value of Judaism. The degradation of *any* man to the level of "an animated machine" is unthinkable in the Jewish setting. To the Jew, every human life is sacred because every man partakes of the holiness of God. This is why all commandments of the Torah must be ignored when human life is in the balance.

Judaism has that regard for the infinite value of man which contemporary social engineers postulate as the *sine qua non* of civilized society. Unlike the Greek philosophers, Judaism does not postulate "abstract man" as the crown of creation but singles out each and every individual for this dignity. Every human being represents in his person both mankind and God, hence there can be no trifling with any human life. The Sages expressed this fundamental truth as follows: "The plants and the animals were created in multitudes. Man alone was created singly, so that he should know that he represents the whole world and is invested with the full value of the totality of life. And thus every human being may say: 'The world was created for my sake.' Consequently, he who preserves one human life really saves the world, while he who destroys a single human life really destroys the world."

The respect for the worth and dignity of human life inspired the social legislation of the Bible and Talmud, which equate charity with justice. The poor, the weak, the aged, the stranger, the man-servant, the maid-servant, the orphan and the widow have been the perennial concern of Judaism. The test of genuine humaneness in the Jewish realm is the mercy extended to the underprivileged and poor. The great nations of antiquity made no provision for the weak. Their idols were the gods of the strong and powerful, in contradistinction to Israel's God Who singled out the poor and suffering as "His people." An ethics of human relations, based on the brotherhood of mankind, had not even dawned upon the Greeks and the Romans. The social suffering in the plutocratic societies of antiquity was therefore of vast dimensions. The world belonged to the strong and powerful—the poor and weak were left to shift for themselves, and suffer and die unaided. Life was cheap in Greece and Rome, for it was not evaluated in terms of the dignity of man.

Throughout the ages Judaism has been vitally concerned with the ethics of human relations. Possibly as a result of this preoccupation with the fundamentals of civilized living, the Jewish contribution to abstract philosophy, science, technique —not to mention art—has been modest. To be sure, standard works on "The Jewish Contribution to Civilization" adduce commendable evidence that Jews have contributed their due share to all departments and spheres of culture and civilization. But the fact remains that collectively the Jews have made only one truly great contribution: they have evolved the ethics of human relations and have taught mankind all that ever will, or can, be known of the theory and the practice of the good life. Judaism has not excelled in the sensate realm of art and technique, but it has created, single-handedly almost, the art of living together. Judaism has not inspired beautiful statues and imposing structures of architecture. In fact, it has been all but indifferent to the fine arts, for it has invariably concentrated its efforts and given its strength to the cultivation of the arts of peace and social justice.

The second commandment, "You must not make an image for yourself in the shape of anything that is in the heavens above, or that is on the earth below, or that is in the waters under the earth," is often cited as an extenuating circumstance for the paucity of the Jewish contribution to art. No doubt this commandment has had a blighting effect. Yet it should not be overlooked that Jews remained inactive even in artistic realms not touched by this prohibition.

The German historian Treitschke asserted that one statue of Phidias, the master sculptor of ancient Greece, was worth the suffering of masses of slaves. In this postulation he succinctly expressed the attitude not only of his countrymen, but that of antiquity as well. The Greeks and Romans callously sacrificed human beings to artistic and political ambition. It was not so in Israel, for there the question was pondered, "How do you know that your blood is redder than your fellow man's?" Human happiness, not statues of marble and abstract theorems, was the perennial concern of the thinkers and sages of Israel.

The Hebrew prophets and sages did not live in secluded ivory towers. They stood in the thick of life's struggles, always espousing the cause of the weak and upholding "goodness" at any cost and risk to themselves. As a result, Judaism early achieved and has held fast ever since to that concentration upon the spiritual ends to which our contemporary would-be healers point as the salvation from "The Bomb." The human being as the concern of the God of ethics is the center of Judaism and of all endeavors and aspirations in the traditional Jewish realm. This is the true reason of the Jewish apathy to artistic splendor and technical triumph. Judaism does not celebrate the human form and it knows that even the most solidly constructed temples will ultimately crumble, even as the splendors of the most exquisite art will finally fade. Only God is eternal—God and ethical man ennobled by the spark of the Divine.

It was not ascetic renunciation in obedience to the second commandment which made Judaism choose the espousal of the spiritual meaning of life in preference to the fostering of the arts and technique. It was a conscious and purposive choice flowing from the conviction that the spiritual ends are worthier than the means of matter.

This concentration upon the spiritual ends of life is also to be credited for the unique phenomenon that in Israel nationalism was not perverted into the kind of imperialistic aggression which has been the bane and terror of mankind. Thanks to their awareness of the unity and brotherhood of men, the Jews never lost sight of mankind while pursuing their own national interests. In Israel alone among all nations was developed "the first sound formula for saving nationalism from itself" by interpreting the history of the nation as a chapter of the history of the human family. Yet this was far from a sacrifice of nationalism on the altar of universalism. Jewish patriotism has always been fervent and steady. But nationalism in Israel was not an end. It was a means and instrument for the unification of mankind.

## IV

All diagnosticians of the "atomic crisis" are agreed that the only effective prophylaxis against total doom is total humane regeneration. The humanizing forces must be strengthened; the ethical goals must be enthroned above technique; the dignity of man must be proclaimed inviolable; the machine must be made subservient to man and technique be subjected to the control of ethics. The brotherhood of mankind must be acknowledged as the logical corollary of the Fatherhood of God. Fellow man must be respected and not be degraded to a mere means toward an end.

Judaism, which has forged all these postulates of *ethical reason* on the anvil of age-old suffering and has made them the norm of its rationale, is preeminently suited to lead mankind out of its present confusion. The armory of Judaism contains all that is needed to save us from doom. But in order to bring its healing powers and salutary message to a world in which the humanizing forces have been eclipsed, Judaism must recapture the courage and certainty of the Prophets who preached justice, righteousness and peace in the midst of injustice, unrighteousness and war. The Prophets were men of singular courage: they were ready to lay down their lives for the Word which seared their hearts. They were not men of compromise. They demanded the full measure of justice and righteousness for they knew that compromise in ethics is—impossible.

Nikolai Berdyaev, one of the thinkers who subjected the crisis of Western civilization to critical scrutiny, singles out "the superficiality of the process of humanization" as one of the chief factors of the breakdown of our moral values. But if the humanization of the Christian world is superficial, it is largely due to Christianity's traditional readiness to sacrifice principles for the sake of temporal power. From the time of Paul, Christianity has been essentially a whittling down of the maximal ethical program of Judaism, which it nominally adopted but curtailed in order to enlarge its sphere of influence.

The Prophets knew that there can be "no peace with the wicked." Christianity, in its quest for world supremacy, has often dealt with the wicked, thus placing its legacy from Greece and Rome above the heritage and testament from Jerusalem. As a result of this orientation, it was inevitable that the humanitarianism of Jerusalem was eclipsed.

Judaism is not a missionary religion in the sense of being eager to win converts for the confession of specifically Judaistic beliefs and the observance of ritualistic commandments. It is, however, definitely missionary in the broader aspiration of leading all mankind to ethics and humaneness. When envisioning and dreaming of the days of the Messiah, the Prophets did not look forward to a time when all of mankind would be observing the dietary laws.... They yearned however, for the ideal future when justice and peace would rule supreme.

Some may argue that in these crucial days of acute challenges to Jewish existence we cannot indulge in the luxury of concentrating on the ultimate problems of man. Those who would argue thus should, however, consider that, even in times of doom and crisis, Judaism invariably rallied its resources and raised its voice in the defense of the eternal truths transcending the national sphere.

That the young State of Israel will rally and strive for universal human betterment is apparent from the utterances of Israeli leaders and, especially, from the Draft Constitution. The key-phrase of the Draft Constitution occurs in Section 2, Article 12. It reads: "*The State shall insure the sanctity of human life and uphold the dignity of man.*" In making *the dignity of man* the concern of the State of Israel, the authors of its Constitution have served notice that the State of Israel means to link itself to the tradition of Israel which made possible the national rebirth. *The dignity of man* is the rock on which this tradition rests and its touchstone as well.

The Israel Constitution is infused throughout with the traditional Jewish regard for *the dignity of man*. Experts on constitutional law will point to numerous details for which the Constitution and Israel is indebted to the French Constitution and to the American Constitution. However it should not be overlooked that the incentive of both the French and the American constitutions was supplied by—the Prophets of Israel. Fortunately, the Preamble of the Israel Constitution acknowledges in full its indebtedness to the Prophetic inspiration.

Judaism, despite its all-pervading national character, is yet inherently cosmopolitan and universalistic. The Jewish salvation is indissolubly intertwined with the salvation of the world. In ages past—and especially in the biblical period—Judaism boldly and courageously confronted the world with the message of the One God Who demands the brotherhood of mankind. Two thousand years of exile and persecutions at the hands of the dominant faiths and regimes inevitably have weakened the Jewish fighting spirit—but it is far from dead, as recent events in Israel have proved.

With the authority and pride of having first proclaimed "the cluster of moral ideas" for whose realization the Western world is yearning, Israel and Judaism should, and must, rally for the formidable task of coping with the atomic challenge, which is not a political but a moral and religious issue. This makes it obligatory that Israel and its intellectual-spiritual spokesmen attack in earnest their prophetic duty "to be a blessing for all the families of the earth."

## V

Students of primitive man know that there is something in the human being which will not let him rest satisfied with existence as an end in itself. To be human means to seek an end and a meaning for existence. In point of fact, there is only one measure for man's progress from the animal realm, from which he started out, to the human realm, where he has not yet fully arrived, namely, the amount of effort spent on making existence more than an end in itself.

To Jews existence was never an end in itself. Sociologists and historians who explain Jewish survival with secularly oriented theories, couched in terms of "national existence as an end in itself," are oblivious of the most important and harrowing fact of Jewish history in the Diaspora, namely, that the life of the Jew was so dismal and hopeless on the "existence as an end in itself" level, that if not for the extra-existential sphere which he had created for his *real* life, the spiritual life that counted, Jewish survival would have been cut short centuries ago. The steady flame of the Jewish will to live, and live as a nation in the Land promised to the Fathers, would have been extinguished ages ago if it had had only the goal of "national existence as an end in itself" to feed it.

We are an exceptional people—*am echad ba'aretz, a people sui generis*. As a result, our national problems and aspirations cannot be defined and understood in terms accepted by and valid for other nations. We are a unique people, if only because we have endowed the Western world—the only part of the globe which has made universal history thus far—with its entire stock of religious beliefs, ethical ideals and moral norms. One simply cannot understand Jewish history unless one keeps sight of the *sui generis* nature of those who made it. It is a history without analogy and the greatest injustice which has been done to it was inflicted by historians attempting to explain the Jewish road of the ages with generally valid terms and laws. It cannot be done! One cannot explain why we survived and why we wanted Palestine, and only Palestine, with cold reason, for to suffer and sacrifice what we have suffered and sacrificed, individually and collectively, for the return to our Land is—unreasonable. It is as unreasonable in time and as right in eternity as were the paths of all those who opposed and oppose the stream of what is accepted as "reasonable" in the market-place.

Why, then, do we want the Jewish State?

To provide a refuge for homeless DP Jews? They might find refuge elsewhere. If we had tried as hard to provide homes for the DP Jews in the Americas, or in some other "territories," the DP camps would have been vacated long before Israel's open doors liquidated them.

To show the world that we are a nation like the rest, with a highly efficient and skilled army, with thriving industries and prosperous farms, with modern cities and model hospitals? The game is not worth the candle, for national existence as an end in itself is as senseless, though perhaps as instinctively right, as life on the level of the individual lacking incentives except those connected with the satisfaction of physical needs and desires.

To solve "The Jewish Problem?" Israel will not be able to solve it in the foreseeable future, for under the most auspicious conditions it will not be able to take in more than another two million of the twelve million Diaspora Jews.

Why, then, do we want this Jewish State newly born? And why do we tremble for its welfare? To be reassured about the military progress of Haganah? Of course. To be reassured that Israel's government is functioning efficiently? Naturally. But above all and everything, I believe, our thought, interests and emotions revolve about what happens in Israel because we look forward to the day when the Jewish State and its people will give attention to the areas where there is something more than national existence as an end in itself.

It is unfortunate that the idea of the "Mission of Judaism," variously referred to as the "Jewish Mission" and the "Jewish Burden," has been all but neglected by Zionist thinkers, as the result of its having been claimed as the central idea of the anti-Zionist Reform Judaism of yesterday. Yet the "Jewish Mission" to the world is inseparable from Jewish nationhood. This mission, and nothing else, led Abraham to forsake his native country and go to the Land God would show him. He was promised greatness and prosperity there, so that in him "all the families of the earth be blessed." There has never been, and there can never be, another justification for Jewish existence except the extent to which we are a blessing for all the families of the earth by sharing with them our religious-ethical insights flowing from the good life on our *own* soil.

There is no inherent flaw in the idea of the "Jewish Mission" as first enunciated in Genesis and reiterated and elaborated by the Prophets. This idea is neither anational nor anti-national. On the contrary, its center of gravity lies in Jewish nationhood. It does not supplant or displace Jewish nationhood but complements it. It does not proclaim the superfluity of Jewish territorial nationhood but, on the contrary, presupposes Israel in its own land, free and its own master, for effectively discharging the "Mission."

Far from detracting from Jewish national awareness, the idea of the "Jewish Mission" has been its strongest prop. For it was the unshakable belief in our appointed purpose and "Mission" which sustained us. We bore the unbearable because the Prophets had taught us that there was meaning and purpose in our agony and travail. We suffered not in vain but for a goal, a mission—our "Jewish Mission." We were the suffering servant whom the Lord pleased to crush by disease to see if his soul would offer itself. . . .

The Prophets who enlarged the scope of the "Jewish Mission," until it became coextensive with a program of ethical universalism—the One World ideal—were ardent Jewish patriots. Indeed, they dreamed of the One World and the One Mankind, but they took it for granted that Zion and Jerusalem would be its focal points, from where Torah and God's word would go forth.

The Prophets never viewed their nation's destruction and exile as anything else but a tragedy. They argued that the penalty was deserved, but they never relinquished hope that the day would dawn when Zion's guilt would be paid off and good tidings would ring out from Jerusalem.

This day is now upon us and with it there has been renewed and intensified the challenge, first flung out to Abram (he was still "Abram" and not yet "Abraham" when the Call came to him): To be a blessing for all the families of the earth. Obviously, we shall have to keep our own vineyard and cultivate it well before assuming the burden of looking after the vineyards of others. But the two tasks are not mutually exclusive; on the contrary. We became the provider nation for the spiritual-religious needs of the Western world precisely by cultivating our vineyard so well and thoroughly. The wisdom of Hillel, "If I am not for myself, who will be for me? But if I am only for myself, what do I amount to?" has been our sure guide throughout ages. Thus we were guarded against such irrational mistakes as that of orthodox Reform Judaism, which defined the Jewish Mission as self-expropriation for the sake of "the others," as well as against the pernicious type of national egotism, the bane and terror of our time, which persuades a people that its own greatness and power is all that matters.

The authors of the many recent "guides" to the solution of the atomic predicament are agreed that Christian ethics and love must be marshalled against the perversion which made possible the abuse of atomic power. Toynbee, Trueblood, Sorokin, Cousins, MacLeish and numerous others, despite their differences, are united in the call for a new Christian humanism which would enable mankind to build a lasting peace and an enduring ethical order on the shambles of despiritualized technology.

Maimonides already pointed out that Judaism's daughters, Christianity and Islam, have exerted a civilizing and restraining influence. Yet Maimonides was aware of it that the thinned down Jewish ethics, on which Christianity and Islam are reared is, in absolute terms, too weak to complete the process of the spiritual education of mankind. This conviction was more fully elaborated by Yehudah Halevi who, in his *Kuzari*, provided a remarkably fair and objective comparative study of Judaism, Christianity and Islam.

Christianity has been the uncontested spiritual force of the Western world for more than a millennium and a half. During the major part of this stretch of time the Church was enthroned superior to any and all temporal powers. Christianity had, and still has, at its disposal all the physical instruments, as well as the psychological-strategic position, to bring nearer the Millennium. Yet, all Christian thinkers and theologians who have participated thus far in the discussion of the moral debacle of the 20th century, have admitted that—Christianity has failed to civilize the old Adam.

Today, as two thousand years ago when Roman imperialistic corruption, abetted by the idolatries of the Empire, had aroused a yearning for a better order of justice, men are again questing for a "savior." Two thousand years ago Judaism, indirectly, provided the savior who was incapable of bringing salvation because he insisted that his kingdom was not of this world. It is to this basic other-worldliness and disdain for *this* world that the failure of Christianity is largely due.

Judaism is too spiritual to consider the here-and-now as the epitomy of being. The world-to-come has an important place in the Jewish pattern. But it was never permitted to displace this world. "If not now—when?" is the Jewish attitude. Justice must well up like water—here-and-now. Peace must be enthroned—here-and-now. Brotherhood must make life better and sweeter—here-and-now.

In the explosives-laden air of the storm which is now gathering, the yearning for "a new humanism" is being intensified by every one of the many steps the West and the East are taking toward the abyss which threatens to engulf both. Coupled with this yearning there is a deep sense of frustration born of the failures of the long past. This frustration can be detected in the books of even the firmest believers in "Christian moral rearmament."

Where, then, shall we look for guidance? Whom, then, shall we entrust with searching for the ethical formula which will neutralize the threat of atomic power misused?

Our answer is: To Israel and to Judaism we must look for guidance—and the reconstituted Jewish nation we shall charge with the task of searching for the badly needed formula for the solution of the atomic predicament.

CHAPTER 2

## *The Long Vigil*

I

THE MIDRASH has it that when Israel was thrust into exile, the Divine Presence went along to comfort them in their homelessness. In point of fact, however, the Jewish people never really left Eretz Israel, for wherever they went they carried with them the tangible memory of Zion and the love for Jerusalem. In a thousand different ways the memory of Zion and the ardent desire and impatient hope for its restoration have become part of the Jewish way of life so that, spiritually and ideationally, the Jew never stopped breathing the air of Eretz Israel. The Jews went into exile, but they carried along the blessed spiritual harvest they had gathered on their own soil as the "portable fatherland" of which no enemy could deprive them. In due course, this *"portable* fatherland" became for them a potent mainstay which upheld and infused them with the strength to survive until the day when their "portable fatherland" would again strike roots in the rockbed of its real, tangible soil.

The much-debated chimerical question whether the Jews are "a nation" or "a religion" would have been regarded as stark madness by virtually all Jews of the pre-emancipation era. To them the organic and indivisible unity of the confession of the religious truths of Judaism and the avowal of the hopes for Jewish national restoration was axiomatic. It was only when the Jew entered the orbit of Western civilization that two schools of Jewish thought emerged which, for the sake of their own specious reasons of ideology, laid the axe on the organic Jewish unity of national consciousness and religion. The founders of Reform Judaism, zealous to secure for the Jew a place in the sun, but cognizant of the fact that cultural assimilation and the divestation of all Jewish national characteristics, such as the Hebrew language and the hope for political restoration, was the price demanded for Jewish emancipation, declared that Judaism had religious connotations exclusively. The postulation of Judaism as a religion only had a curious parallel in the ideology of the Russian Jewish socialists and radical irreligious Jewish nationalists who flourished about the turn of this century and insisted that the Jewish community is a national unit, a people like all the rest and not bound to the Jewish religion.

We have, then, the curious phenomenon of two Jewish factions, each disputing the genuineness of that element regarded by the other as the touchstone and only cohesive force of the Jewish community. But neither the "Jews by religion" only, nor the "Jews by nationality" do justice to the essential nature of Judaism which fuses the national and the religious elements in an organic and indivisible amalgam. There is neither a de-nationalized "Jewish religion" nor a secular "Jewish nationalism," except in the wishful thinking of the proponents of these lopsided and fragmentized definitions of Jewishness.

Judaism is a national religion. The idea of separation of synagogue and state is not only foreign but contrary to it;

membership in the synagogue *eo ipso* implies identification with the Jewish people, and a member of the Jewish people belongs automatically to the religious community of the synagogue. National hopes and aspirations are part and parcel of Jewish religious expression and, on the other hand, many Jewish religious ideas are embodied in Jewish national aims. Moses, the liberator of the people from the Egyptian bondage and its political leader, was also the founder of the Jewish faith.

Jewish ethics is rooted in Jewish nationalism and Jewish nationalism derives its unique tolerance from being nurtured by Jewish ethics. The history of Judaism is identical with the history of the Jews and the fate of the Jews has always been coextensive with that of Judaism. Judaism is a national religion and the Jews are a nation "by virtue of the Torah," i.e. their religion, as Saadia Gaon pointed out a thousand years ago. Notwithstanding the protestations of a minority of Reform Jews, the Jew who renounces Jewish peoplehood and no longer prays and hopes for Jewish national restoration, places himself in eternal opposition to all authentic Jewish teachings. On the other hand, and despite the protest of the consistent "secular nationalists," a Jew who renounces his faith therewith also relinquishes his share in Jewish peoplehood.

Artificially constructed ideologies and wishful thinking cannot change the fact, written large in Jewish literature and history of three thousand years and more, that *the Jews are a nation by virtue of their religion and that Judaism is the religion of the Jewish nation.*

## II

An examination of the basic sources of "the Jewish religion," especially of the Bible, proves conclusively that, although studded with universalistic ideals and goals, Judaism is yet, first and last, the faith of one nation: the Jews. Professor Cadbury, a Christian Bible critic, aptly observes, "we are wont to speak of the Jews as the people of a book, but it is no less true that the Bible is the book of a people.... Its historical parts record the history of the Jewish people; its didactic and hortatory books address themselves to the Jewish people; its poetic books derive their imagery from the natural scene of the Jewish land and the social setting of Jewish society. Indeed, this Book of one people has become the Bible of the Western world but this is no detraction from its thoroughly national character."

The Hebrew Prophets looked beyond the narrow horizon of national frontiers and encompassed all mankind in their visions of a regenerated human society. But the fact remains that the universalism of the Prophets was firmly rooted in the love for their own people and their concern over its destiny. The Prophets were far from desiring the dissolution of their people in "mankind." Their universalism was not as shallow as the philosophy of those who labor under the delusion that the establishment of universal human brotherhood must be preceded by the extinction of all national differences. As true democrats, the Prophets did not demand *gleichschaltung* but broad tolerance, predicated on the conviction that all those created in the Divine image are brothers. The Prophets, therefore, in delineating the ideal future could not but hope and believe that this better day would witness the restoration of the Jewish nation on its own soil and under the sway of its own law — the Torah. Being farsighted and cosmopolitian oriented universalists, the Prophets also hoped that their own reconstituted nation would not form an island of ethics and religiosity in an ocean of corruption, but extend its light to all the nations. This is why they looked forward to the time when "the mountain of the Lord's house shall be established as the top of the mountains, and shall be established above the hills; and all nations shall flow unto it. And many peoples shall go and say: 'Come ye, and let us go up to the mountain of the Lord, to the House of the God of Jacob; and He will teach us of His ways, and we will walk in His paths,' for out of Zion shall go forth law, and the word of God from Jerusalem."

Here, for the first time in the history of mankind, fervent nationalism is interpreted not as a narrow, particularistic program but as an instrument for achieving salvation for all mankind. The redemption of their own people was of paramount importance to the Prophets, but they did not stop there. "It is too slight a thing for you being my servant that I should but raise up the tribe of Jacob and restore the survivors of Israel; so I will make you a light of the nations, that My salvation may reach to the ends of the earth." As Hans Kohn so well put it, "Israel's nationhood, its selection by God, was recognized and proclaimed, not as an end in itself, but as the means to a greater universal end. Nationalism became relativized, subservient to a goal embracing the whole of mankind, but it remained dominant with the Jews and determined even their universalistic conceptions."

The Jews achieved that, in their realm, "nationalism was saved from itself" by the high ethical-religious standards applied to the national aspirations. Nationalism is not an end in itself, but a means to realize the good life with the guidance of the *Torah*. Judaism is universalistic *because* it is nationalistic. Far from detracting from common human concerns, Jewish nationalism intensifies them, for nationally minded Jews never conceived of their people otherwise than as a link in the chain of mankind.

To deny the national character of Judaism is tantamount

to going counter to the facts of thirty-five centuries of Jewish experience. Throughout the Bible, the Jews are never referred to otherwise than as a nation. They are freed from Egypt as a nation; the Torah is given to the Jewish nation; they enter upon the possession of the Promised Land as a nation; they sin as a nation and are chastised and warned by the Prophets as a nation; they are punished as a nation and the ultimate restoration is held out to the nation. But the religious element is inseparable from the national drama. The sin of the Hebrew nation was religious transgression: idolatry and the emulation of the ways of the pagans. Analogously, the consummate national restoration is contingent upon the religious regeneration of the people.

The extent to which the awareness of the organic unity of the national and the religious elements is part of the Jewish fabric is evident especially from post-biblical Jewish literature —the Talmud, the *Midrash,* the great commentaries and rabbinic compendia and codes, the philosophical treatises and countless liturgical poems. This vast body of Jewish religious and cultural expression furnishes ample proof and testimony that Jewry never conceived of its role otherwise than as that of a nation, a nation without a country, but still possessed of all non-territorial national characteristics: a language, a common history, a shared destiny and hope for the future. All the available evidence proves that even in exile the Jews were still living on the soil of their country, as it were. In a thousand and one different ways the prayers, the observances of the festivals, and the rules governing their private lives made Eretz Israel, the lost, beloved homeland, a living reality in the life of every Jew integrated into the tradition of his people. At all joyous and sad moments of life, "the memory of Zion" has stood by the side of the exiled people. The bridal couple, under the *Huppa,* remembered Zion in her desolation and upon establishing their new home, they left some corner of the house unfinished as a constant reminder of Zion in her sorrow. Men and women alike would refrain from wearing especially treasured adornments, for were they not bereaved and mourning for their homeland? And when death and tragedy strike, the best consolation that can be offered to a Jew is: "May God console you, together with all those who mourn for Zion."

## III

Spiritually the Jews never left Eretz Israel. In the Diaspora they live according to its calendar, celebrating the spring and the harvest when it is spring and harvest-time in Eretz Israel. They toast the Sabbath and the Holy Days with wine pressed from grapes of the Homeland and forego necessities to be able to afford the *Ethrog,* whose sweet aroma is to them synonymous with the air of the Holy Land. A little soil from Eretz Israel is among the most precious possessions of Jews who dread nothing more than being buried in foreign soil without the comfort of a bit of Eretz Israel earth under their heads. Even in the grave their faces are turned toward Zion.

The undying Jewish love and attachment to Eretz Israel is the most unique example of loyalty and devotion. From the time of the first exile in Babylon, through the long night of the Middle Ages, down to our own day, every worth while Jewish effort, every spark of Jewish creativeness, every Jewish joy and every Jewish sorrow have stemmed from and been inspired by Eretz Israel. This tiny land, which had been home to the Jewish people for less than one-third of their historical career thus far, has been and is enshrined in the heart of every Jew deserving the name. In all countries and under many skies, for twenty-five centuries, day by day, Jews have thrice daily prayed for the restoration of their ancient Homeland, shedding tears of woe while remembering the vanished glory of Zion.

Eretz Israel is the inescapable destiny of the Jewish people. Our Sages were aware of this preordained and inseparable tie of fate between the Jewish people and their country when they mused about this unique relationship as follows: "God measured all the countries and found only Eretz Israel suitable for Israel." Another Rabbi found the iron bond between the people and their land in the love of God, Who said: "I love Israel and I love Eretz Israel. I shall, therefore, give my beloved country to my beloved people."

Jewish literature, of all times and all countries, is to a very large extent a paean singing the praises of Eretz Israel in keys and notes of limitless variety. Singer and sage, rabbi and scholar, rationalist and mystic, statesman and financier, and the large mass of anonymous though not inarticulate Jews have built monuments to Zion fashioned of verse and prose.

There is not a trait or quality of beauty, goodness, and excellence but has been woven into the tributes paid by generations of imaginative and creative lovers of Zion to their dearly beloved. Nor did this exaltation of the qualities of the Homeland begin in the *Galuth*. The Bible describes Eretz Israel as "a good land, a land of brooks of water; a land of wheat and barley, and vines and fig-trees and pomegranates; a land of olive-trees and honey; a land wherein thou shalt not lack a thing." It is "a pleasant land, the goodliest heritage of the nations... a land which the Lord thy God cared for; the eyes of the Lord thy God are always upon it."

The Talmud and rabbinic literature elaborate and add to these biblical tributes to *the* Land. "Ten measures of beauty were given to the world, nine of these went to Jerusalem and one to the rest of the world." Another Rabbi commented enthusiastically, "Eretz Israel does not lack a thing!" Even its "fruit is easier to digest than the produce of other countries." Small wonder, therefore, that the Rabbis felt that "happy are those who live in Eretz Israel" where, according to the Zohar, "all the splendor and all delight are found."

The spiritual qualities and the inspiration of Eretz Israel were even more elaborately exalted. Nahmanides, the famous scholar and Bible commentator, who stimulated powerfully the "love of Zion" among 13th century Jewry, summed up the conviction of every Jewish scholar in stating that "Eretz Israel is destined for the Torah—and the Torah can be complete only in Eretz Israel." To other Rabbis it was "the holiest of all countries" and the abode of the *Shechina*—the Divine Presence—which, according to Rabbi Yosi Ben Halafta, rests upon him who combines the study of the Torah with living in Eretz Israel.

According to the Talmud, "the air of Eretz Israel makes wise", for "ten measures of wisdom were given to the world, nine to Eretz Israel and one to the rest of the world." The spokesmen of the later generations, who knew life in the Galuth, praised especially the release of the pent-up creative Jewish faculties and emotions in Eretz Israel. A full critique of Jewish religious life in the Galuth is contained in the short statement of the Zohar: "In Eretz Israel God is worshipped in joy—in other countries in fear," and in Yehudah Halevi's assertion that "none of the commandments can be perfectly practised except there."

Some Hasidic Rabbis even identified Eretz Israel with the Divine Presence, the very boldness of this identification of pure spirituality with a concrete and real country attesting their mystical idealization of the Holy Land. It was but a modern rephrasing of the traditional conviction of the universally curative and vitalizing power of Eretz Israel when Ahad Ha'am stated: "No vital thought, no great national ideal can be created in the Galuth."

The intense love for Eretz Israel which inspired the Sages of the talmudic era has been expressed in many passages of touching fervor and in stories of great emotional quality. In order to give concrete expression to their love for Eretz Israel, "Rabbi Abba used to kiss the stones of Acco, while Rabbi Hanina would mend the roads, and Rabbi Hiya the son of Gamda would lie down in the dust of the Holy Land. All this to fulfill the passage, 'For Thy servants take pleasure in her stones and love her dust.'"

Elsewhere we read: "He who is born in Eretz Israel is especially favored, for why did the *Shechina* dwell in Benjamin's territory? Because the ancestors of all the other tribes were born abroad—Benjamin, however, was born in Eretz Israel." Another Sage held that "he who dwells in Eretz Israel and speaks Hebrew is assured of his share in the world-to-come." And elsewhere it says, "it is better to dwell in the deserts of Eretz Israel than in the palaces of other countries." In fact, God Himself is said "to prefer a small group of scholars in Eretz Israel to the Great Sanhedrin abroad."

He who adds to Eretz Israel's glory thus atones for his sins. The Rabbis illustrated this with the following homily about Omri, one of the idolatrous and unrighteous kings of Israel. Wondering at the fact that Divine Providence led him to the throne, despite his many transgressions, they explained it, "He added one town to Eretz Israel," namely he bought the site and built the town of Samaria. On the other hand, because one should not leave Eretz Israel, even in time of famine, Elimelech, Mahlon, and Chilion, whose story is recorded in the Scroll of Ruth, were punished, although they were "the foremost men and leaders of Israel" in their generation.

In later centuries, as the Galuth dragged on and weighed ever more heavily upon those who were longing and hoping impatiently for the promised return to Eretz Israel, the country became the idealized beloved of Jews everywhere. Nearly all of the great thinkers, commentators, and poets of the Middle Ages confessed the unquenchable desire which was burning and searing their hearts to behold Eretz Israel and its glory—Jerusalem. Many left home and family to journey to the Holy Land, notwithstanding the hazards and difficulties they would encounter. Yehudah Halevi, whose pilgrimage to Eretz Israel is often held up as a shining example of the love for Zion, was but one of many celebrities who embarked on the perilous and yet so much desired journey. Nahmanides, who agitated feverishly for the resettlement of the Holy Land, expressed the sentiments and feelings of all medieval Jewish pilgrims, the famous and the nameless ones, when in the introduction to his Pentateuch commentary he wrote that the separation from his family and friends, the hardships of his lonely life far from them, the sufferings and perils of the journey to Eretz Israel are "easy to bear and it is easy to give up all the good that may be my share, for it is agreeable to dwell even one day within your precincts, to visit your destroyed palace, to behold your forsaken sanctuary." He, as all other lovers of Zion, felt that "abroad, even if everything is done to conform with God's honor, complete purity is still lacking." And so he, and all the many who were of his bent, went in search of this purity—the consummation of their Jewishness.

Even those who were divided on the interpretation of Judaism felt alike where Eretz Israel was concerned. The "Besht," the founder of Hasidism, saw the fulfillment of his life in a pilgrimage to Eretz Israel, and his opponent, the rationalist "Mithnaged," the Gaon Elijah of Vilna, wrote to his family upon leaving for the Holy Land, "I beg of you, do not grieve over my departure for Eretz Israel—may it be rebuilt and re-established! I am, thanked be God, on my way to the Holy Land which all are eager to behold. It is the desire of all Israel, yea, the desire of God for which all are yearning in heaven and on earth."

There is very little difference between the tenor and mystical fervor of the Gaon's letter and the Hasidic Rabbi Nahman of Bratzlav's touching prayer: "Please God, may it be Your will to grant me in compassion and love—and as a special favor—to become speedily worthy of reaching Eretz Israel—the Holy Land which our fathers inherited, the country desired and longed for by all those who are truly pious. And most of them came there and improved and accomplished whatever they were capable and worthy of—all this thanks to the sacredness of Eretz Israel, the holiest place on earth."

The lovers of Zion demanded that she be desired for her own sake, and not for ulterior motives. "Only he merits to dwell in Eretz Israel," remarked the Bible commentator Moses Alshach (16th century), "who journeys there out of love for the country and not because of ulterior motives." Three centuries later the Hasidic Rabbi Shneiour Zalman of Ladi declared: "The love for Zion must be like a fire burning in the heart of every Jew. He who wants to live truly as a Jew must go to Eretz Israel. If there are obstacles in his way, he must overcome them—go he must."

The fact that in the desolation of destruction Zion had lost her beauty and glamor did not diminish the tender love of those who worshipped at her shrine. In practically all letters and descriptions of pilgrims to Eretz Israel it is stressed that, notwithstanding the destruction, the land's beauty and holiness are undiminished. Thus, for example, Jacob Emden, the 18th century opponent of pseudo-Messianic movements, wrote: "Every Jew must firmly resolve in his heart to journey to the Holy Land and live there. He must desire to become worthy of praying in the Sanctuary of the Lord, for although it is destroyed the Divine Presence has not departed from it."

If they could not be united with their beloved in life, the lovers of Zion wanted at least to be joined to her in death. Already in talmudic times it was customary to bury those who died in the Galuth in Eretz Israel, and this again was but in accordance with the tradition that prevailed in the days of the Patriarchs. Some Rabbis, however, frowned upon being joined to Eretz Israel in death and remaining far from her in life, as may be seen from this Midrashic account: Rabbi Berokya and Rabbi Eliezer the son of Pedath were walking near the gates of Tiberias when they met a train of coffins that were brought from abroad. Said Rabbi Berokya to Rabbi Eliezer: "Of what good is it that those who rejected her in life come to her when they are dead? I apply to them the passage 'ye defiled My land' while you were alive, 'and made My heritage an abomination'—when you are dead."

Replied Rabbi Eliezer: "This is not correct, for those who are buried in Eretz Israel are forgiven by virtue of its soil. It says, 'And its soil makes expiation for his people.'" Most of the Sages shared the view that "to be buried in Eretz Israel is like being buried under the altar."

Because of a statement in the Jerusalemian Talmud that "those buried in Eretz Israel will be resurrected first in the days of the Messiah," burial in the Holy Land was coveted especially by the Kabbalists and the later mystics who speculated a great deal about the temporal differences in the resurrection of the dead of Eretz Israel and those of other countries. To enable the largest number to share in the salvation bestowed by the precious soil of Eretz Israel, it became customary to put a little earth from the Holy Land under the heads of those who were buried in the Galuth—a custom which still prevails.

The unique place Eretz Israel occupies in Jewish life is perhaps most conclusively shown by the fact that the two most important commandments—the sanctification of the Sabbath and the honoring of father and mother—may be infringed upon for the sake of dwelling in the Land. The duty to purchase soil and houses in Eretz Israel is regarded as so important that, if it would be impossible to postpone the drawing up of the deed of sale, it is permitted to have it done on the Sabbath in order to redeem the land of Israel. "He who buys a house in Eretz Israel may have the contract drawn up even on the Sabbath."

Although children owe obedience to their parents, they may act contrary to their commands if they interfere with their settlement in Eretz Israel. To dwell in the Holy Land is a "positive" commandmant which brooks no interference whatsoever. A husband or a wife may sue for divorce if his or her mate refuses to settle in Eretz Israel. Likewise, a husband has no legal right to ask his wife to move from the Holy Land abroad for "the commandment to live in Eretz Israel outweighs all other commandments of the Torah."

## IV

Jewish history has been written from the vantage points of diverse interpretations of the meaning of the march of the Jewish people across time. But whether one views Jewish history as "*Leidens und Gelehrtengeschichte,*" as Graetz did, or as the unfolding of social and economic processes, as Dubnow and his followers did, the fact remains that Jewish history is to a very large extent the record of the "Love for Zion" translated into action. For Jews did not only *pray* for the return to Zion and the advent of the Messiah to bring about the redemption. From the first "Zionist movement," led by Zerubabel, Ezra and Nehemiah, half a century after the First Destruction, (586 B.C.E.), to the proclamation of the Basle Program (1897), the hope and desire of national restoration have been the most potent elements shaping Jewish destiny.

In keeping with the promise of the Prophets, elaborated by the Sages of the Talmud, the Jews of all countries and all centuries looked forward to the coming of the Messiah, who would lead the dispersed and homeless sufferers back to the ancestral home in Eretz Israel. As the persecutions and tribulations grew fiercer and more difficult to bear, the genius of the Jewish people became ever more preoccupied with speculations and dreams about the days of the Messiah when Israel's bondage would be broken and its ancient glory be renewed. Feverishly eager for the redemption, it was inevitable that the people and their spiritual leaders should seek consolation by means of calculating the date of the advent of the Messiah and the redemption. But when time and again the calculations proved wrong and disappointing, the Rabbis legislated against such dangerous and idle speculations. Yet, notwithstanding the rabbinic admonitions and prohibitions, the people continued to seek in the texts of certain biblical books, especially "Daniel," clues concerning the date of the advent of the Messiah.

According to biblical and talmudic lore, the redemption of Israel will be preceded by severe afflictions. "The birth-pangs of the Messiah" will be agonizing and excruciating—there will be persecutions of great cruelty and harshness, coupled with the breaking of all moral bonds and ties. It was not least due to the tradition of "the birth-pangs of the Messiah" that the Jewish people managed to survive two millennia of persecution unparalleled in the annals of mankind. They did not succumb to despair because their very sufferings were proof to them that redemption was in the offing. And so, instead of trying to escape afflictions, they readily submitted to them in the hope that by intensifying the pains they could expedite the birth of the Messianic redemption.

Throughout Jewish history the Messiah has been conceived of as the redeemer of the nation, who will lead dispersed Israel back to its Promised Land. To be sure, the early and latter day mystics associated a variety of supernatural events with the Messianic era, but, from the authoritative teachers of the Talmud to Maimonides and his successors, the prevailing opinion has invariably been that the Messianic era will be characterized primarily by the cessation of Israel's servitude and dispersion. In keeping with this Maimonides warns, "do not imagine for a moment that the King Messiah will have to perform wonders and miracles, create new phenomena in nature and cause the resurrection of the dead ... the world will go on in its usual course."

As a result of the popular preoccupation with Messianic speculations, in which even Maimonides himself was not altogether disinterested, it was inevitable that from time to time —and especially in periods of great suffering—men should arise and lay claim to the crown of the Messiah. Those who thus came to the people, arousing their hopes, their enthusiasm and their readiness for action, are judged by history as imposters. From an objective point of view the pseudo-Messiahs, who created havoc in the Jewish communities, were definitely imposters. But viewed from a different vantage point, they were only self-deluded fanatics who were victims of the obsessive notion that they were destined for the role of Messiah and redeemer.

The cavalcade of the more important pseudo-Messiahs opened with Bar-Kochba. He led a popular uprising against Roman tyranny but was defeated (135 C.E.) when the enemy destroyed his last stronghold, Bethar. The intensity of the craving for national liberation in the days of the Hadrianic persecutions may be gauged from the fact that Rabbi Akiba, one of the most astute Sages of all times, enthusiastically acclaimed Bar-Kochba as Messiah, and this over the protest and opposition of his colleagues.

While Bar-Kochba did not operate in the sphere of the miraculous, Moses of the Isle of Crete, which in the 5th century when he pressed his messianic claims boasted many flourishing Jewish communities, attempted to prove his authenticity by leading his followers dry-shod through the Mediterranean to Palestine. The result was that many who took the self-styled Messiah at his word perished in the sea.

Two centuries later, when Persian Jewry was in the throes of persecution, Abu-Isa proclaimed himself as the forerunner of the Messiah. He attempted to prove his authenticity by instituting various religious reforms and by attacking the authority of the Talmud. Believing in the might of the sword, he led his adherents against the Abbasides with dire results. Abu-Isa and many of his haphazard army were killed, but the survivors were not discouraged. They founded a sect (Isavites or Ispahanites) which remained fairly active for three centuries after Abu-Isa's death. Another pseudo-Messiah who presented himself in the Mohammedan orbit and promised to free his people from Islamic oppression and restore them to Palestine was Yehudah Yughdan of Hamadan, Persia (8th century), whose messianic pretensions, unlike those of the other pseudo-Messiahs of the Moslem countries, found a response also among the Jews of the Christian countries.

The ascendancy of the mystical lore of the Kabbala, at the end of the 12th century, greatly stimulated the messianic hopes. The first major pseudo-Messiah influenced by the Kabbala was Abraham Abulafia, who was born in Spain in 1240 and died at the age of fifty-one, after a stormy life, in the course of which he even attempted to convert the Pope to Judaism. He authored over a score of Kabbalistic books and proclaimed the year 1290 as the date of Israel's redemption.

No less spectacular and adventurous were the careers of David Reubeni and his follower Solomon Molko, whose messianic pretension, in the early part of the 16th century, found for a time a hearing even at the Vatican, until Molko, as a "relapsed Christian," was burned by the Inquisition and Reubeni was put out of the way, probably by poison.

While the pseudo-Messiahs thus far considered exerted only local influence, Sabbatai Zebi, the Smyrna youth, who in the bloody era of the Thirty Years' War fraught with cruel persecutions for Israel electrified his weary fellow-sufferers, created a stir in Jewish communities the world over. Tens of thousands of Jews in Europe and in the Near East forsook their homes and their belongings to follow him. Never before had the messianic urge clamored so insistently for fulfillment. In the end, Sabbatai, to save his life, adopted Islam and the Jewish communities were thrown into unprecedented gloom and disappointment. Yet even this sobering experience did not put an end to the messianic dream. While Moses Mendelssohn and his fellow "enlighteners" were engaged in leading their fellow-Jews into the wide open spaces of modern enlightenment, Jacob Frank, the Polish pseudo-

Messiah held court at Offenbach, near Frankfurt on the Main, and taught the most shocking perversions of Jewish mystical doctrines.

The messianic longing and the speculations born of it were, however, not merely restricted to dreamers. The desire for redemption and national restoration was a potent force even with the most celebrated Jewish teachers who, despite their logical trend of mind, were so ardently yearning for the advent of the Messiah that they attempted to calculate the date of his coming. Thus Rabbi Hanina held that the redemption was so near that he advised: "If four hundred years after the destruction of Jerusalem, one offers you a field worth a thousand denars for one denar, do not buy it, for the Messiah will soon come and then you will get it for nothing." Even those Rabbis and teachers who discouraged messianic speculations, lest the people would be seized by even greater despair should these hopes not materialize, could yet not altogether refrain from speculating about the advent of redemption. Thus Rabbi Ashi, the famous co-editor of the Babylonian Talmud, advised: "Do not hope for the Messiah before the completion of eighty-five Jubilees, counted from the creation of the world. After that, you may begin to hope for his coming." Even the astute logician Saadia Gaon, disregarded the later talmudic injunction, "a curse upon those who speculate about the date of the Messiah," and attempted to deduce from the biblical book of Daniel clues concerning the date of the redemption. He calculated that the Messiah would arrive about the year 964. Saadia's messianic speculations were severely criticized by many but, significantly and characteristically, they were defended by Maimonides, who argued that the dying hope of the suffering Jewish masses must be sustained by giving them more than merely a general promise of redemption and national restoration. Perhaps this is why in his "Epistle to the Jews of Yemen," Maimonides, while warning them against a pseudo-Messiah who had created havoc in their communities, also mentioned that in his own family there was a tradition that the precursor of the Messiah would arrive in the year 1216.

The intense fascination of messianic speculations extended even to men of profound scholarship, as is best attested perhaps by the strange case of Moses Hayim Luzzatto, the 18th century poet and author of the popular ethical guide "The Path of the Upright." As a result of Kabbalistic studies, Luzzatto believed for a time that he was the Messiah destined to lead Israel back to its ancestral homeland.

When the influence of mysticism was broken, with the advent of the age of "Enlightenment," the Jewish hope for national redemption did not wane. In keeping with the realistic orientation of the time, it assumed again, as it had been originally conceived of by the Prophets and the talmudic Sages, the form of the concrete and realistic hope for national restoration, in accordance with the talmudic pronouncement that the only difference between the era before the advent of the Messiah and the messianic era is "the cessation of Israel's servitude."

The 19th century exponents of the Jewish national idea, who pleaded for Israel's return to its land with political arguments fortified by historical and economic proofs, were in direct line of succession to the pseudo-Messiahs. The hope and the desire for restoration which agitated Hirsch Kalisher, Solomon Gutmacher, Moses Hess, Leo Pinsker and Theodore Herzl and his adjutants was identical with that which had fired the pseudo-Messiahs of a less realistically oriented age.

Modern Zionism, therefore, is no break with Jewish tradition but, on the contrary, its *only* logical continuation. All generations, throughout the millennia of the Jewish dispersion, expressed in terms commensurate with the tenor of the convictions of their times the hope for national restoration. Zionism is thus but the continuation of a firmly rooted Jewish tradition. The Jewish national hope, in its many diverse forms of expression, and even its perverse vagaries, has kept the Jewish national will alive. Judaism could survive after the loss of the land because the physical Jerusalem was transformed into the spiritual Jerusalem, "the chiefest joy" and the greatest love of every Jewish heart. Spiritually the Jews never left their ancestral soil and so the physical separation had no serious repercussions on their will to survive. They breathed, and continued to breathe, "the air of Eretz Israel" in all countries of the dispersion.

## V

Among the possessions a group must own to qualify as a people, language ranks first. Webster places the birthright of "a common language" well before "a more or less compact territory" in the definition of the ingredients of nationhood. And justly so, for history knows of nations that lost their ancestral territories, exchanged their creeds for new faiths, and yet remained conscious of their peoplehood. But there is no case on record of a people divesting itself of its language and retaining its national identity. On the other hand, nations contrived to preserve their identity in the midst of majority populations outnumbering them hopelessly as long as they remained faithful to their national tongue.

The Sages of the Talmud anticipated by many centuries the findings of modern sociologists when they stated that the "Israelites were redeemed from Egypt because they did not forsake their Hebrew language." That is to say, they held fast to their national identity and thus were saved from assimilation and its concomitant, national extinction.

The one hundred generations of Jews, who lived since the Second Destruction, have not forsaken our national language either. Throughout the centuries of the dispersion the Hebrew language has been the cement and unifying force which has kept our people conscious of our oneness and common destiny. This was largely due to the fact that Hebrew has always been infinitely more than merely our language of prayer. Although for many centuries the "Holy Language" was not actually spoken, most Jews commanded a perfect reading knowledge of Hebrew. Thanks to the high standards of Jewish education, illiteracy was unknown in Jewish communities, even in the "darkest" centuries of the Middle Ages. Shut away in ghettos, the average Jew of the pre-emancipation era had only a limited command of the vernacular. As a result, Moses Mendelssohn and his fellow "enlighteners" translated the Bible into German, not to make the Book accessible to those who knew no Hebrew, but to teach them the language of the country where they, their parents and their parents' parents were born.

But we need not go back almost two hundred years for evidence that the ghettoized Jews were "illiterate" in the vernacular while being highly and truly academically literate in their own Hebrew language. In Eastern Europe, up to the First World War, only an infinitesimally small number of Jews had a reading knowledge of the vernacular. To be sure, they knew enough Russian or Polish to get by in the market place, but truly literate they were only in Hebrew and, of course, in Yiddish, *the* vernacular of the teeming Jewish communities of the Eastern Europe of yesterday.

Partly as the result of the average Jew's limited contact

with the majority population, but largely by common consent and studied effort, Hebrew was, up to our own century almost, not only the medium of prayer but also the language of Jewish life. All official documents were written in Hebrew. The registers or vital statistics in all Jewish communities were kept in Hebrew—and in marking the dates of births, marriages and deaths, the Hebrew calendar was exclusively used. Contracts of betrothal and marriage, as well as writs of divorcement, were, as in fact they still are, written in the peculiar Aramaic-Hebrew idiom reserved for such documents.

Businessmen, too, employed Hebrew to a very large extent. Deeds of sale, contracts, receipts and notes of indebtedness were more often than not drawn up in Hebrew. Even if they were not couched in Hebrew, they were certainly written in Hebrew characters, for up to our own time, almost, Jews wrote the vernacular in characters of the Hebrew alphabet. Thus Rashi wrote several hundred French-Provencal "glosses" in his commentaries in Hebrew script, while the luminaries of the "Golden Age of Hebrew Literature" wrote Arabic with Hebrew characters. The Jews in Spanish-speaking countries wrote their vernacular in Hebrew characters, and the German Jews did the same with German. Even when they forsook the Hebrew speech, they still retained the Hebrew script. The Jews of yesterday never completely left the domain of their ancestral tongue.

It is a mistaken notion that Hebrew was a dead language until Eliezer Ben Yehudah restored it to life and spoken naturalness. To be sure, Eliezer Ben Yehudah and his fellow enthusiasts made Hebrew a language "like all the rest." They and their successors, and especially the proficient "Vaad Ha-lashon" (Hebrew Language Board) provided the linguistic material for ordering an ice cream soda in the language of the

Bible and writing Hebrew titles for Hollywood films exhibited in the cinemas of Tel Aviv. This is how it should be, but this does not mean that, before Ben Yehudah and his followers created a modern technological Hebrew vocabulary, Hebrew was "dead." In point of fact, it was far from that.

Throughout the centuries of Jewish homelessness, Hebrew was *the* vehicle of literary creative and scientific-scholarly Jewish expression. There is no Jewish or general theme in the potential orbit of the scholar of the pre-technological era on which volumes in Hebrew are not available. Jews wrote commentaries without number on the Bible and the Talmud in Hebrew; they grappled with the perennial problems of philosophy in Hebrew; they wrote voluminously on mathematics, physics, algebra, geometry, medicine, zoology, botany, astronomy, navigation and nautical instruments in Hebrew; their histories and martyrologies, their memoirs and letters, and their wills and testaments, too, were written in Hebrew. Whenever a Jew of yesterday would commit something to writing, be it a business contract or a moral homily for his children, he almost certainly chose Hebrew as his medium of expression, because it was the language which he mastered perfectly in writing, even if he spoke it only haltingly.

This will seem incongruous to those who, by studying a foreign language, have discovered that the mastery of the written word is much more difficult than that of the spoken word. But to the Jew of yesterday Hebrew was not a foreign language; it was the language in which he lived his better life, as it were. It was not merely the language of his prayers, but also the medium of his thoughts and meditations. The Jew of yesterday, if he was at all literate—there were no actually *illiterate* Jews—read Hebrew and Aramaic works exclusively. Only in the later Middle Ages, there emerged a popular Yiddish literature in response to the needs of those who possessed only an elementary Hebrew training, sufficient to follow the synagogue services.

## VI

Hebrew ceased to be used in everyday speech, except by small sections of our people, about the time when the Second Jewish Commonwealth came to an end. But throughout the ages Hebrew has remained the natural medium of Jewish literary expression. Average Jews of average learning, to say nothing of rabbis and scholars, corresponded in Hebrew exclusively. It was taken for granted that every Jew knew enough Hebrew to understand proclamations of the rabbinate, which were never couched in any other language but Hebrew. When shy *Yeshiva* students essayed their pens, they quite naturally wrote in Hebrew; they simply had no other means of literary expression. Their command of the vernacular was restricted to the vocabulary of the market place.

To be sure, in some countries and during periods of exceptional tolerance to their group, Jewish intellectuals were happily integrated into the cultural scene of the majority population. This integration had disadvantages, however, as it often led to the weakening of Jewish ties and loyalties. Because of widespread linguistic assimilation, Saadia Gaon, Yehudah Halevi and Maimonides, among others, found it necessary to write their philosophical and apologetic works in the Arabic vernacular, so as to reach those of their brethren whose Hebrew knowledge was fragmentary.

In the span of the century and a quarter which opened with the publication of Leopold Zunz's fanfare call on behalf of the cultivation of "The Science of Judaism" (1817) and which came to a close with the burning of the Synagogues and the suspension of all Jewish cultural activities in Germany (November 10, 1938), thousands of books, pamphlets and learned papers on varied aspects of Jewish scholarship had been written by those who followed in the footsteps of Zunz, Graetz, Steinschneider, Frankel and other distinguished pioneers of the *Wissenschaft des Judentums*. Only a fraction of this literature has been translated into other languages. Some of those volumes, printed during the years of the First World War and after, are already crumbling away under the touch of the student. Matter is perishable—we have very few ancient Hebrew manuscripts, and not too many late ones either. Yet all major works written in Hebrew and considered important for Jewish survival by the sound instinct of our people have been preserved. In the Middle Ages, many wagon loads of sacred Hebrew manuscripts, each representing not only a cultural value but also a large fortune, were burned. Yet, the more avidly the Church confiscated and burned Talmud foliants and rabbinic works, the more diligently were they copied and ineradicably inscribed upon Jewish minds and hearts. The perennial truth proclaimed by Rabbi Haninah ben Tradyon was confirmed over and over again: the parchment was burned—but its letters soared on high inviolate.

German Jewry, that is to say those who were German Jewry for some fifteen centuries, has run its course. The history of the Jews of Germany has come to an end. Today there are still large numbers of emigré German Jews who read and speak German, but their children already are estranged from the native tongue of their parents. Who, then, will read the learned and the popular volumes which add up to the imposing edifice of "German Judaica?" Scholars will consult some of those volumes, but already a voluminous and comprehensive

"Jewish Science" literature is emerging in English, which seems destined to take the place of German Judaica in the period of Jewish history we are now entering. There is no future for the vast literature of "Jewish Science" written in German. Its volumes will turn yellow and crumble; they will be forgotten, except for stray references that will become more rare as time will pass.

Ahad Ha'Am's thesis that "our national literature is only that which is written in our national language and does not include what Jews write in other languages" is sound. In his essay, "The Spiritual Survival," Ahad Ha'Am arrived at rather harsh, yet correct, conclusions concerning Jewish literary efforts in languages other than Hebrew. "If Jews write on subjects which concern other nations as well, or other nations only, their books belong to the literature of the nation in whose language they were written," Ahad Ha'Am stated. "If they write exclusively on matters concerning the Jewish people and its national life, they are building for themselves a ghetto in a foreign literature. This ghetto, like any other, is regarded by the native population as of no account, and by the Hebrew community as a merely temporary product, which is not destined to endure as part of its national life ... Thus, for example, we have already nearly forgotten the name of Levanda; his sketches of Jewish life in Russia, which twenty years ago were still among the most popular in Russian Jewish circles, have now very few readers left. But Smolenskin's stories, very similar to those of Levanda in subject, and much inferior to them in ability and taste, are still as widely read and as popular as though they had been written only yesterday. The only reason that I can find for this difference is that Smolenskin wrote his stories in Hebrew, and Levanda his in Russian. This example, which is not unique, proves that the

Jewish nation recognizes as its national literature only that which is written in its own language."

There is no eternity for Jewish cultural and literary expression, except in Hebrew. In the Hellenistic period and, later, in Mohammedan and Christian Spain, there were considerable Jewish literary efforts in the Greek, the Arabic and the Spanish vernaculars. Little or nothing of this literature has come down to us. If Philo's and Josephus' works were preserved it was not so much due to the Synagogue as to the Church. For the progress of Judaism and its survival Josephus and Philo were irrelevant and so our people by-passed them, or rather ignored them.

All of Jewish literature which has stood the test of the millenia and the centuries was written in Hebrew, or a Hebrew-Aramaic idiom dominated by the spirit of the Hebrew language. Jewish books written in other tongues, be it Greek, Arabic, Spanish or German, have never been invested with the peculiar sanctity associated with Hebrew books by whose very touch the Jew is inspired. It is significant that only those medieval philosophical works written in Arabic have influenced Jewish thought that were early translated into Hebrew and subsequently regarded as Hebrew books. Maimonides must have been aware of the certainty of the inevitable and ultimate doom of Jewish books in languages other than Hebrew when, in a letter to his favorite disciple, he deplored that he had written his "Commentary on the Mishnah" and his "Guide for the Perplexed" in Arabic, and informed his friend that he was planning to translate them into Hebrew. Maimonides, who had written these works in Arabic so that those not sufficiently familiar with Hebrew might be instructed and guided by them, eventually came to see that the builders of the Jewish eternity dare not forsake life eternal for temporal advantages.

Jewish history proves conclusively that there is no security for Jews in any country of the Diaspora. Wherever Jews were finally cast out, they had at one time been eagerly welcomed. If Germany were the only country that cast out its Jews, men and women who were completely integrated into the cultural and political life of the German nation, we might perhaps hope that Jews could find security in adoptive homelands. But what has happened in Germany had also occurred centuries before in Persia, Spain, England, France and Poland, that is to say, in practically all countries with representative Jewish population groups.

No country has ever been more to us than a *Nachtassyl*—a stopover, not because we would not call it "home," but because the nations have refused to grant us more, and, in many cases, even this was denied us. And as our adoptive countries, so their languages, too, which we loved and enriched, were inexorably wrested from us in the end.

Jewish survival is bound to Hebrew to an even higher degree than to the Jewish homeland, for Hebrew has always been with us in our territorial homelessness. It has blessed us, under many strange skies, with a sense and feeling of home and belonging, while infusing us with the indomitable will to go on—despite the frustrations and sufferings that are our lot in exile. There can be no Jewish survival without Hebrew! The strengthening of our ties with Hebrew is therefore imperative.

CHAPTER 3

*The Partial Consummation*

I

ZIONISM GROWS organically from Jewish history and so we must turn to the past for guidance to the solution of the many problems besetting Zionism now when it has entered upon its fulfillment. The question which agitates most Jews these days is: "What about *our* relationship to the Jewish State?"

To answer it intelligently, without preconceived notions and prejudices, requires first of all a glimpse at Jewish history. This leads us to discover that the problem of the relationship of Yishuv and Diaspora is anything but new. It dates back more than two thousand years, to the time when the Second Jewish Commonwealth was established by a small group of "Zionists," led by Zerubabel, Ezra and Nehemiah, while the majority of Jews remained by the waters of Babylon and in other focal cities of the ancient Near and Middle East.

As long as the Second Temple stood, and for some eight centuries after its destruction when Eretz Israel Jewry was not even a shadow of its former self, the question of the relationship of Diaspora and Yishuv vigorously agitated creative

Jewish minds. And when, in the sixth century political conditions reduced this question to a mere theoretical speculation, it was yet not muted. On the contrary. The ideological implications of the relationship of *Golah* and *Yishuv* occupied Jewish thinkers most profoundly when there was altogether no practical point in their theoretical discussions.

In modern Zionist literature the controversy of the *mehayevey hagolah* (affirmers of the importance and legitimacy of Diaspora Jewry) and the *sholleley hagolah* (negators of the Diaspora) takes up much space. In recent years, especially, the two camps have become increasingly articulate.

The *Golah* has been the permanent counterpoint of the Yishuv since very early times. As a result, Jewish law and custom evolved already in pre-exilic times (by "pre-exilic" we refer in the present context to the interlude before the Second Destruction) *a modus vivendi* between the Jews of the Diaspora and those of the Homeland. It was a happy relationship, successful and fruitful for both the Diaspora and the Homeland.

The long distance alliance of *Golah* and *Yishuv* was predicated on a few sound and axiomatic premises. They were:

a) The recognition of the equal *human* importance of *Golah* and *Yishuv*.

b) The postulation of the supremacy of Eretz Israel—the country and the soil—over any other country of Jewish settlement.

c) The recognition that "the air of Eretz Israel imparts wisdom." This led to the conclusion that the Jews of Eretz Israel were endowed with superior spiritual faculties—and the authority flowing therefrom—not by dint of their own personal achievement but because of the merit of the Holy Land.

d) The acceptance of special obligations to the *Yishuv* on the part of the *Golah*. The obligations were both material and spiritual, the levying of taxation for the upkeep of the religious institutions of the Yishuv—and submission to the religious authority of its rabbis and teachers.

Alternatives are usually painful and fraught with heartache—and remorse. Fortunately, the juxtaposition of *Yishuv* and *Golah* is not an alternative pressing for an either-or-choice. It is rather a harmonization. *Yishuv* and *Golah* are not two irreconcilable opposites, but two parts of a whole which complement each other. This has been true in the past and is still the case today. The *Yishuv* depends for support in certain areas upon the *Golah*, while the latter leans upon the *Yishuv* in other respects.

Unfortunately this basic fact has been frequently disregarded by Zionist ideologists. The *Golah* cannot be "negated," in the manner of Berdichevsky, Brenner and Klatzkin, for this would mean to sign the death sentence for millions of Jews and for vast and significant areas of Jewish creativeness. Nor can the *Golah* be legitimately "affirmed," as Nathan Birnbaum, the most articulate of the "affirmers" did. The only sound approach to the problem of *Yishuv* and *Golah* is the pragmatic attitude of Ahad Ha'Am. Every Jew is *naturally* a negator of the *Golah*, Ahad Ha'Am argued, for no Jew filled with Jewish awareness can regard exile otherwise than as a misfortune. Individually and collectively, we pray and hope for the redemption from exile. *But* there remains the iron fact that the bulk of the Jewish people are in the *Golah*—so how can we "negate" the *Golah*? Facts cannot be negated—they *exist*. Facts, however, can be changed by actions.

Applied to the problem of *Yishuv* and *Golah* this means that instead of "negating" the *Golah* we must attempt to lift its curse by spiritually integrating Diaspora Jews into the *Yishuv*

THE PARTIAL CONSUMMATION 59

and by carrying something of the spirit of the *Yishuv* and its culture into the Dispersion.

Cooperation between the *Yishuv* and the *Golah* is the only practical solution. Cooperation and mutual sharing, under the terms of which *Yishuv* and *Golah* will contribute according to their respective capacities and receive in keeping with their needs.

This was how *Yishuv* and *Golah* blended into an organic whole in the remote past—and this is how we, the generation of the Third Building, must solve the problem of *Yishuv* and *Golah*.

As most slogans the glib assertion that "history repeats itself" is unprecise. History *never* repeats itself, but men usually react alike to identical challenges. It is therefore beneficial to study the past. It gives one perspective and a vista for comparison. It shows how our forebears solved the problem of *Yishuv* and *Golah* and thus we, too, may find ways and means of coming to grips with its difficulties.

At the present time the bulk of the Jewish people live in the Diaspora. In precise figures, 92% of world Jewry live in countries of the dispersion and 8% are settled in the Homeland. These figures will come as a shock to many, but they need not cause despair. The record of *Yishuv* and *Golah* proves compellingly that the size of the *Yishuv* was unimportant as far as its creative influence upon the *Golah* was concerned. Palestine has always been a small country. When the Jewish people increased and there was no room for expansion, it was inevitable that large numbers of them settled abroad. About the time of the destruction of the Second Jewish Commonwealth (70 C.E.), the Jewish nation numbered between $4\frac{1}{2}$ and 5 million souls, of whom only about one million lived in Eretz Israel. In other words, already before the eclipse of the Jewish State, about 80% of Jewry lived in the Diaspora.

The most optimistic blueprints for the Jewish State do not envision an immigration of more than 2 million Jews over the next ten or fifteen years. In other words, the disproportionate ratio of *Golah* and *Yishuv* will not change much. Even at best we cannot hope for a better "score" than that which obtained at the time of the Second Destruction: 20% of the Jewish world population in the homeland and 80% in the Diaspora.

How did the Diaspora Jews of 1900 years ago fit Eretz Israel into their personal and communal patterns of living? The answer to this question is especially pertinent now when the challenges and impacts converging upon us are similar to those which confronted our ancestors at the time when the problem of the relationship of *Golah* and *Yishuv* first presented itself.

There was then, as there is now, the all-important matter of reconciling the "loyalty" to the Jewish Homeland with allegiance to the country of one's birth. This topic is hotly, though frequently not very intelligently, discussed. The very posing of the question reminds one of the amorous lady who asked her lover whom he would save in a shipwreck, his mother or her, his sweetheart. Such questions cannot be answered.

But this will not keep certain Jews from raising the specter of "dual loyalty." By now even the most stubborn members of the American Council for Judaism should have become aware of the fact that *normal* persons are capable of several non-conflicting loves and loyalties. Only a man emotionally tied to his mother's apron strings will ruin his marriage by a "mother fixation." Normal husbands love their wives while cherishing their mothers. Justice Brandeis merely paraphrased psychological axioms when he stated that an American Jew becomes a better American by identifying himself with Zionism, that is to say, by taking on an additional non-conflicting loyalty and obligation.

It can be argued, of course, that now with the Jewish State on the political map, matters are different from what they were in Brandeis' days, when Zionism meant identification with an idea rather than with a political unit—a country. But this argument holds no water, for the Jewish State is not likely to clash with the democratic nations of the world.

Obviously, the Jews of the *Golah* will take a livelier and more personal interest in the fate of Israel than in that of any other country of which they are not citizens. But this interest and concern will in no way conflict with their loyalty to the country of their birth and citizenship. Our relationship to the Jewish State will probably be very similar to that of the Jews of the Greco-Roman world in the century before the Second Destruction. During this period, the Jews of the Roman-Hellenistic and Parthian orbits enjoyed a large measure of freedom and security. They were ardent Parthian or Hellenist patriots and model citizens of their countries. Yet, at the same time, they regarded themselves as extensions or "colonies," as it were, of the *Yishuv*.

Philo, their most illustrious thinker and spokesman, described the Jews of the Diaspora as "colonies of the Jewish population in Judea." They looked to Jerusalem as their "mother city," while giving their loyalty and devotion to their native cities. The Jews of Palestine and of the Diaspora constituted, according to Philo, one nation. "The unity of all the scattered Jews rests according to Philo on two facts; first, their common racial origin, on which account he describes them by the term 'nation'; second, their common religion, on which account he describes them as a 'universal polity' or a 'divine ecclesia,' that is to say, a number of individual communities, geographically and politically dispersed, but united by a common law, a common form of organized life and a common way of living.... In this conception of Jews as constituting a nation which transcends race and local citizenship, Philo thus formulated a new conception of nationality, one expressed not in terms of race or territory or political government, but rather in terms of religion and culture. Palestine, symbolized by its capital city Jerusalem, was looked upon as the mother country of all the Jews, and this because it was the home from which the various Jewish colonies in the Diaspora had originally migrated and because it had the Temple which was recognized as the center of Jewish religious worship and also because it was the place to which they hoped to return ultimately, when the looked for redemption came" (Harry A. Wolfson).

In other words, Philo and his contemporaries were loyal patriots of their respective countries and cities while looking to Jerusalem, "the spiritual-religious center of the entire Jewish people", for the cultural and religious guidance and inspiration —and for that feeling of Jewish solidarity of destiny which the countries of their birth and citizenship could not give them.

Ahad Ha'Am's philosophy of "cultural Zionism," proclaiming Eretz Israel as the "Spiritual Center" (*merkaz ruhani*) of the entire Jewish dispersion was therefore not an altogether new formulation. It is to a certain extent a paraphrase of Philo's theory of the relationship of *Yishuv* and *Golah*. Ahad Ha'Am compressed into a felicitous formula the history of this relationship over a span of a thousand years during which the Yishuv was the uncontested *merkaz ruhani* of the dispersion. For notwithstanding the fact that from the time of the First Destruction (586 B.C.E.) and throughout the entire period of the Restoration, the bulk of Jewry lived in the Diaspora, the small *Yishuv* was the head, as it were, of all the far flung members of the Jewish people.

## II

An important manifestion of the *Golah's* recognition of the authority of the rabbis and teachers of the *Yishuv* was the payment of the Shekel on the part of *Golah* Jewry. The history of the Shekel, the first democratic tax-system on record, is a fascinating chapter and one which epitomizes the democracy of Judaism. Introduced by Pentateuchal legislation, the Shekel —or rather the Half-Shekel—was the tax every Jew above the age of twenty had to contribute in the early biblical period toward the upkeep of the Tent of Assembly and, later, for the support of the Temple, and, then, for the religious institutions of the *Yishuv*. The Half-Shekel was the only direct tax levied and the indigenous democracy of Judaism speaks from the fact that this levy was exacted from the poor as well as from the rich. The law provides, "The rich shall not give more, and the poor shall not give less than the Half-Shekel, when they make the offering of the Lord." The Half-Shekel was a nominal sum which even the poor could afford. The fact that the very rich were not permitted to give more for this particular purpose proclaimed eloquently that all are equal before God, Who judges man not according to what he *has* but by what he *is*.

The first attestation of the Diaspora's eagerness to be identified with the *Yishuv* is written into the Books of Ezra and Nehemiah. There it is recorded that those who stayed in Babylonia contributed liberally to the building of the Second Temple. After its dedication, the equivalent of the Half-Shekel was levied as a yearly tax for supporting the central Sanctuary of the nation. Even the Priests, exempted from all levies by the Mosaic legislation, and minors, without means of their own, were obligated to contribute the Half-Shekel to the *Yishuv*. In this manner, the sound survival instinct of our people effected the identification of *every* Jew, from the cradle to the grave, with the spiritual and religious center of the nation.

Moreover, the payment of this tax was not left to the discretion of the individual. The Talmudic tractate *Shekalim*, which deals with all the laws and implications of the Shekel, authorizes the community to exact security from those who failed to pay the tax, and compel them to remit double the amount the following year. Every member of the Jewish community had to pay the Shekel for the support of the Temple and, after its destruction, for the academies. The duly constituted Jewish authorities invariably saw to it that this tax was collected.

How eager Diaspora Jewry was to be identified with the Yishuv through payment of the Shekel is attested by the fact that when the Romans decreed that the collected sums were to be turned over to the imperial treasury as the *Fiscus Judaicus*, the Jews submitted to the inevitable decree but raised the same sum all over again for the support of the Yishuv. The Patriarchs (*nesi'im*), upon taking command of the leaderless *Yishuv* after the Second Destruction, organized the Shekel system so perfectly that the proceeds adequately covered the needs of the academies and their students.

Emissaries of the Yishuv chief rabbinate travelled to all countries of the dispersion to see to the proper collection of the tax and its safe conveyance to the Holy Land. If not for the Shekel-tax, the Yishuv could not have maintained its academies—and so the Mishnah and what was reared on this foundation might not have come into being. In other words, the Second Destruction would have been a definitive destruction had the *Golah* not come to the assistance of the *Yishuv*.

We have gone into these details because we believe that a definite system of Jewish taxation will have to be evolved in the Diaspora so as to see the State of Israel through the difficult period of the expansion ahead. The United Jewish Appeal, despite the fact that the bulk of the funds collected is applied to the needs of Israel, does yet not provide that close feeling of identification with the *Yishuv* which was part of the ancient Shekel system. There should be created a special Shekel Union (altogether independent from the present Shekel Boards of the various Zionists groups) for the purpose of mobilizing the Jews of the Diaspora and organizing them for the Shekel-tax payable to the *Yishuv*. This tax should not be "sold" by means of a "charity appeal." It should become the tangible expression of the Diaspora's spiritual-religious identification with the *Yishuv*. This ancient system of taxation may be obsolete as far as details go, but the principle as such is sound.

Another means of the Diaspora's physical identification with the Homeland was the religious custom of making pilgrimages to the Holy City on the Three Pilgrimage Festivals. During the time of the Second Temple, Jerusalem was crowded on Pesach, Shevuot and Sukkot, when large numbers of Jews came to the Holy City from all corners of the Diaspora to offer their sacrifices as prescribed in the Torah. But even after the Destruction of the Temple, the Holy Land, and especially Jerusalem, continued to hold a powerful attraction for the *Golah*. Such eloquent and articulate pilgrims as Nahmanides and Yehudah Halevi expressed not merely their own personal feelings, but the sentiment of the Jewish masses when they proclaimed that their hearts were in the East and that life in the wilderness of Judah's destruction was more agreeable to them than the comfort of their homes and the loving solicitude of their family and friends. . . .

Even as pious Jews continued to pay the Shekel-tax after its official abolition (in some congregations it is still customary to remit the equivalent of a Half-Shekel on Purim, before the reading of the *Megillah,* and dispatch the sum collected to the Holy Land), so the lovers of Zion continued to make pilgrimages to the Land of Splendor (*eretz zvi*), even after the splendor was turned into squalor. Until the era of emancipation and assimilation, practically *all* Jews lived and breathed the spiritual air of the Homeland. The name of the Land was ever on their lips and the love of Jerusalem warmed their hearts. They rose at midnight to mourn for the Destruction, drawing strength and consolation from the mention of the beloved Land and the cherished City.

Thanks to the survival genius of our people, Eretz Israel never ceased to be a living reality. In joy and sorrow, in the drab daily round of life and at its high points of climax, Eretz Israel was interwoven with routine and worship. Thrice daily and after every meal, the Land and the City were remembered. On joyous occasions one prayed for the renewal of the joy of the Land and the City. When tragedy struck, the quest for personal consolation was identified with the collective need for consolation of our people, mourning for the Land and the City.

One cannot turn back the clock and the calendar. There is no use sighing nostalgically for the time when Jews left bare a spot in their houses as "a reminder of the destruction" and rose for *Hazot* (midnight) mourners' services in its commemoration. We shall have to devise new means of identification with the Yishuv, which will imbue our generation with the feeling of oneness with the Land and the City. But some of the old techniques are still adequate. With the easy accessibility of Israel, by sea, air and land, it should not be difficult to "sell" a trip to Palestine to large numbers of Jews who can afford it. At present, a few American organizations are sending a handful of young people to Israel on scholarships, hoping that upon their return they will bring with them a whiff of Hebrew air and diffuse it in the Diaspora. This is an auspicious beginning—but only a beginning. Facilities should be provided for enabling youths of the Diaspora countries to spend at least one of their summer vacations in Israel. With the summer vacation schedule of American schools, it is possible for children to spend six weeks in Israel. This is not at all fantastic. We would like to see some enterprising Jews enter the "vacation business" and take young boys and girls for summer trips to Israel. It also would be worth while were Zionist groups to establish vacation camps in Eretz Israel and make them accessible to campers on scholarships as well as to campers who can pay their way.

### III

Notwithstanding the role of centrality Israel will command in the Jewish world of tomorrow, the *Golah* must not be undervalued, for the bulk of our people will continue in the Diaspora. Only the supernatural resources of the Messiah could achieve the feat of settling our present twelve million Jews (and we are growing!) in Israel's borders, to say nothing of making them acquiesce in this transplantation. To all intents, the Diaspora is here to stay—and we must face this fact squarely. Moreover, the Diaspora is important for its own inherent values, too, and not merely as the reservoir of human material and economic resources for the Yishuv.

Despite its many ties with the *Yishuv*, the Diaspora will have to be independent and stand on its own feet. This is no contradiction in terms. The Golah of the centuries between the two Destructions and that following upon the Second Destruction were closely bound to the *Yishuv*, submitting to its authority as the head of the Jewish people, as it were. But this did not keep the Jews of Babylonia from being supremely creative. There is no basis in facts for the apprehension that the Diaspora is Jewish culturally sterile. In point of fact, the bulk of Jewish culture is the product of the Diaspora. It is important to realize all the implications of this fact. The Babylonian Talmud and many of the Midrashim were created on Babylonian soil. Saadia Gaon wrote in Egypt and in Babylonia, Rashi in Northern France; Maimonides created eternal Jewish values in Spain, Morroco and Egypt. "The Golden Age of Hebrew Literature" had its setting in Spain and the modern Hebrew renaissance first flowered and bore fruit in Eastern Europe.

It is patently untrue that the physical climate of the Diaspora arrests Jewish creativeness. *Of course,* there is a magic link between Land and Nation. *Of course,* we look to the Land as a special stimulus and inspiration. But this in no way minimizes or precludes the creative potentialities of Diaspora Jewry. In the two centuries before the Second Destruction and the two or three centuries thereafter, both the *Yishuv* and the *Golah* were supremely productive. Thus, in the earlier period, while the *Yishuv* was writing the later books of the Hebrew Bible and some of the Apocrypha, the Diaspora was producing other Apocryphical books, the first Bible translation (Septuagint) and the first attempts of Bible exegesis (Targumim and Philo.) Later, when the *Yishuv* academies produced the *Talmud Yerushalmi,* the Babylonian academies reared the *Talmud Bavli* on the foundation of the Mishnah.

The intensive creative spiritual activity of the *Yishuv* did not keep the Jews of the Diaspora from the pursuit of Torah. On the contrary. There was a lively give-and-take between *Yishuv* and *Golah* in the course of which the *Golah* sent to the *Yishuv* not merely the "Shekel of gold," but also the gift of the spirit.

"The secret" of Jewish survival in the two-thousand-years' dispersion is largely centered in the conviction that "when Israel went into exile, the Divine Presence (*Shechinah*) accompanied them." Because the essence of their soul's constitution did not forsake them in the tragic near-eternity of national doom, the cold and hostile countries of exile were yet suffused with the air of the Land where the *Shechinah* is at home.

Diaspora Judaism retained its vigor and creative powers because it was able to build on foreign soil citadels of the spirit that were of the same mold as those reared earlier in the Homeland. Until the time of Moses Mendelssohn, that is to say, until less than two centuries ago, *all* Jews breathed their own spiritual air. Judaism has never hermetically closed itself to trends of other peoples and cultures—but the rod of measure for their evaluation were Jewish standards exclusively . Thanks to this catalytic power, even the foreign elements assumed a Jewish character.

There are some "negators of the *Golah*" who argue that although the Jews of the Diaspora did not sink into intellectual and spiritual stupor, still their cultural creations do not compare favorably with those of Israel on its own soil, such as the Hebrew Bible and the Mishnah. They justify their position saying that Diaspora Jewry excelled in exegesis—commentaries and, again, commentaries, but not in original creations. While it is true that the bulk of Hebrew literature, up to the time of Mendelssohn, was of an exegetical nature, it is not fair to generalize that no novel and original values were created in the Diaspora.

Among the new cultural areas opened up by Diaspora Jews, philosophy (starting with Isaac Israeli and Saadia Gaon) and poetry, liturgical as well as secular (there is a pronounced difference between the "poetry of the Bible," as exemplified by Song of Songs, the Psalms, Proverbs, Job, etc. and the verse of the exponents of the Golden Age of Hebrew Literature in Spain, to say nothing of modern Hebrew poetry which was likewise born in the Diaspora,), are sufficiently important and original to be placed on the same level with the creations of Eretz Israel Jewry in the olden days. Those who hope to raise the honor of the Homeland by deprecating the Jewish values which have been created on foreign soil err sadly.

Sociologists know that, notwithstanding its prime significance for a healthy and balanced national existence, the national territory is the possession a people can most easily do without—provided it retains on the foreign soil its *language*, its *culture* and its *mores, especially those with religious associations,* fostering them with zest and devotion. There is no other nation which has achieved this feat with the same success as the Jews. The law of history is that the loss of country inevitably leads, sooner or later, to the extinction of the national individuality of the nation without a country. The strategy of such great conquerors of antiquity as Assyria, Babylonia and Rome, to which the first and second Jewish States fell victims, was predicated on the premise that the best method of subduing a conquered nation was to deport its leading citizens and upper classes, and fill their places with members of other conquered nations or with occupation forces. Deportation and transplantation proved highly successful in levelling the vassal nations of Babylonia to the Babylonian norm and, later, in the Hellenistic and Roman periods to the Hellenistic, respectively, to the Roman norms. These measures worked everywhere but not with the Jews, for when they went into exile they took along their national beliefs and ideals, and the books that gave expression to them. *Israel went into exile with the Shechinah!* This was the decisive factor. Wherever a Jew pored over the Bible, wherever a Jew proclaimed the *Shema,* wherever a Jew remembered the Land and the City, in any of the many contexts and ways in which they are interwoven with the daily routine, there the *Shechinah* rested and Jewish creativeness could flower.

We Jews are a unique people. This recognition is already written into the early books of the Bible. We are unique not merely respecting our religious-spiritual faculties of cognition, but also in the down-to-earth aspects of daily life. We are a "unique people" and so we managed to build and sustain in all countries of our dispersion abodes for the *Shechinah.*

## III

"Jewish alienation" and "alienated Jews" have become household words of Jewish intellectuals in this country. "Jewish alienation" is a variety of Jewish self-hatred which, unlike the more virulent type of the disease described by Theodor Lessing in his famous book *"Der Juedische Selbsthass,"* expresses itself in passive melancholy over "not belonging" and "having been left out," rather than in aggressive attacks against the "hated" Jewish group to which "the hater" knows and feels himself inextricably bound by "the accident of birth." Up to the era of Emancipation and Assimilation there were no "alienated

Jews." To be sure, there were defections from the fold, for there will always be men who prefer a pottage of lentils to a non-edible birthright. By and large, however, the Jews of the pre-emancipation centuries and millenia were *integrated* Jews, who lived their entire lives, from the cradle to the grave, within the Jewish community, physically as well as spiritually.

It would lead us too far afield to examine the forms of Jewish Self-Government in the Diaspora. But besides the officially and politically recognized central Jewish authority that regulated life in the Diaspora (the *Resh Galutha* and his "court" in Babylonia and the various *Kehilla* systems that operated in all countries with a sizable Jewish population), there was always a supreme religious and spiritual authority—the authority of *Torah*—to which all Jews were pledged in voluntary fealty and from which they derived reassuring and comforting security. Although *physically* in exile, the Jew of the pre-emancipation centuries was not "alienated." He was "at home," wherever a *minyan* congregated and wherever he opened a sacred Jewish tome.

Of course, he longed for redemption from the *physical* exile and its harrowing persecutions. Yet this longing for the Return to Zion was not primarily a yearning for deliverance from the political disabilities of life in Exile. It was equally a surging desire for complete Jewish self-fulfillment, which is possible only when the "three-fold thread" of People, Land and Torah are organically united. It is mistaken to assume that yesterday's pilgrims to Eretz Israel forsook their homes only because of physical necessity. The letters of Nahmanides and Yehudah Halevi, to cite but two of the best-known medieval "Zionists," prove that theirs was not a "crisis motivation." They left the "West" because their hearts were in the "East" and, being sensitive men, they could not endure this split-existence indefinitely. Yet this did not inhibit their creativeness while they were longing in the "West" for the "East." Yehudah Halevi wrote his inspired "Zionides" in Spain (only legend associates "*Tzion Halo Tish'ali*" with his dying hour in Jerusalem.) Neither Yehudah Halevi, nor Nahmanides, nor Moshe Hayyim Luzzatto, nor the galaxy of other Jewish creative minds who journeyed to Eretz Israel for the ultimate consummation created there anything comparable to the quality of their books written in the lands of exile. Possibly they settled in Eretz Israel too late, when their creative powers had become exhausted. These case histories, as well as that of Bialik, the greatest Hebrew poet of modern times, who upon settling in Eretz Israel stopped writing poetry almost completely, goes far to prove that "the air of the Galut" is not inhibiting Jewish creativeness.

If we were to excise from Jewish culture the great books created in the Diaspora, Judaism would be reduced to lamentable proportions. It would be a Judaism without the Babylonian Talmud; it would lack the works of Saadia and Rashi, Gabirol and Maimonides, Alfasi and Yehudah Hasid, the Baal Shem Tov and the Gaon of Vilna, Bialik and Tchernichovsky, Leopold Zunz and Ahad Ha'Am. It would be a Judaism of narrow confines and even narrower vistas, for it would lack the vision of the many hundreds of major Hebrew works and the many thousands of minor Hebrew books.

We have seen that there can be no physical "liquidation" of the *Galut*. But there cannot be a spiritual "liquidation" either, for to liquidate the spiritual "baggage" of the Galut would mean to discard the very values for whose sake *alone* it is worth while to seek a new beginning in the Homeland.

It might be argued, of course, that Galut Jewry, as constituted at present, is not likely to be Jewishly creative in the manner previous Jewish generations were. No doubt, linguistic assimilation, has blunted Jewish creativeness. As Ahad Ha'Am succinctly argued, authentic and eternity-geared Jewish books (and what other authentic Jewish values are there except ideas, expressed in writing as form-giving inspiration for the good life of the nation and mankind?) *must* be written in Hebrew. *But* Hebrew is not bound to Eretz Israel, although there is no doubt that only there where it is the spoken, living language it can unfold to the fullest. Throughout the millenia of the dispersion Hebrew has remained the soul-language, as it were, of our people. Even today Hebrew is far from being a dead language in the Diaspora. In this country, to cite but one instance, Hebrew has gained considerably in popularity and impetus in recent years. Of course, most of that gain is on the elementary level—but it is also a fact that there are about two-score established and budding Hebrew writers born or raised in America. It is also a fact that the branch of Jewish scholarship cast in the traditional mold of the exposition of Jewish law is gaining a strong foothold in this country—and of course this literature is written in Hebrew. Moreover, the prospects for the future are encouraging. The growth of the Jewish Day Schools, with a maximum Hebrew program, augurs most auspiciously for the development of Jewish culture in the authentic Hebrew form on American soil.

Before our eyes the contours of the Jewish world of tomorrow are rising. The Jewish world of tomorrow will have a political center of gravity—the Jewish State. It will have a unified cultural-religious base, anchored in the Jewish State but with ancillary bases in all the countries with Jewish communities. The Jewish world of tomorrow will be dichotomous—there will be the center, the Jewish State, and the periphery, the Diaspora. Neither will aspire to be independent from the other, for their salvation will lie in making the most of their interdependence. The Jewish State will be built not at the expense and sacrifice of the Galut, but with its cooperation and for its strengthening and more meaningful and creative survival.

The Jewish State will not solve—at least not in our and our children's and children's children's time—the problem of Jewish physical homelessness. The bulk of our people will, or rather must, continue as "strangers" on "strange soil." But the Jewish State will solve the plight of spiritual Jewish homelessness as contained in the lack of a national center of Jewish cultural integration. Again, as in the fruitful and creative era of the creation of the Talmud, there will be a strong spiritual center and a strong spiritual periphery—each creating, creative in giving and creative also in receiving, notwithstanding all difficulties.

## IV

The chief hindrance to Jewish creativeness in the Diaspora is that unlike the Jews of yesterday, contemporary Jews are not exclusively guided by and geared to the spirit and temper of Jewishness. They strive for at-homeness in "two civilizations" and extol the ideal of the fusion of Western culture and Jewish culture, to which each will contribute equally and in which neither will be obliterated.

In reality, however, the union of Western culture and Judaism has not materialized, due to the circumstance that Judaism, as a "minority civilization," quite naturally lacks the physical power "to compete" with the dominant "majority civilization." This, of course, in no way implies that Judaism is inferior to Western civilization. It goes to prove, however, that in order to hold its own a civilization must have relevancy, power and *status* as guarantees of other than merely metaphysical compensations and rewards.

The Diaspora was creative until emancipation and assimialation propelled large sections of our people into selling their Jewish birthright for "equality." Jewish history of the past 150 years is in large parts the record of the tragedy of Jewish groups divesting themselves of Jewish peoplehood associations in order to qualify for admission into the community of the emancipating state. It was a *tragedy* because they cut themselves adrift, forsaking their own without yet being fully accepted by "the others." The result was a special type of spiritual *malaise* born of insecurity, despair over rootlessness and the craving for safe moorings.

"Jewish education" is rightly prescribed as the proper cure for the spiritual *malaise* of the modern Jew. But schools for children and adults, even schools with maximal programs, can only foster but not *create* the unique spiritual climate which permeated the pre-Emancipation Jewish community and made it a focal point of Jewish creative energy. The Diaspora can be a setting for Jewish creativeness only when the Jewish community regards its unique distinctiveness as a treasure of value to be jealously guarded.

The exhibits of botanical gardens and zoos prove that flora and fauna from tropical and arctic countries can prosper in our temperate zone. But—and this is of paramount importance—these plants and animals must be provided with a man-made setting of soil, climate and food identical with that of their natural habitats. In the past, the Diaspora managed to be creative by providing for its members an atmosphere of Jewish spiritual self-sufficiency and autonomous purposiveness. In this self-contained setting of ideas, ideals and values, the integrated and well-ordered Jewish community experienced a unique spiritual prosperity. It gave its members physical, spiritual and psychological stamina and filled them with pride in the relevancy of the people of Israel. The modern Jewish community in contradistinction, by "escaping" from the extraneous position created by these preconditions of Jewish creative survival, has lost its soul in flight and, with it, the *raison d'etre* of Jewish continuity.

On the mass level of superficiality it may be possible "to live in two cultures," flirting with both while being wedded to neither. On the level of the intensely creative individual, however, "life in two cultures" is impossible. Jewish history knows of no creative Jew of major stature who "lived in two cultures." Indeed, most creative Jews, especially those in Mohammedan countries and not subjected to the special variety of the Church's hatred of its "mother," owned a solid stock of general knowledge. But, as is well illustrated by the case of Maimonides and his attitude to Greek philosophy, the non-Jewish culture was of peripheral interest, and ancillary, as it were, to the Jewish areas.

Some time ago this writer was consulted by a Jewish author resident in England about a likely American publisher for his latest book on a very specialized Jewish theme. "But please note, I do not want a Jewish publisher for this book." An inquiry as to the motive of the strange request, resulted in this explanation: "The imprint of a Jewish publisher stamps a book as of interest to Jews exclusively."

Such an attitude would have been incomprehensible to a Jew of the pre-Emancipation era. Judaism was never narrowly parochial. Throughout the ages, Jews cherished the hope that the Torah from Zion and God's word from Jerusalem would become the possession of all mankind. But this Messianic expectation did not deflect yesterday's creative Jews from creating for their own people, first and last. Many of the Hebrew commentaries and philosophical works projected by their authors for the spiritual benefit of their own people eventually scored spectacular triumphs among the Gentiles. But this was purely coincidental and unintentional. When Rashi wrote his Bible commentaries he was only concerned with his fellow Jews' need of a tool opening up the understanding of Scriptures. He did not anticipate, to say nothing of hope for or expect, that, through the mediation of Nicholas Lyra, his commentary would become one of the sources feeding the Reformation. Similarly, when Solomon Ibn Gabirol wrote his *Mekor Hayim* (The Fountain of Life) he projected it as an exposition of Jewish ideas and beliefs. That it was subsequently rendered into Latin and became as Fons Vitae a classic of the Catholic Church, which venerated its author "Avicebron," unaware of his identity with Solomon Ibn Gabirol, would hardly have been pleasing to the author.

The disparagement of Jewish distinctive uniqueness and the concomitant loss of Jewish self-sufficiency and self-respect have wrought havoc also in the realm of modern Jewish scholarship couched in the vernacular. Non-Hebraic and non-Yiddish *Jewish* literature of the past century has become *de-Judaized* to an alarming degree. Notwithstanding the great achievements of the *Wissenschaft des Judentums*, it yet remains a fact that, in its entire German phase, it was geared not so much to the spirit and essence of Jewishness as to the apologetic prestige aim of proving that Jewish ethics, Jewish poetry, etc. can hold the candle to other ancient and modern systems of ethics and canons of literature. Graetz's contribution to Jewish historiography, besides other specialized fields of Jewish research, will endure. But, in passing judgment on men and movements of the Jewish past, Graetz applied German standards rather than methods of evaluation oriented by Jewish principles. As a result, he failed to understand the organic and live nexus between the Jewish survival instinct and the Kabbala, the Pseudo-Messiahs, and Hasidism. He was as purblind to the great significance of the East European period of Jewish history as he was insensitive to the dynamic messianic surge of those who *made* Jewish history in the millenia and centuries of the past.

While the early exponents of modern Jewish scholarship studiedly concentrated on "Westernizing" Judaism, to their heirs this "Westernization" came natural. They could not be anything else but apologetic scholars and researchers, writers and pamphleteers pathologicaly concerned with "order," "system" and "the reaction of Christian scholars" to the texts they edited, elucidated and compressed into learned treatises.

The contemporary Western Jew—alas, there are no more East European Jews in the traditional sense—lives from the cradle to the grave in a non-Jewish environment. The United States may not be a Christian nation in the technical scene, but Christianity certainly dominates the American scene. As a result, Christian categories of thought determine much of Jewish expression. It is amazing to what extent Christian terminology dominates our speech and platforms. The ethics and thought world of the American Jew is hardly different from that of his Christian neighbor. As he sees it, Moses and the founder of Christianity taught the same ten commandments and the same golden rule. That Moses preceded the founder of Christianity may add to the hollow "pride in being a Jew," but it does not lead to an intelligent differentiation between the two faiths and the articulation of a distinctive Jewish philosophy.

This levelling of differences constitutes a serious threat to Jewish continuity. Jewish survival is possible only when Jews assume the burden, and thus qualify for the compensations of being "a people dwelling alone." The present trend, however, is to stress alikeness. American Jews do not want to be different...

Obviously, to be "a people dwelling alone" is a difficult assignment for a minority whose safety and prosperity, as the safety and prosperity of all minorities, are bound up with assimilation to the majority, that is to say, the renunciation of distinctiveness. This is the core of the modern Jew's problem and the indications are that he will continue to solve it along the line of ease.

It is not the Diaspora situation *per se* which poses the problem but the modern Jew's reaction to it. "We do not wish to go back to the ghetto," is a gauntlet which is frequently flung out to the Jewish maximalist. To the *average* modern Jew, Jewish distinctiveness and self-sufficiency spell "Ghetto." As a result, the average modern Jew is frustrated in creatively coming to grips with his Jewishness.

Zionist educators and would-be engineers of American Jewish survival have insistently stressed, especially of late, that in order to invigorate our cultural scene, the literary and artistic resources of Israel must be made available to American Jewry to the fullest extent. As it cannot be expected that the rank-and-file of American Jews will be turned into proficient Hebrew scholars, it has become almost an axiom that the literature of Israel must be brought to the English speaking Diaspora in translations.

Reaching for the stars is futile. It is certainly preferable that American Jews read Bialik's poems in an English translation than not at all. It is doubtful, however, whether a five-foot bookshelf of translations from Hebrew literature will appreciably change our spiritual predicament of the renunciation of Jewish distinctiveness. It seems unlikely that Hebrew literature in translation can basically change the prevalent view that the "Jewish civilization" should be an addendum to, but not the dominating force in, the American Jew's personality.

While politically mankind is still far from realizing the "One World" ideal, culturally and religiously the Western nations have long been "One World." They profess the same religion, venerate the same sacred books and recite the same prayers. All significant French, Russian, German, Italian and Spanish books of the past and present are available in English. But does this mean that American readers of the great European books forsake their American pattern of life and thought to adopt French, Russian or German mores? The literary production of our time is so prodigious and the amount of print consumed by the average person—to say nothing of the word diet of the radio—is so staggering that for modern men the printed word is a medium of information and entertainment rather than an incentive of personality and character formation.

Formerly, when book publishing was not geared to book clubs and Hollywood and when there were fewer but better books produced, people read for self-improvement and inspiration. These days inspirational literature—if thus it may be termed—takes the form of self-help books. The prevailing attitude to books as a source of entertainment and information, rather than as a catalyst of new thought, justifies a certain amount of reserve and pessimism respecting the potential effect of Hebrew literature in translation on the authentic Jewishness of the American Jewish community. The most that we can hope to achieve is to arouse in the intelligent American Jew the same interest in Hebrew life and trends which are awakened in him by the reading of translations of European books. A more basic and intimate rapport than sharing Israel's culture by means of translations is called for if American Jewry is to survive creatively—and there is no life without creation, i.e. the propagation of the stock endowment in new and variegated forms of expression.

## V

The central idea of the Kabbala was "Redemption." As a consequence, the Kabbala inspired in the practical deed realm the "Zionist" efforts of the so-called pseudo-messiahs. The Kabbalists conceived of the "National Redemption" which, they held, would automatically bring about individual redemption as consisting of three stages. To quote from Moses Alshach's commentary on Isaiah: "The redemption consists of three stages: The redemption of Israel by means of the deliverance from oppression and death; the redemption of Zion and Jerusalem; and, most important of all, the deliverance of the Divine Presence (*Shechinah*) from the Galut, as it were." Kabbalistic literature proclaimed the unity of God, Israel and Torah as the basic axiom of Jewishness. But it also stressed emphatically another triad: the unity (*yichud*) of the *Shechinah*, Israel and Eretz Israel.

Ahad Ha'Am was not the first to point up the dual nature of the Jewish problem in the Diaspora as "the plight of the Jews" and "the plight of Judaism." In manifold variations, Kabbalistic, Hasidic and rationalistically geared Hebrew literature of the post-Talmudic era elaborates on the urgency of spiritual redemption, i.e. the redemption of the *Shechinah* as the presupposition of the political redemption. Herzl was never more authentically Jewish than when he insisted that the return to Judaism must precede the return to the Land. Rabbi Israel Baal Shem Tov, the founder of Hasidism expressed this thought by counselling his Galut-oppressed brethren to think less about their physical afflictions and worry more about "the Galut of the *Shechinah*." Although there was bitter ideological warfare between the Hasidim and the Gaon of Vilna and his heirs, they were united in the conviction that Eretz Israel held the only solution for the physical Jewish homelessness and the plight of Judaism, i.e. "the Galut of the *Shechinah*." Rabbi Hayyim of Wolozin, the Gaon's most distinguished disciple and, like his master, an uncompromising foe of Hasidism, became an ardent mystic when he focussed his analytical mind upon the problem of Israel's two-fold homelessness. Like the early Kabbalists and the Hasidim, Rabbi Hayyim, too, saw in the Galut of the *Shechinah* the core of the Jewish affliction, and thus he ventured: "If we concentrated in our prayers primarily on sorrowing for the plight of the *Shechinah*, we would deserve to be heard and fully redeemed. However, we are sinning against our own interest by not taking to heart the sorrow of the *Shechinah*, and by praying only for the relief of our afflictions and economic difficulties. This is why we are not helped."

According to the prevailing opinion of the talmudic Sages, "the air of Eretz Israel imparts wisdom." What they meant was that only in the normal national setting of the union of people and land can the Jewish spirit unfold and create the best. Although the same talmudic Sages, and their heirs, were concentrating their efforts on establishing creative Jewish centers in all the corners of the dispersion, they yet never stopped longing for and emphasizing the ideal union of the Land, the People and the Torah. As Ahad Ha'Am, studiedly and reflectively, they were "natural Galut negators" while, impelled by insuperable difficulties and the imperative necessity to insure Jewish survival at all costs and in all circumstances, they accepted the Galut as an inevitable evil. It is therefore no contradiction but rather a harmonization of freedom and necessity that the very architects of the many Jewish fortresses in the Galut looked to Eretz Israel for the replenishment of their spiritual reservoirs.

Men like Nahmanides, Yehudah Halevi, Solomon Alkabetz, Joseph Karo, Isaac Luria, Eliezer Askari, Isaiah Hurwitz, Moses Hayyim Luzzatto, Nahman Bratzlaver, and many of their peers and followers did not "ascend to Eretz Israel" in the hope of adding there to their factual Jewish knowledge and scholarship. It was well known in the Diaspora that Jerusalem and the Holy Land lay in ruins and that the spiritual desolation, too, was great. With the exception of Safed and Tiberias, which in the late Middle Ages became important focal points of Kabbalistic studies, Eretz Israel had no centers of Jewish scholarship to match those in the Diaspora. And yet, the many distinguished pilgrims who came to Eretz Israel echoed Nahmanides' conviction that "consummate purity and absolute holiness can be achieved only in Eretz Israel."

Throughout the ages, Jews settled in Eretz Israel not merely to rebuild the land but also to be rebuilt by it. In the words of a popular song of the Halutzim, *Anu banu artza livnot ul'hibanot ba*—"we have come to the Land in order to build and be rebuilt." Different generations of Jews variously articulated this desire to be restored to Jewish normalcy, but the quest for it was common to all of them. What else but reverence for the soul-restoring quality of the Land made Rabbi Nahman Bratzlaver refer to his teachings from the years before his pilgrimage to Eretz Israel as "vain and wild fruits?"

Rabbi Nahman was poignantly aware of the Galut estrangement of the Jewish spirit from its source of strength centered in Eretz Israel, as may be seen from his prayer: "Merciful and gracious God, may it be Your will that I and all Israel will yearn, long and earnestly desire to come to Eretz Israel soon and very speedily. You know my great personal need, how urgent it is that I dwell in the Holy Land, so as to remedy my immense and profound estrangement from You, and to heal the thick grossness and twistedness of my heart, and the confusion of my mind. For all these reasons I must dwell in Eretz Israel, where the very essence of our holy faith abides. The sum total of everything Jewish is bound up with Eretz Israel, the land which God has chosen for His chosen people, Israel."

Rabbi Isaiah Hurwitz (Shela), the eminent 17th century ethical teacher and pilgrim to Eretz Israel, held that "all the countries are sustained by the substance of Eretz Israel." Considering the origins of Western civilization, which is co-extensive with Christianity, Shela's estimate was an accurate statement. It is equally correct to say that, throughout the ages, the Diaspora has drawn its sustenance from the substance of Eretz Israel. The source of Galut creativeness has invariably been *shechinta bigeluta*, the substance of Jewishness carried from Eretz Israel into all the ends and corners of the dispersion.

The culture of the State of Israel is still aborning. Its "substance" is as yet not clearly defined. But everything points to it that a creative renewal and renewed creativeness are surging forward to the fructifying consummation. Galut Jewry will share in this process or—go under. But this sharing must amount to more than the perusal of translations and the enjoyment of art works made in Israel. It must be infused with the awareness of our *need* of Israel, not because Jewish values cannot be created or appreciated in the Diapsroa, but because the Diaspora has distorted our sense of Jewish values and undermined our self-sufficiency to such an extent that the *Shechinah* can no longer dwell there.

## VI

Relationships of dependence—physical, spiritual or emotional—cannot be easily and completely reversed and recast into a pattern of independence. Even if it could be achieved, this would hardly be an ideal, for the "protest" accentuation would ever remain its principal dynamic momentum. The real alternative to dependence, therefore, is not independence but interdependence, a mutual give-and-take, a community of sharing and responsibility. Our Sages compressed these insights admirably into the formula: *kol yisrael areivin zeh bazeh*—all Jews are responsible for one another.

Zionism is a "historical movement," that is to say, its program is based on the hope of "the renewal of our days as of old." The "historical" character of Zionism was most powerfully demonstrated at the "Uganda Congress," when the movement rejected Herzl's Uganda project with the argument that Zionism is not the quest for a *territory* for Jews but the concerted effort for a new beginning in the Jewish Homeland. Despite its adherence to the basic historical line, however, Zionism has not infrequently flaunted the wisdom of history. Obviously, the past cannot serve as an unfailing guide for future generations. It is dangerous, however, to attempt the solution of *historic* Jewish problems without studying how those who preceded us solved them successfully.

The problem of the relationship of *Yishuv* and *Diaspora* did not newly emerge on May 14, 1948. It dates back more than two thousand years when, as we of today the Jews of the Hellenistic and Babylonian diasporas had to define their relationship to their countries and to the Yishuv, and come to decisions as to their places in the total Jewish pattern and concerning the *Yishuv's* role in keeping the periphery of the Diaspora properly alligned to the center.

The Jewries of the Diaspora outnumbered the Yishuv from the time of the First Destruction, through the era of the Second Jewish State and the following four centuries when Jabneh filled he place and most of the functions of Jerusalem. During this entire period the Yishuv and its duly constituted rabbinical authorities had the final and decisive say concerning all matters pertaining to the religious-cultural unity of *Yishuv* and *Golah,* while the Diaspora Jewries were autonomous in the administration of their local affairs. In due time, however, a large measure of spiritual-intellectual autonomy and independence was achieved by the Diaspora as well. Yet, for the organic integration of all their far-flung groups, Jews continued to look to the leadership of the Yishuv.

Even when the rabbis of the Babylonian Talmud academies emerged as equally proficient, if not superior, in scholarship to their colleagues in Eretz Israel, they still deferred to them in decisions affecting the lives of Jews everywhere. Thus, for instance, the Eretz Israel rabbinate retained the prerogative of the calculation and determination of the calendar and the Holy Days. Long after error-proof methods of calendar calculation had been developed and Babylonia boasted rabbis who, like Samuel, knew the paths of the sky as well as the streets of their native towns, Jews everywhere continued to rely upon the rabbinate of Eretz Israel for authoritative information on the dates of the special days of the Jewish year. It was only when Christian interference made it impossible for the Jews of the Roman Empire—the Yishuv which survived in Eretz Israel after the Second Destruction was under Roman rule—to communicate with Jews abroad, that Hillel II issued the rules guiding the calculation of the calendar. Only then the spiritual leaders of Babylonian Jewry assumed the responsibility for the calendar. Still, as late as the tenth century, an Eretz Israel rabbi, Ben Meir, challenged the Babylonian Gaonim in this realm and it took the acumen of no less a man than Saadia Gaon to defend and uphold their authority.

The human factor can never be entirely eliminated from human affairs. Jealousy and competition inevitably becloud the interaction of groups and individuals. There was also a certain amount of rivalry between the *Yishuv* and the *Golah* of olden days. It expressed itself in the *Yishuv's* bid for recognition as the head of the Jewish people, as it were, while the Golah, eager for independence and self-sufficiency, strained at the leash of its dependence on the Yishuv. Still, this rivalry between *Yishuv* and *Golah* was beneficially fruitful by contributing to the survival of Judaism. For had a new Jewish center not been established in Babylonia, during the centuries when the Yishuv was still spiritually intact, the final eclipse in the Homeland might have spelled the end of the Jewish drama.

As *Yishuv* and *Golah* are constituted now it would seem that a certain amount of spiritual authority should voluntarily be vested in the *Yishuv*. This does not imply that American Jews should take orders from Tel Aviv. Good judgment, however, dictates that our *Golah*, which is after all tragically estranged from organic Jewishness, defer in certain realms to the Yishuv because it thrives in a 100% Jewish climate. Naturally, this will not keep the *Golah* from evolving its own expressions of Jewish experience, but it will bring a certain basic unity and coordination, though not uniformity, into the Jewish world. Although the *Golah* should look to the *Yishuv* for the enrichment of its Jewish spiritual-intellectual climate, there need not be a slavish *dependence of the Golah* upon the *Yishuv*.

The *Golah* will look to the *Yishuv* also for the sorely needed authentic and tradition-attuned interpretation of Jewish law in terms of the needs of *our* generation. But this again does not rule out the possibility of the evolution of *Halacha* (and the very name *Halacha,* which is derived from a root signifying "to go, to proceed, etc." points to what it is meant to be) in the *Golah*. Jewish law is a composite of "Palestinian Halacha" and "Babylonian Halacha" and, significantly, they grew side by side.

The Babylonian *Golah* of the centuries after the Second Destruction evolved numerous customs and observances differing from those of the Yishuv. There were altogether some fifty differences between Eretz Israel and Babylonian Jewish observances in the centuries when the Talmud was in the making. For example, the Jews of Eretz Israel would be standing during the reading of the *Shema,* while Jews in Babylonia would remain sitting. In Eretz Israel, the full mourning ritual was observed even for an infant of only one day, while the Babylonian Jews did not ritually mourn infants who had died before their thirtieth day. In other mourning customs, too, the Babylonian Jews were less exacting than the *Yishuv*. Eretz Israel Jews refrained on the half-holidays (*Hol Hamo'ed*) from strenuous work—in Babylonia there were no such restrictions. Generally, the Babylonian Rabbis tended to be lenient in areas where Galut conditions made observance difficult, if not impossible.

Obviously, the differences in minor observances were not sufficiently important to set the Jewries of Eretz Israel and Babylonia apart. They merely enabled them to cope with their environments. Nor must it be overlooked that the Rabbis who sanctioned certain deviations from the customs and observances of the Yishuv were—the Makers of the Talmud. It is mistaken to believe that Judaism is averse to "change." In point of fact, up to, and in our time, too, traditional Judaism is in flux and evolution. There is no opposition to "change," but only to "reform" not based on the fullness of Torah knowledge and authority.

At the time when Rabbi Yehudah Hanasi put the finishing touches to the Mishnah, Rav established the Yeshiva of Sura (ca.200), which in a remarkably short time led to the fullest development of Jewish scholarship in Babylonia. But, simultaneously, the Eretz Israel academies continued their activities. Both, the contributions of the Babylonian and the Palestinian academies were gigantic, but there was a marked difference in their methods and, consequently, there is a marked difference in their legacies, the Palestinian Talmud and the Babylonian Talmud.

The Palestinian Rabbis excelled in *Aggada,* the Babylonians in *Halacha.* There is no point in trying to determine the cause of this phenomenon. And it is mistaken, to say the least, to make a case for the superiority of the Babylonian Rabbis because of their predilection for the abstract-logical realm of law, in contradistinction to the Palestinian Rabbis who emersed themselves in the poetic depths of folklore. What matters is that both *Yishuv* and *Golah* were creative and in different realms. What matters even more is that in due time wise judgment defeated jealousy, so that each group looked to the other for expert guidance in its speciality. Notwithstanding the pride of the *Yishuv* and its conviction that "a small group of students of the Law in Eretz Israel is preferable to the Great Sanhedrin abroad," and despite the fact that decisions of even one authoritative Rabbi of the Yishuv were automatically accepted by Babylonian Jewry, when weighty legal problems were on the agenda, the Rabbis of the Yishuv would send to Babylonia for expert opinion. Thus, for instance, Mar Ukba, the eminent Sage from Babylonia was consulted by the Sanhedrin at Tiberias, and other leaders of the Babylonian *Golah* were similarly called upon. Yet this did not affect the respect in which Babylonian Jewry held the Yishuv because of its organic connection with the Land.

In the past, *Yishuv* and *Golah* were not *in*dependent but *inter*dependent. Their correlation was organic and based upon the premise that the connection with the Land gave the *Yishuv* a certain spiritual preeminence which, in turn, elicited the voluntary deference of the *Golah* to its authority.

It would seem that in the era of the third Jewish commonwealth, too, the relationship of Israel and the Diaspora must take the form of an *inter*dependent exchange and correlation, under the terms of which both *Yishuv* and *Golath* will give, receive and share according to their respective capacities and needs.

## VII

THE CONTROVERSY on the place of "religion" in the Jewish State is of more than mere academic interest now when religious Zionists demand that "the Torah become the basis of the constitution of the Jewish State," while Labor and General Zionists insist upon complete separation of religion and state, as a guarantee of democracy.

It is a truism that modern Jews live spiritually, and not only physically, in a Christian climate. We breathe the Christian air and so, despite our Jewish "island within," we think and speak in Christian images and terms. It this were not the case, the problem of the place of "religion" in the Jewish State would not be acute, for the juxtaposition of "religion" and "state" is altogether foreign to Judaism. The much-hailed "democratic achievement" of the separation of Church and State is, to the Jew and translated into the Jewish realm, an illogical abstraction, for the separation of religion and state subverts the basic facts of Jewish existence and survival.

To be a Jew means to belong to a people that achieved and sustained nationhood by means of a religious culture. Whatever else Judaism be, it is, first of all, the *national* religion of the Jewish people. This does not imply that Judaism is narrowly chauvinistic and lacking in universalistic vistas and hopes. From the beginning, our Prophets and teachers were infused with the conviction that the ethical truths of Judaism are meant to be the common property of mankind. Toward this end, a special legislation was devised, consisting of seven basic ethical rules by whose observance the non-Jew can qualify as a "Son of Noah" and claim his share in the world-to-come.

The religious and the national spheres are inseparable in the Jewish realm. Each and every "religious" observance and law has national significance, and each and every national occasion is suffused with "religious" associations. Is there a dividing line between the purely national aspects of Passover and its religious-spiritual associations? Can one delimit the religious and the secular elements of the Sabbath? Obviously, the dietary laws are "ritualistic," yet can their contribution to Jewish national survival and consciousness be overestimated? Ahad Ha'Am was far from being a "religious Jew." He knew, however, that "more than Israel has preserved the Sabbath, the Sabbath has preserved Israel."

The attempt to separate "Jewish religion" from "Jewish nationhood" bespeaks alienation from Jewish thinking. It is

## THE PARTIAL CONSUMMATION 93

proof of the sway of Christian concepts in our midst to the extent that, even when we are about to shape anew our destiny, we remain under the curse of "slavery in freedom."

Th separation of Church and State was the inevitable consequence of the Church's attitude to the temporal powers. Christianity started out with the claim to universal rule and sway over all of mankind. The early Church stepped into the void left by the decline and fall of the Roman empire. It inherited its ambition to supplant national territorial loyalties by a supra-national loyalty. That Rome claimed this loyalty for Caesar and the Church for "Christ's Vicar on earth" made little difference as far as national self-determination was concerned.

Rome failed and could not maintain its totalitarian sway. But the Church managed for a considerable span of time "to rule the world." From the middle of the fourth century to the Reformation, that is to say, for over a thousand years the Vatican was the uncontested ruler. Emperors and kings ruled with the consent of the Pope. If they rebelled, they found themselves on the road to Canossa. The controls of the Western world were switched in Rome.

The world which was ruled by the Vatican was a realm of one religion—Catholicism. It established a totalitarian rule never equalled since, not even by the Nazis. All men had to profess Christianity—or be damned in *this* world. There were many forms of damnation and all of them were visited upon the Jews, the only organized "opposition" to the Church.

Then came the Renaissance. Men harked back to the spiritual freedom of antiquity. The era of the great discoveries did not merely lead to the discovery of new continents, but also to the rediscovery of the individual and his right of self-determination. Men began to rebel against the fetters imposed upon free thought by the Church. They rose against the Catholic brand of asceticism which decried the joy of the senses as wicked.

The time was ripe for Luther, and he succeeded. The might of Rome was broken and a new day dawned. No longer did kings and princes bow to the Pope. No longer were the political destinies of a dozen countries decided in the Vatican. National self-determination became the slogan of the Reformation. Henceforth the national ruler, and not the Pope in distant Rome, made the law! It was a great gain, no doubt, but there remaied a bleak spot: the individual conscience remained fettered, for the principle which regulated the relationship of the individual to state and church was *eius regio eius religio*— the religion of the ruler is *eo ipso* the religion of the population of his realm. Men continued to be persecuted on account of their beliefs, although Protestant religious intolerance never equalled that of the Catholic Church.

Then the Age of Reason dawned and in its wake followed the French revolution. Religion was pilloried as a force of dark superstition and government was "emancipated" from its sway. In the first triumphant surge of the French Revolution even the Christian calendar was abrogated. The "Separation of Church and State" was enthroned supreme.

Separation of Church and State is, in historical perspective as well as factually, a protest against the militant aggression of the Catholic Church directed against all who dare dispute its claim to universal and absolute domination. According to Catholic doctrine, temporal rulers derive their authority from the Pope. "The Pope can do what he wants" was a current adage in the Middle Ages—and the Popes fully lived up to it.

Separation of Church and State became an issue of democratic survival, because the Catholic Church continued to press for recognition as State Religion in all Christian countries. In the Encyclical *Immortale Dei*, Pope Leo XIII stated in 1885: "States cannot without crime act as though God did not exist, or cast off the care of religion as alien to them or useless, or out of several religions adopt whichever they please, but they are absolutely bound to the worship of God in the way that He has shown to be His will." The implication, of course, is that rulers and their subjects may not follow the religion "they please" but must confess Catholicism. There is no other way of dealing with claims of this sort than—denial by means of an institution. And "Separation of Church and State" is the institution opposing Catholicism's, or any other religion's, interference with self-determination in the realm of religion.

The Catholic Church has remained the implacable foe of democracy. It is no accident that the Vatican has accommodated itself with such ease to Fascism at home and abroad. "Authority" is the Catholic ideal and "authority," as interpreted by the Church, means spiritual submission to "superiors."

In the Encyclical from which we have quoted, Leo XIII, also militated against "that fatal and deplorable passion for innovation" which led to the promulgation of new principles. "Amongst these principles," the Encyclical continues, "the chief one is that which proclaims that all men, as by race and nature they are alike, are also equal in their life; that each is so far master of himself as in no way to come under the authority of another; that he is free to think that no man has any right to rule over others. In a society founded upon these principles, government is only the will of the people.... And since the people is said to contain in itself the source of all rights and of all power, it follows that the State does not deem itself bound by any kind of duty towards God; that it makes no public profession of religion; that it does not hold itself bound to inquire which of the many religions is the only true one, nor to prefer one religion to the rest, and to show it special favor."

"Individualism" was branded as evil by Pius XI as recently as 1931, in the Encyclical *Quadragesimo Anno*. "Individualism" is in Catholic interpretation synonymous with freedom of speech. Catholicism has never relinquished its opposition to freedom of expression. Even in its own inner circle, no opinion may be expressed unless *nihil obstat,* as "duly constituted" hierachical authority defines it.

This cursory inquiry into the Catholic attitude to the state and, especially, to the democratic foundations of the United States, explains the prevalent apprehension of governments not pledged to uphold "Separation of Church and State." In truth, however, this Separation is little more than a prophylactic measure against assaults upon religious freedom. It is not a positive ideal. There is no independent value in the Separation of Church and State. All it does is—remove an obstacle. This is no small matter, of course, for all that is subsumed under modern thought, literature, art, music, etc. could not have come into being without the emancipation of the indidual from the tutelage and the domination of the Church.

The Churches, and not merely the Catholic Church, have not readily and complacently accommodated themselves to this restriction of their sway. The current American scene provides ample proof that the various Protestant denominations, as well as the Catholic Church, are eager to regain lost ground. President Truman's matter-of-fact statement that "America is a Christian nation" proves that even our American variety of Separation of Church and State is rather superficial. Separation of Church and State was born of the needs of the individual in Christian society. Its presuppositions lie in Christian history and it is exclusively fitted to the Christian climate.

## VIII

Those who suggest Separation of Religion and State as the norm for the Jewish State attempt to graft something utterly foreign to the Jewish spirit upon Israel. Separation of Religion and State is an antidote to Christian totalitarianism. What purpose, then, is it to serve in the Jewish State? Already in the days of Solomon's monarchy, some three thousand years ago, the religion-centered Jewish State was free from religious intolerance. The historical books of the Hebrew Bible attest that the Jewish State always had contingents of foreign residents, who enjoyed full equality. Jewish law guarantees the *ger* (foreigner) all basic human and political rights. As a result, there never was felt a need for delimiting the religious authority.

The extent to which "the stranger" was considered the *human* equal of the Jew may be gauged from Solomon's prayer at the dedication of the Temple. He did not merely petition that Israel's prayers be heard, but also asked that God answer the prayer which "the stranger" will utter in Israel's sanctuary. Occasionally this tolerance led too far, thus, for instance, when Solomon built idolatrous shrines and altars for his foreign wives. It underscores, however, the fact that a religiously oriented government need not be "intolerant." The religious quality of the Jewish State in the past did not deteriorate into religious totalitarianism. On the contrary, it gave rise to a legislation which guaranteed to the fullest the liberties of "the stranger," who benefitted from the "Jewish religion" without being obliged to confess it.

The broad tolerance of Judaism obviates the need for separation of religion and government. Is it then conceivable that the Jewish State will interfere with the religious freedom of its Moslem and Christian minorities? Separation of Religion and State is in place only where there is danger that either of the two will invade the realm of the other. Such an over-reaching, however, is altogether unthinkable in the Jewish sphere, for here nation and religion are identical. There simply cannot be a clash of Jewish national and Jewish religious interests! They are entwined and interlinked, so that it is impossible to say where "religion" ends and "nationalism" begins. Up to our own time, almost, the Hebrew prayer book was the most important tract of Jewish nationalism. Could "secular" Zionism have come into its own, if Jews had not prayed for two thousand years for the return to Zion ? Could Jerusalem in ruin and ashes have fired the imagination of our people, if there had not been on our lips the cry, *Leshanah haba'ah bi-Yerushalayim?*, which was sounded not merely on the "national" festival of Passover but also on the "purely religious" Day of Atonement?

"Jewish culture" attests the organic fusion of the national and religious components. Is it possible to separate the "religious" from the "national" parts of the Bible ? Is there a "secular Jew" who would want to excise Rashi's commentaries from "Jewish culture" because of their predominant "religious" topics? For that matter, can the national note be isolated from religious associations in modern Hebrew and Yiddish literature? Is it possible to draw a line between the national and the religious elements in Peretz's stories and Bialik's poems?

Judaism's greatest asset is its organic continuity. There

is no departmentalization in the authentic Jewish realm. The Jewish definition of God, as Unique Unity, quite naturally led to a unitarian interpretation of the world and Israel's place in it. But this blueprint does not provide for a totalitarian world governed by Israel and its law. It merely envisions a time when the basic Jewish program of peace, justice and humaneness will be realized by all men. The motto of Judaism has always been: "Let all peoples walk in the ways of their gods, and we shall walk in the ways of the Lord our God." A nation thus committed need not enact "legal separation" of religion and government, for the espousal of its national religion will not turn its goverment into a tool of armed intolerance.

## IX

To separate "religion" from the "government" of the Jewish State is impossible, for Judaism is not a religion in the Christian sense. With Jews, religion is not a "private affair," but the nation's cultural-spiritual assertion. The ideal Jewish prayer is not uttered in secluded privacy but recited in the community of the Minyan. Every Jewish religious act has Jewish national significance. Individual salvation, as Judaism interprets it, is merely an aspect of the national redemption. Judaism is far from underestimating the worth of the individual. On the contrary, it considers one life the equivalent value of the collective life of the nation. But Jewish wisdom also knows that the individual can only fulfill himself in the nation, even as the nation must become fused with and see itself as a part of mankind, while yet remaining true to its own self.

Secular Judaism is an abstraction of the wishful imagination. All of authentically Jewish culture, not merely of the past but of the present as well, is infused with religious motives.

A secular Jewish State would be a freakish monstrosity, for it would resuscitate the Jewish national body without the spirit. Unless the Jewish State will be not merely a country for Jews but a base for Judaism, in its fullest connotation, one may well question whether the game is worth the candle.... Throughout the ages Jews have looked to their national restoration as a healing of the spirit restored to creative vitality in a Jewish State patterned along Jewish lines. Can this be achieved in a setting that is foreign to the spirit of the nation and its values?

What is needed, then, is a *Jewish definition* of the relationship of religion and government. Fortunately, our history abounds in precedents proving that the law and government of the Jewish State can be identified with the essence of Jewishness, i.e., the awareness of the religious basis of Jewish nationhood, without prejudicing in the least the rights of religious minorities. Obviously, the Jewish State will not compel its citizens to observe the Sabbath in the Shulchan Aruch fashion, nor will it presume to dictate their diets by enforcing state-wide observance of the dietary laws. But the Sabbath should be the official day of rest in the Jewish State and the dietary laws should be the guiding principles of the pertinent sections of the sanitary food code.

It would be calamitous were the government of the Jewish State to interfere with the private lives of its citizens. Let those who wish "desecrate" the Sabbath and the dietary laws. But the government of the Jewish State must be the official guardian of Jewish law. The tenor of the Jewish State must be Jewish. Its calendar must be the Jewish calendar and its festivals the holy days of this calendar. Sabbath must be the official day of rest and it must be the Jewish *Shabbat*, and not a version of the Christian Sunday.

There will be room in the Jewish State for Jews of all

ideologies, for "religious Jews" and "secular Jews." Although the Jewish State may not endorse certain philosophies espoused by its citizens, it will uphold their right to profess and propagate them. In other words, the Jewish State will be a democratic state in the Jewish tradition, which enabled the Prophet Nathan to reprove King David and point at him an accusing finger: "Thou art the man." It will be a state built on the Jewish principles of human equality and democratic freedom, where men will be free to think and express their thoughts. It will be a state where freedom of religion will not be a mere phrase but the pattern of life.

"We are a nation solely by virtue of the Torah." Saadia Gaon's definition of Jewish nationhood remains valid also today. Without our culture, which is religious and ethnical in equal parts, we cannot qualify as a nation. We are a people because, after nearly two thousand years of territorial homelessness, the *Torah*, in all its many connotations and their associations, remains the *terra firma* of our national existence. All this has no bearing whatsoever upon "belief." The importance which certain Jewish groups and their leaders attach to "belief" is another sympton of our assimilation to Christianity. Belief is the touch-stone and acid test of Christianity. One becomes a Christian by "believing in Jesus." To be a Jew, however, is not a matter of belief—it is an act of historical affirmation and national identification. We have survived as a religious community and as a nation. Only thus could we hold on to life—either bond alone would have been too weak. We entered the stage of history as a national-religious people; we wrote history as a national-religious people; we survived exile and persecution as a national-religious people; and our hope for the future, too, lies in the fusion of Jewish nationhood and Jewish religious consciousness.

The idea of "Separation of Religion and State" is foreign to Judaism as the differentiation between "life" and "religion." Judaism cannot conceive of "religion" apart from "life," as little as it can differentiate between the "national" and "religious" components of Jewish culture. They are of the same woof and warp.

There is no likelihood that the religious emphasis and orientation of the Jewish State will give rise to conditions similar to those that led to Separation of Religion and State in the democracies. A Jewish government, guided by the principles of the *Torah*, will coerce neither its citizens nor the members of minority groups in the Jewish State. The constitution of this government will be informed by the spirit which motivated the Jewish proclamation: "The righteous of all the nations will share in the life to come."

"Religion" cannot be "separated" from the government of the Jewish State. On the contrary, this government must be guided by "Judaism" in its organic wholeness.

"The return to the Jewish country must be preceded by the return to Judaism." Herzl's program also implies that upon returning to Eretz Israel, we forsake the foreign ideas and concepts of the Galut. One of these alien fetishes is the Separation of Church and State. Judaism is *not* a "Church" and "Church" categories cannot be applied to it. The formula "Separation of Church and State" falls deaf on Jewish ears. It is meaningless in the realm of a nation consolidated by faith and of a faith which is the mark of identification with the nation.

CHAPTER 4

## Toward a Definition of the Jewish Genius

### I

"JEWISH ART" ranks prominent among the panaceas prescribed by many would-be healers of the spiritual deficiency diseases afflicting the modern Jew. "Jewish art," it is argued, if given half a chance, will stir and arouse the modern Jew to identify himself with the Jewish past and present on which the Jewish future hinges.

Upon closer scrutiny, however, the popular cult of "Jewish art," is discovered to be but another symptom of the assimilation which Ahad Ha'Am, succinctly and inimitably, termed "slavery in freedom." This type of assimilation is characterized by the levelling of the distinctive characteristics of Jewish culture. The ideal of its proponents is "let us be like all the nations." And as art plays a very important role in Western civilization, the slavery-in-freedom type Jew feels impelled to apologize for "the paucity of Jewish art" by pointing up "the villain," i.e. the second commandment, and to adduce "evidence" that, notwithstanding "the crippling effect" of this villain, Jews have always contributed to art.

The apologetic devotees of "Jewish art" mean well, no

doubt. Their arguments, however, are hollow because they ignore the significant circumstance that the second commandment was the result of the primary Jewish rejection of art, and not its cause. In point of fact, the basic tenor of Jewish culture is antithetical to art as commonly defined. In the biblical period our ancestors concentrated on literary creation of a special type rather than on the art efforts in which their Egyptian, Babylonian, Hittite, Phoenician and other neighbors excelled. Their preoccupation with the creative word in its ethical connotations was not due to the second commandment, but to the distinctive twist of the Jewish soul which sensed in this commandment spirit of its spirit.

Art is static, unchangeable for all eternity. Once the artist has given his painting or statue the final touch, the object of art is forever removed from the impact of life and change. Moreover, the limitations of the materials with which the painter and sculptor work lend themselves only to the fixation of one moment, arresting this moment in eternal immutability. Art, as Lewis Mumford has shrewdly observed is "life arrested."

As the Jew sees it, "life arrested" is death. Not *being* but *becoming* is the Jewish ideal of perfection. God is *ehye asher ehye,* not static *being* in the present but *dynamic becoming* and unfolding in the future. Not static *perfection* but dynamic *perfecting* is man's destiny and choicest portion, as Judaism envisions it. "The *tzaddikim* rest neither in this world nor in the world-to-come but proceed from valiant achievement to valiant achievement."

All civilizations distinguished by notable success in art evolved their metaphysics by gazing nostalgically backward to a "Golden Age." Their fondest hopes were centered in the return to a "Paradise Lost" or, as in the case of the Egyptians, in "the arresting of life" on the pinnacle of physical might and splendor.

Altogether different is the Jewish version of *aharit hayamim,* which is inadequately rendered into English as "the end of the days." Not complacent indolence and gross enjoyment of wine, women and song, but zealous exertion for "the word of God" dominate the panorama of the ideal future as limned by the Hebrew Prophets. Respecting after-life, Jewish folklore, deposited in the Aggadah of the Talmud and the collections of the Midrash, spun fantasies centered in a heavenly banquet with Leviathan as the *piece de resistance.* Among the great molders of Jewish thought, however, there was none who did not insist or imply that "in the world to come there will be neither eating, nor drinking, nor procreation." This dictum should not be taken as proof that Judaism is ascetic. On the contrary, it disparages asceticism in the strongest possible terms. It insists that man claim his due portion of physical joy and castigates those who reject the good things of this earth which rejoice the flesh. But, and this of of paramount importance, Judaism is ever cognizant of the evanescence of physical joy. Indeed, the Sages conceded that "these three approximate the future world's delight, namely: the Sabbath, the sun and the embrace of man and woman,"—but they did not equate these earthly pleasures with the bliss of the world-to-come which consists in the enjoyment of the spiritual light of the nearness of God (*siv hashechinah*).

Judaism neither disparages nor distrusts matter. It knows, however, its limitations. Matter *is* destructible. Moreover, matter is "heavy" and all that is created of it is bounded by its limitations of perishability and static localization. The sober inventory of the limitations of matter—and proof that this inventory was taken by all generations of Jews is found in

Hebrew literature and, especially, the Bible—inspired the quest for a more satisfactory medium and vehicle of creative effort. The quest led to the discovery of the word as the most adequate medium of creative endeavor, for the word is imperishable and universal. Light and winged, as it were, the word is not circumscribed by time and place. This is why only the word is the adequate medium for the creativeness of a people on the road to Eternity.

The recognition of the superiority of the word over matter is at the root of the paucity of Jewish art. Jews became the People of the Book intentionally and purposively. The word was their first choice of perennial ardor, and not a makeshift substitute. The assertion of the superiority of the word over matter is perhaps most powerfully and pathetically, too, sounded in the account of Rabbi Hanina ben Tradyon's martyrdom. Sentenced to death by the Romans for the defiance of the prohibition of Torah study, the executioners wrapped him in a Torah scroll, the *corpus delicti,* and burned him as a living torch. And such was the fortitude of the Sage that *he* consoled the disciples who broke down watching his agony. "Only the sheets of the scroll are consumed," he cried amidst the flames. "The letters soar into space!"

This wisdom did not spontaneously erupt from the death-seared martyr. It was the age-old wisdom of his people, the wisdom Israel acquired in Egypt amidst the Pyramids and towering statues of the Pharaohs. For Judaism is essentially a "protest movement." Throughout the Pentateuchal code there occurs the refrain "because you were slaves in Egypt" you shall do thus and not thus. A principal motivation of Jewish law and ethics is the protest against un-Jewish ways and morals. The Pentateuchal code shows that the Hebrew slaves were their Egyptian masters' most penetrating critics.

They knew the Pyramids and temples, the glory of Egyptian art, for what they really were—"life arrested" at the sacrifice of life and its meaning.

## II

Archaeologists conducting excavations in Palestine invariably are disappointed by the paucity of the material remains of ancient Israelite culture. In view of the literary achievements and the depth and acumen of ancient Hebrew ethics, the crudity of the few artifacts of indisputably Israelite origin is extremely puzzling. In comparison with the yields of excavations in Egypt and Babylonia, or in Palestine proper but of foreign make, the simple crudeness of ancient Hebrew technique is puzzling. If not for the literary heritage of ancient Israel, one would have to conclude, on the strength of its material legacy, that the Hebrews of old were a people of uncivilized nomads, insensitive to the beauties of life and culture.

Even the most radical Bible critics and the most rabid Jew-haters could not venture to propound such a thesis without exposing themselves to ridicule. The Hebrew Bible, our "patent of nobility"—to borrow a felicitous phrase of Solomon Schechter's—demonstrates conclusively that its creators belonged to the spiritual aristocracy of all times.

The real cause of the archaeologists' disappointment who hoped for worth while remains of material culture and civilization under the rubbish of the "Tels" of Palestine is that the Jews, from their very first beginnings, concentrated on the "voice" and neglected the "hands," to wit the antithesis of the "Voice of Jacob" and the "Hands of Esau." As a result, the "voice" spoke the books of the Prophets, the Psalms—and all the spiritual and ethical glory of the Bible, while the "hands," as the hands of all those who fashion the world out of their minds, became increasingly awkward and unskilled.

One of the most characteristic Jewish traits is the disdain for the artistic product of the "hands." Thus the Midrash has it that it was extremely difficult for God to teach Moses the details of the making of the Menorah for the Tabernacle; yet, in purely spiritual and legal lessons Moses proved invariably a talented pupil.... With equal candidness the Bible records that King Solomon appealed to Hiram, king of Tyre, for "servants" because "there is none among us that has skill to hew timber like the Phoenicians." The Bible critics who are zealously charging the ancient Hebrews with "unacknowledged" borrowing, should reflect on the integrity of the Hebrew conscience which did not hesitate to admit that the Temple, the Holy of Holies of the nation, was built with the collaboration of foreign workmen, namely: "And Solomon's builders and Hiram's builders and the Gebalites did fashion them (the stones of which the Temple was built), and prepared the timber and the stones to build the house."

From the dawn of history, even until our time, Jews, rooted in the tradition of their people, have been rather disdainful of the material culture, which we term "art and technique." The Hebrew ethical genius, which discovered virtually all of the social and ethical truths that man will ever know, perceived early that beauty embodied in matter is vain and—often wicked.

In antiquity (and in the Middle Ages, too) art was primarily religious in character. The statues were statues of the gods, or of the kings worshipped as gods. The temples and their magnificent splendor were dedicated to the glory of the idols, and the Egyptian Pyramids, representing the blood and sweat of an enslaved and exploited country, likewise owed their origin to idolatrous ideas of the hereafter that required the Pharaoh and the mighty men of his realm to amass in this life the gold, the raiments and the food they would need in the netherworld.

The cult of the many deities supplied the *raison d'etre* for ancient oriental and antique art. By prohibiting this kind of worship, the Hebrew genius broke with the conventional idea that beauty is pleasing to the deity. Instead it postulated the eternal verity that what God requires of man is "only to do justice, and to love mercy, and to walk humbly with thy God."

In recent years the literature on the "Jewish Contribution to Civilization" has grown to stupendous dimensions. Unfortunately, however, the term *"Jewish contribution"* is usually interpreted as the *contribution of Jews* to various branches of culture and civilization. When a Jewish chemist discovers an important new formula, or a Jewish physician a new test or cure it is as little a characteristically Jewish contribution as the discovery of the principle of lighter-than-air aviation, or of the telephone by engineers who happen to be Jews. These inventions and discoveries could have been made just as well by Frenchmen, American, or Chinese. There is nothing specifically Jewish, or French, or American, or Chinese about them— and the very fact that similar or comparable inventions and discoveries have been made by members of practically all modern nations proves this conclusively.

In referring to the "Jewish Contribution to Civilization" we, therefore, do not think of the Zeppelin and the telephone, the Wassermann and Zondek-Aschheim tests, the novels of Feuchtwanger, Werfel and Zweig—as a matter of fact, we do not even take pride in the "Theory of Relativity" as a

*Jewish* contribution. The Jewish contribution, as we understand it, is ethics and morality in the peculiar and unique connotations as conceived by the Prophets. The Jewish contribution to civilization is the emancipation of ethics—the revolt against the mistaken belief of antiquity that splendor and gold, beauty and perfection of form are pleasing to God. The Jews discovered that not beauty, which is of necessity ephemeral and evanescent, is desired by God, but goodness, kindness, justice and peace.

The Hebrew genius, articulate in the message of the Prophets, perceived clearly and without any illusions the high cost of beauty and material luxury. The living conscience of Israel—the Prophets—denounced and condemned the temples and palaces that were built by the offerings of those "that pant after the dust of the earth on the head of the poor, and turn aside the way of the humble."

The statues of Phidias, which stand for the misery of millions of slaves, are museum pieces. The books of the Prophets are the rod and staff of hundreds of millions of men in our time—and have been the inspiration and consolation of countless billions of men and women and children who preceded us on this earth.

More than three thousand years ago, the Hebrew genius recognized and, what is more, found a solution for the problem presented by the fact of technique outdistancing civilization—beauty eclipsing goodness—esthetics claiming the supremacy over ethics. The solution was to make *man* and not the statue or the machine the highest good. No Jew, nurtured in Jewish tradition, could ever bring over his lips a statement as callously blasphemous as Treitschke's that *one* statue of marble is worth the price of millions of living human being that had to endure misery to make its birth possible.

The Greeks bequeathed to mankind statues devoid of the living breath of ethics—the Jews taught all of mankind, and exemplified that teaching in their own lives, that "one human being is equal in value to the whole of creation."

A people that sets such great value by each and every human life can not sacrifice human happiness to material splendor: it will refuse to sacrifice man to the machine. How long ago is it that children of eight and nine years of age were made to slave fourteen hours in the mines and cotton mills of England? How long ago is it that human beings were hauled across the seas and driven like beasts of burden to make the South a place of heartrending misery for the hundreds of thousands of slaves and a charming island of "Southern Graciousness and Chivalry" for the few? What else has been the "industrial revolution" if not a gigantic application of the thesis that one statue is well worth the misery of millions of slaves? Could this perversion of justice have come about and endured if the world had truly worshipped and followed the heritage of Moses, instead of offering incense before the beguiling statues of Phidias?

One frequently meets in books dealing with Jewish ideological problems verbose apologies for and explanations of the almost total lack of "Jewish contributions" to art. However, are these apologies and explanations really necessary? Should we feel apologetic for the fact that we lived on a plane beyond esthetics—the realm of ethics? Phidias created statues—Moses created human beings. Plato wrote philosophical discourses for the few that never meant anything to the masses of mankind. The Prophets and Psalmist wrote on brotherly love, the love of God for men—they envisioned the "End of the Days" when peace and justice will reign supreme and *all* those created in the image of God will have a share in the good life. This is why the Bible has become *the* book of mankind.

Shortly before his death the eminent Egyptologist James H. Breasted attempted to delineate the cultural forces, described by him as "The Dawn of Conscience," that emerged thousands of years ago as antidotes to the ruthlessness of technique. The motive that led Professor Breasted to undertake his cultural-historical inquiry into "The Dawn of Conscience" was, to quote from the foreword to his book, that "it has become a sinister commonplace in the life of the post-war generation that man has never had any hesitation in applying his increasing mechanical power to the destruction of his own kind. The World War has now demonstrated the appalling possibilities of man's mechanical power of destruction. The only force that can successfully oppose it is the human conscience—something which the younger generation is accustomed to regard as a fixed group of outworn scruples. Everyone knows that man's amazing mechanical power is the product of a long evolution, but it is not commonly realized that this is also true of the social force which we call conscience—although with this important difference: as the oldest known implement-making creature man has been fashioning destructive weapons for possibly a million years, whereas conscience emerged as a social force less than five thousand years ago. One development has far outrun the other; because one is old, while the other has hardly begun and still has infinite possibilities before it."

As an Egyptologist Breasted traces the origins of conscience, that is to say the birth of Western morals and ethics, to Egypt. One of the chief exponents of the "Pan-Egyptian" theory, that would derive most of the religious legacy of Judaism and its daughter religions from the country of the

Nile, Breasted held, as late as 1933, that "it is now quite evident that the ripe social and moral development of mankind in the Nile Valley, which is three thousand years older than that of the Hebrews, contributed essentially to the formation of Hebrew literature which we call the Old Testament. Our moral heritage therefore derives from a wider *human* past enormously older than the Hebrews, and it has come to us rather *through* the Hebrews than *from* them."

It is intriguing and illuminating that Breasted felt constrained to emphasize that these opinions were "based solely on a judicially minded study of the ancient documents; but in a world in which anti-Semitic prejudice is still regrettably evident it seems appropriate to state that the book was not written with the slightest anti-Semitic bias."

Despite his "scientific conviction" of the unorginal character of Hebrew ethics and its force of conscience, Breasted yet was alert to the "extraordinary fact that this great moral legacy should have descended to Western civilization from a politically insignificant people."

The question raised by Breasted, and which he failed to answer, namely, why "this great moral legacy should have descended to Western civilization from a politically insignificant people," is the most conclusive refutation of the thesis that this moral legacy was not the authentic achievement of Israel. If it be true that the "Eternal People" has been endowed with immortality by its moral legacy and the ethical momentum of the prophetic heritage, a fact that is not denied even by the most radical critics, it would be incongruous that the "morally creative nations" should have disappeared. Surely as bearers and originators of "conscience" *they* should have been the ones to survive, *and not the Hebrews.*

But, in point of fact, Professor Breasted erred sorely in

tracing conscience to Egypt. Conscience, ethical awareness and religious responsibility could not have blossomed forth among the Egyptians who enslaved the poor of their own people and the nations they subdued to build Pyramid tombs for their kings and nobles. *Conscience is the Jewish contribution to mankind* — the only *characteristically* Jewish contribution. Let those who would deny the Jews this claim compare the Bible with the so-called ethical literature of the Egyptians, steeped in idolatry and reflecting all the social ills and evils that are its inevitable concomitants and consequences.

The antithesis of technique and humane civilization, in relation to the Greek and the Jewish contributions, has been expressed singularly well by Heine in his *Confessions*: "Formerly, I felt no special affection for Moses," he wrote, "probably because the Hellenic spirit was paramount in me, and I could not pardon the legislator of the Jews his hatred against the plastic arts. I did not see that, notwithstanding his hostility to art, Moses was a great artist, and possessed the true artistic spirit. But this spirit was directed by him, as by his Egyptian compatriots, to colossal and indestructible undertakings.... He built human pyramids, carved human obelisks; he took a poor shepherd family and created a nation from it, a great, eternal, holy people, a people of God, destined to outlive the centuries, and to serve as a pattern to all other nations, even as a prototype to the whole of mankind: he created Israel.... As of the artist, so also I have not always spoken with sufficient respect of his work, the Jews.... I see now that the Greeks were only handsome youths, while the Jews were always men, powerful, indomitable men, not only in olden days but even to this day, in spite of eighteen centuries of persecution and misery."

## III

Works of art are immobile and elusive—they are not outgoing. The would-be beneficiary of the beauty of a statue or a canvas has to seek it out, cross continents and oceans to gaze upon it. As a result, the appeal of art has always been confined to the few. This holds true also today when reproductions make the immobile and elusive statues and canvasses more readily accessible. Today, too, those who would "live with art" must have means. In the past, the influence of art was wholly confined to those who could afford to be patrons of artists.

As to the alleged "revolts" of art, the facts are that, from the very earliest times to the present, art has consistently catered to money and the tastes of the rich. To assert that "modern art" is a revolt against the stuffiness of the Victorian Age is putting the cart before the horse. "Modern art" emerged *after* Victorian stuffiness had been dispelled by technological tastes and morals. The stubborn survival of outworn art styles, centuries after the cultural scene into which they were born and fitted was eclipsed, goes far to prove that art's eye is riveted on the patron who pays the bill.

Art always does the bidding of those who pay the bill. . . . It minimizes their vices and spices their perversities. It clothes with beauty what they wish to appear beautiful and smears with ugliness what they desire to be tainted. For evidence we might point to the glorification of homosexuality by Greek artists of antiquity and to the hideous depictions of the Synagogue and of Jews by medieval and even more recent artists.

Art is congenitally undemocratic. It is created for the few and is contemptuous of the masses. In order "to live with art," one must own art. To be sure, admission to most museums is free, yet most *average* persons working at the *average* kind of jobs are not among the regular visitors of art exhibits. They may visit a museum once or twice in a life time, but this hardly amounts to "living with art."

Art is still, as it has always been, reserved for the aristocracy of money and leisure. This is one of the chief reasons why Judaism is marked by a "paucity of art." For Judaism is wedded to democracy. Its concern is not with the few but with the many. The Torah was not given to a caste but to the entire people—men, women and children. The Torah, the Rabbis explained, was given in the desert, which belongs to no master, to emphasize that the Torah belongs to all men. It is the property of all who desire to claim it.

Unlike works of art, the word of Torah is universally and ubiquitously accessible. The word addresses itself to all men. The humble shack can encompass it as adequately as the palace. Thought and speech through which it is expressed are common human possessions. They are gifts of God, as it were, and God does not "sell" his bounties. Some of the creative giants of the Jewish word were day laborers. Throughout the ages the creative Jewish word has flourished among "the sons of the poor," thus impressing upon every generation the truth of the Sages that poverty, even if it be the kind of abject poverty Hillel endured, is no license for living without the word of Torah.

Works of art are created "singly." Also, they are invested with the exclusiveness of irreplacability, for no matter how good reproductions may be, they are only "copies." It is different with the creations shaped of words. No matter how many copies of a book are printed, the force and flavor of the

## TOWARD A DEFINITION OF THE JEWISH GENIUS 117

original are retained in all of them, on every page and in every sentence.

Works of art are subject to all the frailties of matter. When accidents strike their extinction is final. When a painting is mutilated or burned, when a statue is broken and shattered, nothing except rubble remains. There is nothing left of the destruction to soar free into space.... The end is definitive and irrevocable. It is not so with the creation of the word. Parchments on which the word is recorded may be burned, voices that carry it may be stilled—but the word, Phoenix-like, rises from the destruction of its physical medium of expression and soars free and invincible into its allotted space of eternity.

Because of their perishability, works of art are risky and hazardous survival investments for a people which attained nationhood not by the act of settlement, but by the feat of the Exodus. For Jewish homelessness has a metaphysical significance besides its tragic political connotations. Homelessness has determined Jewish destiny from the hour when Abraham projected the Jewish idea by leaving his home and the land where he and his fathers were born. Obviously, the important and, be it admitted, creative part homelessness has played in the Jewish drama should not lead to the assumption that Judaism considers homelessness anything else but a curse. Ever since Abraham started on *his* road to homelessness, Jews have prayed and fought for a home.

A people carrying the burden of physical homelessness and metaphysical homelessness must be equipped for the journey. It must travel light, though with durable accouterments. The possessions of such a people must be portable, for otherwise they cannot be carried across countries and continents, oceans and deserts.

During the monarchy the Judeans and Israelites invested in

"art." They built temples and palaces and "went astray" with statues of stone and wood. If the Ten Tribes of Israel became "lost," it was because they had too heavily invested in "art" and sent the Prophets, the men of the word, "to the land of Judah, to eat bread there, and prophesy there." When Samaria's temples and palaces were destroyed, no "letters" remained to soar free and imperishable into space. But when Jerusalem fell, a century and a half later, there were "words" and men of words that belied the destruction. These "words" were strengthened, and through strength they increased. After the First Destruction, the victory of the word as the medium of creative Jewish expression became definitive. The Prophets, the bearers of "the word," and the Scribes its faithful recorders, scored this victory through which Jewish survival was entrenched.

## IV

Art has always exacted exorbitant tribute in terms of human suffering. Nor is this astounding, for the sight of human suffering leaves the artist as emotionally uninvolved as the observation of happiness and well-being. Suffering is to the artist not a tragedy calling for amelioration but an interesting phenomenon requiring fixation. For art, it is being asserted, is beyond good and evil. But this is not true. The fact is that art is indifferent to good and evil. A human form contorted in pain is to the artist as "interesting"—and possibly more engrossing—than a figure reclining serenely in a spring-meadow setting. The artist does not want to *change* suffering and evil, for suffering and evil are his most "fruitful" inspirations and subjects.

Judaism is informed throughout by the burning zeal and passion not merely to change but to uproot suffering and evil. Treitschke, the German historian who coined the slogan "the Jews are our misfortune," fathered another oft-quoted pronouncement. "One statue of Phidias," he wrote, "is well worth the misery endured by millions of slaves in antiquity." This is a perfect epitomy of the artist's ethics. To the artist, art is its own end and purpose. "Art for art's sake" —*ars pro artis*—is his slogan. What does it matter if the world goes to pieces, if only the holocaust feeds inspiration to the muse?

Art which is its own end and purpose, refusing to bow to any authority or restraint outside its realm, is of course nothing else but a form of idolatry. A pithy Jewish saying states that he who fears anything except God commits idolatry. Civilizations which conceive of art not as a means toward an end, but as *the* end and purpose, idolize a temporal phenomenon by endowing it with the dignity and sanctity belonging to the Eternity which Jews, at times, equate with God.

Because art is "selfish" it has developed a type of man who is virtually devoid of the humane qualities by grace of which man becomes a human being. Nor need we adduce historical evidence in support of this assertion. Anyone who has had occasion to observe at close range artists "who live for their art" is familiar with their standards. It would seem that "art," like the monster deities of antiquity, feeds on obscenity and immorality. What moral laws and ethical duties are not being flaunted by artists proclaiming that "the Muse" requires freedom from "bourgeois" restraints? Nor is this attitude limited to the mediocrities of Latin Quarter and Greenwich Village flaming youth artists. The biographies of the great artists of all times professing "art for art's sake" as their credo, provide overwhelming evidence that "pure art" thrives most abundantly—on impurity and corruption. These strictures apply also to "creative writers" who abuse "the word" by enthroning it as its own end and purpose. "Poetry for poetry's sake" or "literature for literature's sake" leads to the same dead end annihilation of purpose and ethics as "art for art's sake." When Rabbi Akiba threatened with dire punishment those who would recite "Song of Songs" as a mere love lyric, he intuitively grasped the dangers of the pitfall lying in wait for those committed to "art for art's sake."

Art is predicated on the glorification of the sensuous realm. Indeed, ethics was not foreign to the ancient Greeks who bequeathed to Western civilization its art concept. Their bondage to art, however, was such that they could not perceive of ethics otherwise than as an appendage to the sensuous-beautiful. There is no better summing-up of the Greek philosophy of life than their slogan, "the beautiful is good." Jewish wisdom, on the other hand, knows that all too often the beautiful is achieved through evil. A Greek promenading in the streets of Samaria as a companion of Amos would surely have praised the beauty and artistry of the "ivory palaces." But as Amos contemplated the details of their perfection, he could only think of it that the great houses of ivory were built by men who oppressed the poor and crushed and exploited the needy. And so Amos proclaimed, in the name of God: "I abhor the pride of Jacob, and hate his palaces!" Neither "the noise of songs" nor "the melody of psalteries" are pleasing to God. He delights in the harmony of "justice welling up as water."

Shall we conclude from Amos', Isaiah's and other Prophets' denunciation of beautiful things that the ancient Hebrews lacked the sense for beauty? Certainly this would be a false inference. The care bestowed upon the adornment of the Tent of Assembly and the Temple prove that "integrated art," which was not its own ethics-defeating purpose, had a place in ancient Israel.

More than Bezalel's gold and silver cult objects the pictorial language of the Bible attests that those who spoke it were people of a highly refined and developed appreciation of the beautiful. Thanks to this sense of beauty the ancient Hebrews did create art, although an art which is as distinct and unique as were its creators. It is an art which uses as its medium of expression the word exclusively. *The word picture is the authentic expression of the Jewish art impulse.* The Bible abounds in word pictures which depict the entire sensory panorama of the world with graphic and tangibly realistic images. It is deplorable that the "slavery in freedom" mourners of "the paucity of Jewish art" do not realize that the art impulse may express itself in any of several media. What matters is the idea and its intelligible expression through the medium which the projector of the idea considers most germane. Sculptors resort to stone or clay for expressing their ideals of feminine and masculine beauty; painters use colors. "Song of Songs" limned the Beloved and her Lover with words stringed into metaphors and word pictures which have spoken to a hundred generations of men perhaps more stirringly than Venus of Milo and Rubens' voluptuous nudes.

The Hebrew Bible excels in *word* pictures of nature. Alexander Von Humboldt was but one of many eminent critics who pointed to Psalm 104 as the most exquisite word picture canvas depicting the glories of nature. Commenting on such lines as "Who coverest Thyself with light as with a garment; who stretchest out the heavens like a curtain; who layest the beams of His chambers in the waters; who makest the clouds His chariots; who walkest upon the wings of the wind; who laid the foundations of the earth, that it should not be removed forever, He sendeth the springs into the valleys, which run among the hills ...," Von Humboldt wrote: "We are astonished to find in a lyrical poem of such limited compass the whole universe—the heavens and the earth—sketched with a few bold touches."

The circumstance that the vociferous pleaders for "Jewish art" have altogether ignored the indigenous Jewish pictorial language art of the biblical period is a telling indictment. Moreover, it betrays the pathetic narrowness of their definition of art by recognizing only its tactile forms of expression. Obviously, such a delimitation is absurd, if only because it ignores the "arts" of music and literature.

There are varieties of artistic endowment. He who achieves greatness in painting will not be expected to excel as a sculptor. A poet may be color blind and a composer may labor over a routine letter without prejudicing his reputation. Nor are variations of artistic endowment limited to individuals. Through consistent selective concentration on a certain form of art expression, a nation can "breed" into its members a predilection for a form of artistic expression. Thus, for instance, the Greeks "specialized" in sculpture and the Spaniards and the Dutch in painting.

We Jews made the word the receptacle and the vehicle of our artistic impulse! Why, one cannot help asking, have the self-appointed guardians of "Jewish art" overlooked the fact that the pictorial language of the Hebrew Bible, expressive in thousands of poetic metaphors, is "art" of such dynamic power and response-begetting fruitfulness that the effect of the sum total of ancient medieval and modern art pales before it into irrelevancy?

Phidias created statues of life-like beauty in which the grace of youth is enchantingly caught. Ostensibly, those statues are "art." But *must* artistic expression of necessity resort to a tactile medium?

Is the human form chiselled of stone, or painted, or etched, more "real" and artistic than the human form sketched by the poet's word-picture?

## V

Among the articulate devotees of "Jewish art" and their inarticulate slavish followers the opinion prevails that "Jewish art," in any of the media of creative plastic expression, is a prop of Jewish survival. As many planks of the ideology of the devotees of "Jewish art," this opinion, too, is not supported by facts. On the contrary, an inquiry into the skills of "the art of Jewish survival" proves that "Jewish art" does not figure among them.

Art is exclusively concerned with the sensual qualities of its objects and models. Although the artist invests and endows a model with nuances not perceptible to the average eye, when all is said, a statue or a portrait does not tell the onlooker a thing about the nature of the ideas and ideals, the fears and hopes, he joys and sorrows of the person who sat for it. Art remains chained to the realm of one sense only: visual perception. Inevitably, therefore, art's reflection and portrayal of reality lacks *spiritual* perspective and dimension.

The word picture, too, explores the visual and tactile spheres, but by its very nature the word is less confining than the media with which the artist works. Language, though limited, is yet less limiting than stone and color, and it is a better means than either for conveying abstract ideas. The mind rather than the body is the domain of the word picture. And as the progress of civilization is coextensive with the abstraction of ideas and ideals from sensually perceptible "factual reality," it follows that creative literary expression occupies a higher rung on the ladder of cultural progress than creative artistic expression resorting to stone, clay, color or drawing pencil. Primitive art has been dug up in layers of civilizations which preceded the invention of the alphabet by many millenia. That mankind's urge of creative expression travelled the road leading from primitive tactile manifestation to highly refined abstract thought seems to be proved also by the developmental stages of the child in our civilization. The tot of three or four expresses himself "creatively"—to use the term in vogue—with clay, crayons and finger paints. But from this stage he progresses before long to expressing himself "creatively" by means of language. The average child of three of four is clumsy with the use of words. Usually he will prefer modelling or drawing an elephant to describing it with words. Moreover, his word pictures will be of necessity sketchy and inadequate. Yet, an eight-year old will delight in doing a composition on the elephant and a typical composition of a child of this age group will refer to aspects of elephant life and behavior which a sensual-tactile portrait of the animal cannot convey.

The most primitive form of perception is sensual. Consequently, creative expression inspired not by sensual perception but by the thoughts, ideas and ideals abstracted from it, is superior to art which cannot and does not transcend the realm of the tactile. By concentrating its creative potential on the mind realm, Judaism merely followed the normal path of human progress which proceeds from the sensual to the abstract. We need therefore neither apologize for nor explain "the paucity of Jewish art." It is just one more proof of the distinctiveness which is our true *raison d'etre*.

## VI

Since the Atomic Age opened, in 1945, "the crisis of Western civilization" has ceased to be an exclusive and theoretical concern of philosophers, sociologists and theologians. Multitudes of men *are* worrying about the possible explosion of the crisis which is shaping up fast. The diagnosticians of the dilemma of the West are agreed that the predicament is rooted in the circumstance that man's mechanical acumen and resources have outstripped his moral-ethical fund and efforts, with the result that the Golem of the machine created by man has shaken off his guidance and control. The real threat of the atomic bomb is not its potential of destruction, but the calamity that mankind cannot muster the moral strength required for converting the power potential of the bomb, which is neutral, into a force of good. Our failure is the inability "to beat the swords into plough shares."

Technique which is largely responsible for "the predicament of modern man" belongs wholly to the sensual realm. Significantly, it started on the road to victory with the devaluation of ideational values towards the end of the Middle Ages. Pitrim Sorokin, who diagnoses the crisis of the West as a disease stemming from the overemphasis on the sensate, points to modern art (he should have included ancient and medieval art as well) as one more difficult obstacle to attempts of saving "sensate culture" from itself. He describes "sensate culture" as predicated on the principle "that *the true reality and value is sensory.* Only what we see, hear, smell, touch, and otherwise perceive through our sense organs is real and has value. Beyond such a sensory reality, either there is nothing, or, if there is something, we cannot sense it; therefore it is equivalent to the nonreal and the nonexistent. As such it may be neglected ... In this way the modern form of our culture emerged, the sensory, empirical, secular and 'this-wordly' culture. It may be called *sensate*. It is based upon and is integrated around this new principle value: *the true reality and value is sensory*. It is precisely this principle that is articulated by our modern sensate culture in all its main departments."

Besides all else, the second commandment is also the single strongest disavowal of "sensate culture." Nor is this interpretation an artificial rationalization. The fact looms large that Jewish culture is "ideational" throughout and that Judaism resorts to the sensate only for the indispensable minimum of material support without which the idea cannot become manifest.

The devotees of "Jewish art" have made much of the fact that Jewish law stresses the duty of *hiddur mitzvah*—the beautification of Jewish ritual. Wrongly, they have interpreted the various forms of *hiddur mitzvah* as art expressions. In truth, the quest for the beautification of Jewish rites and cult objects is the very antithesis of the art impulse as commonly understood.

Art is self-centered and proclaims its self-sufficiency. There is no need to repeat what has been said above concerning the egotistical tendendies of "art for art's sake." The emphasis of the quest for *hiddur mitzvah*, however, has always been on *mitzvah* rather than on *hiddur*. Its products, moreover, such as ornaments for the Torah scrolls, finely worked *Kiddush* cups, *Havdalah* spice boxes, *Mezuzot*, illuminated

*Haggadot* and manuscripts of sacred texts are not "art" but properly fit into the category of "arts and crafts."

Until the era of emancipation and assimilation Jewish culture was non-sensate. Its medium of expression was language and its emphasis was centered in the word and the idea. As to the arts and crafts efforts of silversmiths, goldsmiths, embroiderers, calligraphers, and other craftsmen who produced cult objects for the sake of *hiddur mitzvah,* they never conceived of their role otherwise than as a tribute to the idea of Judaism manifest exclusively in the non-sensate realm.

Writing on "Jewish Art" in "The New Judea" (March-April, 1948) Israel Cohen recalls that over forty years ago he interviewed Joseph Israels, the Dutch Jewish artist, in order to learn whether it was correct to speak of Jewish art. Mr. Cohen reports that Israels "at first maintained there was no such thing as Jewish art. He said that he was a Dutch artist, that Max Liebermann was a German artist and that Solomon J. Solomon was an English artist. Then he reflected for a moment and referred to Hermann Struck: 'Him you can call a Jewish artist,' he said. 'I know him well, and his work, especially his studies of Jewish types, may rightly be described as Jewish art.'"

The more recent devotees of "Jewish art" have no such exclusive standards. To qualify as "Jewish art," the canvas or sculpture need not reproduce Jewish types or give plastic expression to Jewish themes. Any piece of art by a Jew is generously dubbed by them "Jewish art" with the weak argument that "the mood" and "temperament" matter more than the theme.

But Joseph Israels' definition of Jewish art is no less unsatisfactory and illogical than that advanced by the contemporary devotees of "Jewish art." For if "studies of Jewish types" represent Jewish art, it can be argued that Rembrandt was a great "Jewish artist." His portraits of "Jewish types" of the Amsterdam Jewish quarter, his unforgettable studies of "Rabbinical types" and, last but not least, his pictorial interpretations of scenes and characters of the Hebrew Bible surpass in quantity and quality the work of any Jewish artist thus far. Still, Rembrandt was not a Jewish artist.

Those who aver that "studies of Jewish types" are "Jewish art" might also reflect on the curious fact that most of the great medieval and modern exponents of Church art went to the Ghetto for "inspiration" and models when portraying Jesus and the apostles. It is a bitter and ironical fact that *Jews* served as models for many of the crucifixion scenes that looked down upon the worshippers from every wall and corner of the Churches, adding venom and impetus to their hatred of the "Christ killers." Are these "studies of Jewish types," too, "Jewish art?"

Art cannot be pidgeon-holed according to the chimerical notions of the racial theory, for it is universal. An artist need not be a Jew to excel in studies of Jewish types, to wit, Rembrandt. Nor need a writer be a Jew to do justice to a biblical theme, as is proved by Thomas Mann's Joseph novels. Creative imagination is not circumscribed by national or geographic boundaries. As is well-known, the German poet Schiller had not seen the Swiss Alps when he wrote his "Wilhelm Tell," glorifying Swiss patriotism and graphically describing the landscape and life of Switzerland. A more recent case is that of Franz Werfel's "The Forty Days or Musa Dagh." Werfel was not an Armenian, yet his novel accurately describes Armenian life and espouses the Armenian cause with a fervor and zeal that could scarcely be surpassed by a member of the Armenian people.

Much has been made of the frescos found in a Dura-Europos (Syria) Synagogue which was built about the middle of the third century (C.E.) Only devotees of "Jewish art" will take these rather crude paintings of biblical scenes as evidence of indigenous Jewish art. The true facts are as follows: Dura-Europos was a focal point of Hellenism. Numerous Jewish communities in the Hellenistic era abandoned themselves to Hellenism as completely and uncritically as 19th century West European Jews rushed to purchase "the entrance ticket to European society." The paintings of Dura-Europos do not prove that already in the third century there flourished "Jewish art," but only that the Jewish community of Dura-Europos, removed from the center of authentic Jewishness in Palestine, had succumbed to assimilation. Hellenism held a powerful attraction for Jews who were not rooted in their own community and its culture. Such Greek diversions as the gymnasium and the amphitheatre were popular with Jewish youths. It would be mistaken, however, to infer from the fact that Jewish youths frequented theaters and sport arenas, that the drama and sports played a role of importance in the life of the integrated Jewish community dedicated to the non-sensate type of culture. To be sure, *shemirat haguf*—keeping physically fit—is an important Jewish principle. In fact, Maimonides, the physician, placed it above all over commandments, for the sick cannot fulfill the commandments and serve God as required. But *shemirat haguf*—the Jewish regimen of physical fitness—is not synonymous with sports. Indeed, Rabbi Simeon ben Gamaliel was a proficient athlete, but this should not be interpreted as proof that he and his colleagues regarded this proficiency as anything else but an amusing curiosity.

Analogously, the paintings of Dura-Europos—and it will still have to be proved that they were painted by Jews—do not attest the existence of early Jewish art. They only prove the depth of assimilation and Jewish alienation of the Dura-Europos Jewish community.

## VII

Although the non-sensate realm of creative linguistic expression is better protected against the hazards of the sensate sphere where art flourishes, literature of the *belles lettres* type is possessed of the same ethical weakness which is "art for art's sake" failure and undoing. Until Jewish literature began to imitate Western ways it was immune to the degenerating influence implicit in "literature for literature's sake" and its cult of self-expression. Self-expression, as defined by Judaism, is discipline in the service of a higher ideal rather than self-abandonment and self-indulgence.

The Hebrew poets, too, sang of love and its delights. But while revelling in their *own* love, they remained cognizant of its larger implications, first, in the Jewish realm, and, then, in the cosmic order of the universe. The traditional interpretation of "Song of Songs" and Hosea's self-interpretation prove that, already in the biblical period, "literature for literature's sake" had as little a place in the Jewish setting as "art for art's sake."

All of art and literature is a form of libido sublimation. Jewish literature is no exception. It is, however, characterized by a unique process of sublimation which is at work in virtually all of classical Hebrew poetry. To trace this process, we can do no better than subject Yehudah Halevi's verse to a bit of closer scrutiny. "The Sweet Singer of Zion" started out as the passionate glorifier of feminine beauty. His verse, according to al-Charizi, was woven of dew and fire. With the ardor Yehudah Halevi loved Zion in later years, he wooed woman as a youth, professing that he was "a slave to love." He knew both the exultation of fulfilment and the agony of frustration. Accustomed to think of Yehudah Halevi in terms of a liturgical poet and religious philosopher, we often forget that as a young man he wrote verse typified by these examples·

> The night when the fair maiden revealed herself to me
> The warmth of her cheeks, the veil of her hair,
> Golden like a topaz, covering
> A brow of smoothest crystal
> She was like the sun making red in her rising
> The clouds of dawn with the flame of her light . . .

> Cheeks of lilies, and mine eyes gathering;
> Breasts of pomegranates, and mine hands harvesting;
> If thy lips be glowing coals
> Then let my jaws be tongs . . .

> If parting be decreed for the two of us,
> Stand yet a little, while I gaze upon thy face.
> I know not if my heart be held back within my frame
> Or if it goeth forth upon thy wanderings.
> By the life of love, remember the days of thy longing as I—
> I remember the nights of thy delight
> As thine image passeth into my dream,
> So let me pass, I entreat thee, into thy dreams' . . .

Yehudah Halevi, the author of these and similar poems, and who also excelled in wine songs and marriage odes, seems to have little in common with Yehudah Halevi, "the harp of

Zion" and philosopher-interpreter of Judaism. But this is a superficial judgment. The two Yehudah Halevis were one and thoroughly integrated. Had the young Yehudah Halevi loved less impetuously the "Fair Maiden," the middle-aged Yehudah Halevi would never have abandoned security for the uncertainty of being united with Zion, the beloved.

At a certain point in Yehudah Halevi's life there started the process of sublimation, which has marked the birth of all great Jewish literature. In the course of this sublimation, the personal emotion does not become extinct. It abides in full vigor, but, and this is all-important, it takes on a new meaning. Thus the temporal becomes expressive of the eternal, and the timely of the timeless. Yehudah Halevi described this transition of which he was thoroughly aware as follows:

Asleep in the bosom of youth, how long wilt thou rest?
Know that boyhood is shaken off like tow.
Are the days of dawn for ever? Rise, go forth—
See, the angels of old age do chasten thee betimes.
Then shake thyself from the drops of the night.
Dart like a swallow to find release from thy trespass,
And from the happenings of the day which rage like the ocean.
Pursue after thy King in the intimate company
Of souls that flow unto the goodness of God.

Yet this sublimation is more than a mere discarding of boyhood. It is rather the translation of boyhood longings into manhood goals.

The analytical study of Yehudah Halevi's style, and especially of his favorite metaphors and idioms, shows that frequently he employed identical metaphors and phrases both for the description of his romantic ardor and for the delineation of the intensity of his love of God and Zion. Yehudah Halevi was a master at investing spiritual longing with the sublimated impatience clamoring for physical consummation. Here are a few examples which illustrate the manner in which Yehudah Halevi, following established precedent as exemplified by the rabbinic interpretation of "Song of Songs," transferred physical love images to the spiritual realm.

In the poem "Parting" he told his beloved:
> I know not if my heart be held within my frame
> Or if it goeth forth upon thy wanderings.

The identical image of the non-localized heart he used later in the Zionide:
> My heart is in the East, and I in the uttermost West.

In "Parting," Yehudah Halevi averred that he desired as his "share":
> Nought but a thread of scarlet from thy lips
> A girdle from thy waist.

In the religious poem "They That Know My Grief," he pointed to "the sweet fruit of Thy Torah" as his "share."

Paraphrasing a line "Song of Songs," he sang to his beloved.
> My sweet wild honey is between thy lips.

In "Beautiful of Elevation," the kissable lips had become sublimated into Zion's earth:
> Shall I not be tender to thy stones and kiss them,
> And the taste of thy soil shall be sweeter than honey unto me?

Pledging eternal devotion to his beloved, he vowed:
> May I forget to discern my right hand from my left, O my doe,
> If I ever forget the love of thine espousals.

Later, he vowed loyalty to God, saying:

Let my right hand forget—if I stand not before thee.

There are many more strophes in Yehudah Halevi's "Diwan" which point up the process of sublimation by which the youthful poet's love of woman became transfigured into the devotion to God and Zion.

The uniqueness of Jewish literature consists in this sublimation of the temporal into the eternal. Those who would doubt this might well reflect on the fact that, from the earliest time to the present, our people honored as "national poets" only those who achieved the sublimation of the temporal by transfiguring it into eternal values of the nation. To attain greatness as a Jewish poet, a writer must be endowed with something else besides lyrical emotions and an exquisite style for portraying the beauty of nature and the passion of the heart. Love lyrics and nature idyls are no valid passports to *Jewish* literary greatness and immortality. Even "modern" Hebrew literature sets more exacting standards, as is best proved perhaps by Bialik's unique place in modern Hebrew letters.

Bialik did not excel as a lyrical poet. His nature poems are pale and liltless, and his love lyrics betray the inhibited *Yeshiva Bachur*. Without doubt, Tchernichovsky's verse is lyrically superior to Bialik's and Shneiour's love pomes glow with an intensity of passion which Bialik, had it smouldered in his heart, would have been hesitant to profess. Even among "the young ones" of Hebrew literature, there are poets who, as lyricists, are superior to Bialik. Yet, only Bialik of all modern Hebrew poets has merited the unique position of "the Jewish national poet."

**Why?**

Bialik's greatness, as Yehudah Halevi's, was that he devoted his gifts not to the glorification of personal emotions and experiences, but to the utterance of his people's hopes and woes. Bialik's love and nature poems, few in number, prove that he was at home neither in love nor in nature. Indeed, he wondered whether there was such a thing as love, and asked: "Love, what is your name?"

Bialik rose to the full stature of a "God-kissed" poet only when he was inspired by Jewish themes. He became a poet "On the Threshold of the Bet Ha-Midrash" and "In Front of the Book Case," not when listening to the birds of spring or when gazing into the eyes of a beautiful girl. The *"Matmid,"* the eternal student of the Talmud, pale, emaciated, yet burning with a sacred fire of enthusiasm, who by his personal sacrifice insures the eternity of our people, rather than the charms of woman, stirred him to rapture. He tasted tragedy not in the disappointments of love but in the martyrdom of Kishineff, "The City of Slaughter." His romantic imagination did not spend itself in dreams of the consummation of erotic desires but in superb poetic recreations of the heroic chapters of Jewish history.

Upon attaining his full stature as a poet and on the pinnacle of spiritual power—Bialik ceased writing poetry altogether, except for occasional stanzas. It would be mistaken to conclude that Bialik had exhausted his creative resources. The essays and epigrams of his after-forty period prove the contrary. Bialik did not "stop" writing poetry, rather he "renounced" it, because he had come to the conclusion that our generation was not in need of new creations but of the appreciation of the legacy of the past. And so there began for Bialik two blessed decades of *Kinus*—the ingathering and popular presentation of the great classics of the past. He projected a Jewish people's library encompassing the wealth of ancient and medieval Hebrew literature. He planned anthologies and text-editions to keep busy a score enthusiasts of his own caliber.

Philological scholarship and critical text editions are usually associated with a specious type of dullness. Bialik demonstrated that the "resurrection" of ancient literary treasures is, first of all, a creative feat. He spent the years of his prime editing the poems of Solomon Ibn Gabirol, Yehudah Halevi, Shemuel Ha-Naggid, and other medieval Hebrew poets. His sensitivity to Hebrew style was fabulous and, added to the intuitive understanding of the poet, it enabled him to produce editions of the works of the medieval Hebrew poets which were not merely sound, but also came as near as possible to the original text. Bialik's decisions on manuscripts are definitive and his ingenuity in restoring mutilated or faultily copied versions was almost uncanny. In this way too Bialik achieved greatness. For "Jewish greatness" is predicated on a special variety of "sublimation." It requires the transubstantiation of the purely personal into meanings of national significance. This trend was already foreshadowed in the Bible, as in the Book of Hosea which transmuted a personal wound into identification with the great festering sore of the nation.

Thus far all great Jewish poets were "national poets," that is to say, their egos were fused with the past, present and future of their people. Even when a "national poet" excelled in the purely lyrical realm to the extent Yehudah Halevi did, he became enshrined in Jewish literature not as the author of rapturous love poems, or of sensitive and powerful descriptions of the raging sea, but as the "Sweet Singer of Zion."

For all *Jewish* poets beauty of expression was but a means toward an end, but not an end in itself. In this respect too Bialik was utterly Jewish. Unlike Tchernichovsky, he did not bow to Apollo, the symbol of youth and strength, but to the ideals of *yisrael sava*—Israel, old, gnarled and, often, physically unattractive, but possessed of eternity.

## VIII

Authentic Jewish creative expression has a national "additional soul" with which the I of the creative individual is inseparably fused. Our analysis of the process of sublimation in Yehudah Halevi's and Bialik's works has shown that their unique position and stature as "Jewish national poets" is predicated on the transubstantiation of their individual egos in the matrix of the "additional soul" of their people.

Lest it be argued that this is a labored rationalization induced by this writer's "antagonism to art," it will be expedient to see how Menachem Boraisha, a distinguished Jewish poet of our day defined "the mission of the Jewish poet." Boraisha who devoted to this theme a chapter in his volume *A Dor* (A Generation), was also the author of *Der Gayer* (The Wayfarer), one of the few great *creative* Yiddish works of our time. Cast in the traditional mold, Boraisha was not merely a "sweet singer" but also a profound thinker and a blazer of new trails in the ideational interpretation of Judaism.

Boraisha's was the spontaneity typical of the creative genius—as his poetic works compellingly attest—but he also was a *traditional* Jewish poet of the pattern of Yehudah Halevi and Solomon Ibn Gabirol. His philosophical inquiries probed deeply and thoroughly also into his own self and explored what strands went into the making of his creative genius. In the course of this analysis, recorded in great detail in the closing chapter of *A Dor*, Boraisha examined the place of "self-revelation and egocentricity" in general creative expression and in the utterance of the Jewish poet in particular. He confessed that his early inner struggles stemmed from his instinctive desire for self-revelation and egocentricity in which his Jewish soul would not permit him to indulge. Already as a youth of eighteen and twenty, Boraisha rebelled against "literature for literature's sake." He could not bring himself to enthrone "man as the measure of all things" while placing his own creative talent "beyond good and evil" in the manner of European artists and creative writers.

Looking back on these early conflicts Boraisha recalled, "I balked at taking this final step toward placing the individual in the center of creation. The ancestral spirit within me shuddered at the thought of man setting himself up as the mirror reflecting both earth and the heavens. Self-revelation aroused a sense of shame within me and egocentricity evoked a painful aversion. Not that I did not share the desire of the generation to write self-revelatory poems. I would conceive such poems, but not write them. Or I would write them in the form of ballads of the people. . . . My small literary output cast in the form of the first person singular cost me a wealth of effort."

This attitude will seem strange to writers swayed by the Western tradition which appraises creative literature in terms of self-revelation and egocentric expression. But this is not the rod of measure of the Jew's evaluation of literature. Boraisha insisted, "We are a people of visionaries, not of troubadours." This pithy sentence holds the key to the understanding of Jewish creative expression throughout the centuries and millenia. All great and abiding Jewish literature has been inspired by the "additional soul" of our people and has collective national meaning besides personal significance. This is why love lyrics and spring songs are no valid passports for securing

*Jewish* literary immortality and greatness. Indeed, "there is a time for everything" and *shira,* lyrical poetry inspired by love and devoted to its glorification, has its legitimate youthful niche. In the mature pattern of Jewish creative eternity, however, there is no room for mere troubadours.

Boraisha proved his genuine Jewish mettle by confessing that, when reading the works of some modern Jewish poets, he felt the need of asking: "What do they mean to me?" He could not help wondering thus, because already in 1912 he wrote: "Of what does the poet not sing? A leaf torn off by the autumn wind, the first snow, the kiss of a maiden, the unfaithfulness of a sweetheart—everything is a theme for a poem. Let a city be destroyed, let a people fall or rise—of these, too, he makes poems..."

In other words, the poet, as the Western world knows him, is not unlike the painter and sculptor. He does not pass judgment but merely records what he sees. He does not want to bring about changes, but merely desires to reproduce reality in word pictures of "life arrested."

We have characterized the current "Jewish art" vogue as a symptom of the assimilation of the "slavery in freedom" pattern. Boraisha went further. He classed also *literature* of the troubadour type and accentuating the self as "art" foreign to the Jew. He clamored for authentic Jewish creative expression born of our Jewish "additional soul," and diagnosed the decadence of certain areas of modern Jewish literature as "the triumph of art over the spirit of Israel."

Boraisha proclaimed proudly "Yes, I stayed outside the temple of art." This means to say that, as all great Jewish poets and writers from the days of the Bible to our own time, in him, too, the spirit of Israel triumphed over art. Not "art for art's sake," but art as the servant of the idea was Boraisha's guiding principle. As his great predecessors, he classed art as *hiddur mitzvah* but never as the important essence of *mitzvah* proper.

Judaism places *na'aseh* (doing) before *nishma'* (audible theorizing). Boraisha did not content himself with merely staying outside the temple of art. He also went to war against those who attempted to introduce alien art standards into Jewish literature. He opened the offensive with a volume "in which the Jewish national idea speaks from every page." The operation was unsuccessful "because the generation would not tolerate this plot against art." But this did not discourage Boraisha. He continued to wage "war against art" as "a battle growing out of the deep-rooted knowledge that the Jewish way in the world is different from that of the others, and that our interpretation of art must therefore be different."

Boraisha's self-analysis and credo as a creative writer strengthens our thesis that the quest for "Jewish art" is a symptom of our assimilated generation's estrangement from Jewishness. His self-revelatory insights bolster our contention that the Jewish contribution to civilization is not to be traced by those who appraise it in terms of its approximation to and imitation of Western civilization.

The *real* Jewish contribution to civilization was not made by painters like Liebermann and Chagall, musicians and composers like Heifetz and Leonard Bernstein, sculptors like Jacob Epstein, and internationally acclaimed writers like Stefan Zweig and Arthur Koestler. Nor is there a distinct note of Jewishness in the achievements of Einstein and Oppenheimer, Bela Schick and Wassermann. Whatever these and other men of Jewish birth but non-Jewish associations and interests contributed to the various fields of culture and civilization did not stem from authentic Jewish inspiration—cast in the mold of the authenticity of a Yehudah Halevi, a Bialik, or a Boraisha—and was not infused with the elements of belief and the quest for salvation, national Jewish and universal human salvation, which are the distinctive marks of Jewish creativeness.

## IX

The *real* Jewish contribution to civilization is manifest only in the creative work of Jews rooted in and inspired by Judaism. This contribution is not to be measured with the rod of "Western civilization" but is to be evaluated as a self-contained feat of creative originality. We are not addicted to the mythology of race and racial genius. We believe, however, that there is a distinct and distinctive "Jewish genius" which is rooted not in physical genes, but in the "Jewish spiritual climate" which has been assiduously fostered by our people for generations.

This "Jewish spiritual climate" permeated the integrated Jewish community of yesterday which was dedicated to the Messianic ideal of recruiting all men to partnership with God in the realization of the perfectability of the world. In this community, man was considered to be not merely the crown of creation but its only absolute value under God. This community honored in man His maker and so concentrated its best efforts not on the glorification of the human form, in color, stone or word, but on *mussar*—the contemplation of man's ethical destiny and purpose in the cosmos of the spirit.

This "Jewish spiritual climate" produced the Prophets and the Sages of the Talmud. It also caused poets and logicians, saints and legalists to flourish, while providing a favorable habitat for *millions* of plain, everyday Jews—laborers, small businessmen, craftsmen—who spent the beginning and the end of every day in the *Bet Hamidrash,* reciting the Psalms, rehearsing the "Ethics of the Fathers," learning and living—actually living—the *Torah* whose ways are the paths of peace and justice. The creative efforts of this integrated Jewish community were concentrated on translating the image of God's ethics, as palpable in the Torah and the writings of the Prophets and Rabbis, into a livable pattern.

Drawing a moral is being decried by contemporary critics as stuffy philistinism, with the result that much of current creative literature is of one-day propensities. Jewish literature of the authentic spirit invariably "draws a moral" and stresses in ever new variations and connections, and in an infinity of contexts, that all and everything which is not dedicated to illumine the ethical meaning of man's existence is hollow and empty.

The Jewish way in the world has consistently and unswervingly pursued the idea and technique of the good life. Not beauty but goodness is the central problem and theme of Judaism. Not the amassing of physical power, but the generation of spiritual energy is the ideal of which the builders of our civilization have dreamed. Not man in his animal strength and expression, but man as the highest ethical purpose has been their perennial theme. Not self-indulgence, but self-control and abnegation in the service of a higher goal inspired the greatest works of Jewish literature. *Thou shalt*—the ethical imperative—is so inseparably interwoven with Jewish creative expression that, deprived of its momentum, "Jewish art" —no matter in what form of expression—cannot succeed for lack of a *raison d'etre.*

Ahad Ha'Am, among others, has rightly stressed that Jewish literary creations which are projected for eternity must be couched in the eternal and undying language of our people—Hebrew. It is important, however, to recognize that the Hebrew medium alone does not suffice to stamp a literary work as authentically Jewish. In addition to the authentic linguistic garb, there must also be in evidence the authentic Jewish idea content. The thirty-nine books of the canon of the Hebrew Bible represent but a part of the literature of ancient Israel. In our Bible there are numerous references to books which were lost. We also know that the Hebrew Apocrypha were denied admission into the canon of the Bible because the Rabbis who edited the canon felt that the idea contents of these books was not of the authentic Jewish grain.

These days when "Hebrew art" (whatever this may mean) is vociferously glorified, it is well to reflect on the standards of those who edited our Bible. Authentic Jewish culture cannot be a mere translation of Western literary trends into Hebrew and the transplantation of Western art into a romanticized pseudo-Oriental setting.

Jews always drew a line of separation between *Chochma* and *Parperoyos l'Chochma*—wisdom and wisdom's ancillaries. Translated into current terminology this would mean that the creations of a Bialik, a Boraisha and others who hark back to authentic Jewishness are *Chochma*—essential and rock-quality Jewish culture—while the rest is trimming and decoration, delightful of a certainty but inessential in the final analysis.

## X

The most striking trait of the Jewish genius is its concentrated and concerted fixation upon "the inner man." The second commandment, prohibiting art except where it is subservient to *mitzvah* and contributes to the beautification of the religious rite and observance, and the declaration, "Not by might nor by power but by My spirit, saith the Lord of hosts," are the credo, as it were, of our people's creative genius.

This concentration upon "the inner man" was regarded as a fault by the advocates of "let us be like all the nations." Apologies were offered for it, emphasizing that the Jewish preoccupation with "the inner man" was a result of ghetto conditions.... The fact that the second commandment and the Prophet Zechariah antedated the ghetto by millenia and centuries, did not trouble the eager and well-meaning apologetes.

Of late, however, the best contemporary thinkers and would-be healers of the malaise of the 20th century have been persistently proclaiming that the root of all the evils is our civilization's preoccupation with "the outer man" and "the sensate realm."

It would be mistaken to interpret the perennial Jewish preoccupation with "the inner man," i.e. ethical being and purpose, as proof that Judaism is essentially ascetic and hostile to matter. Except for short-lived insignificant splinter groups, which disappeared without leaving a legacy, Judaism has been full-bloodedly affirming the sensate realm, "accepting" matter while molding it for a supra-matter purpose. The Hebrew Bible is cogent proof that those who wrote it knew and relished the sweet savor of life compounded of budding spring and romantic love, strong drink and the clank of armor, seedtime and harvest, friendship and the tender devotion of the closely knit family group. Judaism does not reject "the outer man." On the contrary, the Sages of the Talmud held that he who rejects his "outer man," by depriving himself of legitimate physical enjoyments, will be punished in the hereafter.

Judaism asserts, however, the primacy of "the inner man." It insists that matter is meant to help the spirit realize and fulfill itself in the temporal sphere. This is a far cry from the deification of matter which was prevalent in Greece and Rome, and to which Western civilization has become the heir, as well as from the rejection of matter by Christianity. Judaism, ever realistic, early recognized that without the lure of "the evil inclination" men would neither marry, nor build houses and engage in useful activity—and so the world would come to an end. "The evil instinct" of "the outer man" is a precondition of human survival. But it will lead to ruin without the brakes of the control and the purpose orientation of "the good inclination" of "the inner man."

Judaism has invariably identified its ultimate purpose with —Messianism, defined as the redemption of Israel from exile *and* the redemption of the world from evil by the grace of the "Torah from Zion." Thanks to this Messianic orientation, Judaism has been more occupied with "ends" than with "means." Again, this did not imply the neglect of immediate tasks. The Aggadah which records how God reproached Moses, who prayed when he should have *acted,* proves forcefully the common sense Jewish frame of mind, which knows that "there is a time for everything." But it is one thing to use means for an end and another thing altogether to mistake the means for ends and enthrone them supreme.

Virtually all serious critics of standing who have written on the predicament of modern man and his civilization in recent years have stressed that the debacle stems from the exaggerated importance bestowed upon technology and the machine. Although they are mere "means," machines have become the "ends" of our civilization. As a result, we have built bigger and more powerful machines—for producing bigger and deadlier instruments of war.

There are no mathematically precise analogies of men, peoples and their times. But there are striking similarities. Roman civilization, about the time when Christianity emerged as the fighting missionary force into which Paul had transformed it, was in many respects similar to our 20th century civilization. It was a civilization of "means" which were proclaimed as "ends." It was a power civilization glorifying "the outer man" and revelling in bloodshed and sensuality. "Bread and circuses" were its watchwords and they precipitated Rome's decline and fall.

It was at this point that Christianity stepped in, substituting for the hedonistic opportunism of the means as ends the asceticism of ends serving, besides in their own capacities, also as substitutes for means. Christianity eventually emerged victorious. But the victory must be credited to—Judaism, for there is nothing in "Christian ethics" but can be traced to a chapter and verse of the Hebrew Bible and of the "Ethics of the Fathers" which was flourishing at the time when the Gospels were written. "Christian ethics" is Jewish ethics, reinterpreted and cast into a less exacting form than that given to it by the Pentateuch and the Prophets, who based the ethical imperative not on the loose and instable *subjective* support of "love," but on the firm and immutable principle of Justice tempered by love, to be sure, but not supplanted by it.

Despite the gulf of differences which separates Judaism from Christianity, there remains the fact that as the daughter of Judaism—recalcitrant, to be sure, but a daughter nevertheless—Christianity has a Jewish legacy. Nor could the many changes and alterations to which it was subjected obliterate its basic Jewish character. The Nazis were never more right than when they decried and rejected Christianity as an attempt of Jewish world domination.... Judaism became the decisive power in the drama of Western man by giving him—involuntarily—his religion. Because Christianity is *the* decisive spiritual factor in the Western world, medieval and modern Western literature and art, the theater and philosophy, government and law were "sparked" by Christianity. Bible translations ushered in all literatures of the Western world. Biblical figures and scenes stimulated literature and the arts. Biblical ideas and ideals of government supplied the foundations on which all democratic constitutions were reared, and they inspired all movements and revolutions on the road to progressive democratic government.

Much has been made of the fact that the Teutonic tribes who overthrew the Roman empire were assimilated and thus defeated by those who had given way before their physical strength. The Roman victory over the Teutonic barbarians was dwarfed, however, by the Jewish victory over the *entire* Western world. It was a victory so sweeping and momentous in its consequences that to "undo" this victory would be tantamount to obliterating all of Western culture and civilization. This Jewish victory will endure. The Jewish stamp has been pressed too deeply into the life tissue of the Western world to be ever erased.

As most victories, Christianity's triumph left an undefeated area, for it is in the nature of human beings that they resist *complete* penetration and domination. For good or for evil, there is a residuum of individuality in men and nations which will *die*—but which cannot be conquered. When we speak of "the badly Christianized" Western nations, who wage war and persecute dissidents in the name of the "Prince of Peace," we only attest that the Jewish victory, scored through Christianity, over Rome and the barbarians has been incomplete. Seen in this light, the many contemporary appeals for "Christian rearmament" against the paganism of technology are really appeals for stronger infusions of the Jewish potion which dissolved, but did not neutralize in the solution, the ancient Roman quest for power....

What this atomized generation needs, therefore, is another and stronger infusion of the Jewish spirit! Once again, Jerusalem must rise to fight Rome, for the ancient conflict of Jacob and "Edom" remains unresolved—Edom, who lives by the conquest of his sword, and Jacob, the guardian of the word.

The curtain rang down on the first act of this drama nearly two thousand years ago, when "Edom" defeated Jacob. But the political catastrophe did not end Jewish creativeness. On the contrary, the challenge of the tremendous odds and difficulties of the exile proved to be a fruitful stimulus. Jewish cultural creativeness flourished abundantly in the dispersion. Here were written the bulk of Jewish books of the ages. But, and this is important, the Jewish cultural creations of the none-statehood era differ sharply from those of the statehood period. It is not the question of "better," "more important," or "more original" that interests us in this connection, but the complete spiritual reorientation of Jewish exile creativeness.

While before the Destruction overall and universal issues had been the principal themes, after the Destruction the national concerns and problems moved into the foreground. This does not mean that the Prophets and the Psalmists were disinterested in their own people's problems, or that the Rabbis lost completely sight of the existence of "the nations." The Prophets spoke as ardent Jewish nationalists and the Rabbis looked forward to the time when all nations would give heed to the Torah from Zion. Still, the Rabbis' chief concern was with their people's homelessness and the efforts aiming at securing its survival. There is a continuity of Jewish thought and doctrine. And yet, in this continuity, there occurred a break when the Exile commenced and the emphasis of values was shifted to "particulars."

The early Tannaitic ethical teachings influenced Paul and the authors of the Gospels. Later, Rashi's Bible commentary, through the mediating interpretation of Nicholas de Lyra, influenced Martin Luther and the Reformation. Gabirol's *Mekor Hayyim,* in the Latin version *Fons Vitae,* contributed to the crystallization of Scholastic ideas. The same, although to a more limited degree, was true of the philosophical works of Maimonides. Crescas' influence upon philosophical thought, via Spinoza's mediation, might likewise be mentioned in this context. But this about sums up the influence of Jewish works of the post-Second Destruction Diaspora upon Western civilizations. Even those endowed with stronger apologetic instincts than this writer will have to admit that the sum total of this influence is negligible. Scholastic philosophy, the Reformation and pantheist thought would have flowered without the added impetus supplied by Jewish thought of post-exilic origin.

It is different, however, with the all-important "cluster of moral ideas" on which Western civilization is predicated. These ideas and ideals—the infinite value and dignity of *every* person, the equality of all men, regard for the weak and underprivileged, justice, peace and liberty—were *first* projected in the Western orbit by the Hebrew Bible and they stand out as *the* enduring Jewish contribution to civilization.

Tremendous technological progress has been made since the Prophets "saw" in Israel and Judah "the cluster of moral ideas" and the paths to its realization. The ethical insights of the Pentateuch and the Prophets, however, stand unequalled and unsurpassed. Kant's categorical imperative is little more than a cumbersome and weak paraphrase of "And thou shalt love thy neighbor as thyself!" Isaiah's formula for making technology the helpmeet of human progress, instead of its Nemesis, is as adequate for the atomic age as it was for his iron age. Isaiah counselled to "beat the swords into plowshares" which, translated into the 20th century language of Mr. Lilienthal, means to utilize atomic energy for peaceful purposes instead of for wholesale destruction.

The characteristic bent of the Jewish genius is most strikingly revealed in its definition and description of the *entire* ethical idea equipment mandatory for the good life. There is nothing missing from and nothing can be added to the ethics of the Hebrew Bible, which has become the acknowledged but unpracticed code of the Western world.

The ethics of the Bible, which synthesizes "the cluster of moral ideas" into an organic whole, has not infrequently been characterized as "Utopian." But its projectors certainly did not conceive of it as unsuited to the needs and challenges of *this* world. The social legislation of the first and second Jewish Commonwealths was molded by this allegedly "Utopian" ethics, and it proved to be practicable and practical. What with the limitations of man's ethical capacity, there was poverty and rapaciousness, injustice and immorality in ancient Judah and Israel, too. Yet, when all is said, the Jewish Commonwealth *was* an island of justice and decency in the welter of the corrupted civilizations of the ancient Middle East.

We Jews are "the descendants of Prophets." There is no merit in the argument that the Jewish descent of Karl Marx and of other modern proponents of socialism proves that Jews naturally incline toward movements for social progress and justice. Karl Marx was baptized as a child and had no Jewish upbringing—"the voice of the blood" is a fiction of romantic writers and bigoted "racial eugenists." The voice of authentic Jewishness can be heard only from those "descendants of the Prophets" who are claiming their prophetic legacy by identifying themselves with their people and its aspirations, precisely what Karl Marx and his followers failed to do.

The voices inspiring Jews to rebuild their land while pleading with the nations of the world for respect for the inalienable human rights, they, and only they, are the authentic Jewish voices. They speak the spirit of the Prophets as it behooves their descendants.

We, the descendants of the Prophets have now won the first round in the battle for the Messianic age. The Land of Israel has been *partially* redeemed and the Jewish State is a fact. Israel is still embattled and it may therefore be still too early for speaking of ultimate goals and of consummating Jewish genius. It may be too early now, but the day will come when "Prophets" will again speak and teach in Israel. Their voices will reach out not merely to their own people, but to "the nations." It cannot be otherwise, for the Jewish creative genius will clamor for the *universal* meanings fraught expression which was stifled when the long night of the exile began. We could not sing the Song of the Lord on strange soil.... And our *particular* woe made it impossible for us to concentrate on *universal* needs. We kept the treasure and expanded it by means of commentaries and fences, elaborations and rationalizing philosophies. All this is important—and will *always* remain important. For two thousand years, however, we have lived—and with us the Western world—on the idea endowment of Israel on its own soil.

The genius of our people can be trusted not to spend itself merely in ephemeral efforts of "art, literature and culture." As of old, now that our days have been renewed as of old, the Jewish genius will be attracted first of all by the challenge of moral values which give meaning to life by ennobling its purpose. "Ends" and not "means" agitate the center of gravity of the authentic Jewish creative genius. "The bush which burned and was not consumed" is our fascination and our challenge.

CHAPTER 5

# Jewish Survival - Why and How?

## I

THE PHENOMENON of "Eternal Israel" has puzzled the world for close to two thousand years. How could any people, no matter how dogged and virile, survive triumphantly the hardships and persecutions which have been Israel's lot throughout the ages?

The Church "solved" the puzzle with the doctrine that Israel is condemned to be a homeless wanderer for all eternity as punishment for its rejection of the Christian savior. By bearing the crushing burden of persecution, the Christian theologians declared, the Jews are testifying involuntarily, to be sure, to the truth of Christianity. From the viewpoint of the Church the eternity of the Jews is therefore not a blessing but a dire curse, for the Eternal Wanderer must live on, although he would prefer to die, until the end of days and "the second coming of Christ."

"The Wandering Jew" agitated however not only the theologians. He also stirred the imagination of creative artists and writers. The figure of the Wandering Jew, Ahasver, who, in the words of St. Augustine, "like Cain was not killed but cursed through the land which swallowed the blood of his brother," became a favorite topic of medieval poets and dramatists. Nor has he lost his fascination for modern writers. There is an aura of genuine pathos woven about the martyr for whom life eternal is not a boon but a scourge. The Wandering Jew is represented as tired of his charmed life—but, lo, he cannot die. He must go on and on, bearing the curse and sighing in vain, as Wordsworth put it:

> Day and night my toils redouble,
> Ever nearer to the goal,
> Night and day I feel the trouble
> Of the Wanderer in my soul.

As to the Wandering Jew, he has never regarded his charmed life as a curse. To him life eternal is a precious gift, God's blessing, and so he glories in the Divine promise that "the days of Israel are unnumbered." There was, in the very beginning, the "everlasting covenant" into which the Lord entered with Abraham, the father of the nation, pledging "to be a God unto thee and to thy seed after thee." Later, in the days of the Prophets, the very order of the cosmos was drafted as a witness to the Divine pledge of Israel's eternity: "Thus saith the Lord, who giveth the sun for a light by day, and the ordinances of the moon and the stars for a light by night. Who stirreth up the sea, that the waves thereof roar.... If these ordinances depart from Me ... the seed of Israel shall also cease from being a nation before Me forever."

Fortified by such promises, the Jews will not interpret their afflictions as a sign of Divine rejection. They view them as punishments of a loving father who chastises his son in order to lead him back to righteousness. They know the punishment is only temporary, for "the Lord will not cast off

His people, neither will He forsake His inheritance." This promise has braced the Eternal Wanderer and kept him from losing hope.

The Sages of the Talmud, faced with the strident harshness of the exile, firmly entrenched the belief in their nation's indestructibility as a sign of Divine favor. "Israel lives forever," they proclaimed confidently. "It was not forsaken and will not be forsaken. It was not consumed and will not be consumed." The biblical promise that Israel would be like unto "the sand," gave rise to this rabbinic exaltation of Jewish survival power: "As the sand reaches from one end of the earth to the other, so your sons shall be trodden upon by the kingdoms. And as the sand, which even rots metal vessels, endures forever, so also is Israel—all the nations vanish and they endure."

The Sages were convinced that Israel could never be broken. They compared the hardihood and persistence of their people to the strength of the sapphire. For when "placed on the anvil and struck with the hammer, the sapphire remains intact, while the anvil is split and the hammer is broken..." Thus is also the fate of the nations that attempt to crush Israel between the anvil and the hammer: the nations are broken and Israel lives on. The history of the Eternal People bears out the trust of the Rabbis that "whenever afflictions are visited upon Israel, the afflictions pass and Israel endures." And so, elaborating on the prophetic parable of Israel as an olive-tree, the Sages offered the homily that "just as the leaves of the olive-tree do not fall off, either in the summer or in the rainy season, so Israel will never disappear—neither in this world nor in the world-to-come."

Talmudic and medieval rabbinic literature abound in touching descriptions of the indestructible love that binds God to

Israel and Israel to God. Because of Israel's waywardness God could not but chastise it. However this punishment—manifest in exile and homelessness—did not diminish the affection which God bears for His people. As for the Eternal Wanderer, he conceived of his relationship to God not only in terms of the correlation of father and son, but also as the union of lover and beloved. "Song of Songs," the biblical paean to love, was admitted into the canon of Holy Scriptures because the Rabbis saw in it an allegory of the relationship of God and Israel. Midrashic and Kabbalistic literature are rich in pithy commentaries on Song of Songs interpreting the glowing pictures of desire and sensuous delight as symbols of the relationship of God and Israel. Thus the avowal that "many waters cannot quench love" meant to the Rabbis that "were the idolatrous nations of the world to unite in order to destroy the love between God and Israel, they would not succeed." In the same vein there are other authoritative rabbinic utterances on the undying Divine love for Israel, asserting that this affection is "everlasting to the end of eternity" and that "he who hates Israel is like one who hates God."

Thanks to these pledges, the Jews never felt rejected or forsaken. They gloried in the affection of the Holy One of Israel, and thus their very sufferings appeared to them as a seal of Divine Love: "Because God loves Israel He multiplies its sufferings." As if to anticipate later Christian charges that "Israel's rejection" is predicted in the Hebrew Bible, the Rabbis ingeniously proved that for every condemnation of the "sinful nation," there is also a tribute to its ultimate realization of righteousness. For if Isaiah threatened, "Woe to the sinful nation," he also proclaimed, "Open the gates that the righteous nation may enter." And if he condemned Israel as "a people laden with iniquity," he also anticipated a time when "My people shall be all righteous." If the Prophet represents the Lord as threatening the sinners, "Yea, though ye make many prayers, I will not hear," he also knows that God comforts His people, "Before they will call, I will answer them."

This trust in Divine love heartened and sustained the Eternal Wanderer. He did not despair of his ultimate redemption, nor did he ever regard his exile otherwise than as a just penalty and the instrument of atonement and reconciliation with God. Because of this unreserved trust and unshakable conviction in having God by their side, the very tortures of hell on earth could not prevail upon believing Jews to desert their banner. They interpreted their sufferings as a manifestation of God's loving concern for them, and so death and afflictions lost their sting. When the Church tried to convert the Jew by pointing to his distress as a telling sign of Divine wrath and rejection, he did not lack texts with which to refute the claim and prove that God's favorites are tried and refined in the crucible of suffering. The Christian interpretation of his homelessness seemed illogical to the Eternal Wanderer. He ignored it, to concentrate instead on the interpretation of the many biblical passages which testify to God's love for His people and to the covenant under the terms of which He will restore them, as of old, to their ancestral soil.

## II

The standard Hebrew term for Jewish survival is *netzah yisrael*—the Eternity of Israel. It is not without profound philosophical implications that *netzah yisrael*, in the only place where it occurs in the Bible, serves as a metaphor for "God" (I Samuel 15:29). In other words, God is Israel's Eternity as the 10th century Bible commentator, Rashi, succinctly remarks on this passage.

The discovery of the monotheistic truth of one God, one mankind and one justice impelled the discoverers not to rest or relax their efforts until all nations would *voluntarily* worship the Only God and abide by His commandments of truth and ethics.

The postulates of the One God and the one and united mankind are eternal ideals of limitless dynamic drive. By aligning their fate and future with these ideals, the Jewish people became eternal. Thus they no longer were chained to the three-beat cycle of national ascendancy, flowering and decline; instead they went "from strength to strength." Nahman Krochmal, the nineteenth century philosopher and self-taught disciple of Hegel, could therefore justly aver that "the infinite and universal idea" enabled the Jewish nation to pass not once but several times through the three Hegelian cycles of a nation's normal course of life. In other words, his identification with eternal ideals gave the Jew eternity. Their power was such that he defied and defeated all corrosive impacts. It filled the Jew with the awareness of his purposive existence and the certainty that he must not die, for were he to disappear, what would happen to the *Ideal?* Charles W. Eliot was therefore correct in ascribing the indestructibility of the Jews to the fact "that they early embraced certain invaluable ideals, and have struggled towards them indomitably for thousands of years."

These "invaluable ideals" are: God, mankind, and justice. It is surely not without significance that the Hebrew language lacks a present tense and substitutes for it, rather inadequately, the participle. Ahad Ha'am, the philosopher of modern Jewish nationalism, concluded from this philological oddity that the Jewish nation is rooted in the traditions and promises of the past and wholly dedicated to the ideals which are to be realized in the future. This preoccupation with what shall be rather than with what *is,* contributed largely to metamorphosing the people that achieved the remarkable feat of disregarding the present and concentrating instead on the future into the Eternal People. For as the historian Graetz put it: "A nation which makes light of the present and lives only for the sake of the future, living so to say on hope alone, is eternal like hope itself."

The hope eternal of his ultimate redemption from exile, while leading the nations to ethical salvation, would not let the Jew die when according to all logic he should have disappeared from the stage of history. He survived because his *raison d'etre* and purpose are not achieved as long as there remains a single human being who is ignorant of the Only God and His ethics of peace and justice. The Jew must go on and teach the world the will of God, if need be by enduring crushing hardships and excruciating tortures, for the driving force of the Ideal does not permit him to quit. The Wandering Jew has survived not because he *could not die,* but because *he refused to die.* As every genius serving an ideal he refused to rest or resign before he would see it triumphant.

The Greeks, after giving birth to philosophy and science, faded out of the picture. They had achieved their purpose, because their aristocratic and exclusive *Weltanschauung* admitted only the small number of the privileged few to share in the good life of the body and spirit.

The idea of the equality of *all* human beings, a logical corollary of the idea of the One God, never dawned upon the Greeks and Romans. To the spiritual leaders of Israel, on the other hand, theory was but a useless toy. They held that ideas and ideals do not come alive until they are translated into everyday life, not as mere form-giving principles in the Platonic sense but as regulative forces of human behavior and social relations.

Since the purposes and aims of Judaism are directed toward the translation of the abstract ideal into the concrete good, the Jews could not *afford* to die when it seemd inevitable and natural that they should. When the Greeks had fulfilled their *raison d'etre,* they made room for others. To the Jews, however, their *raison d'etre* will only be consummated with the fulfilment of their nationhood in the setting of the one mankind. They cannot abandon this program. It is their destiny!

### III

"Israel is the heart of mankind." Yehudah Halevi's dictum epitomizes the stimulus and support the universalistic strands of the "mission of Judaism" have given to Jewish survival. Israel is universalism incarnate and therefore—imperishable and deathless.

In probing the phenomenon of Jewish survival, it is inadequate to take note merely of the stamina which enabled the Jews to outlive *all* their enemies in ancient times and most of the more recent ones as well. Old age *per se* is no advantage. A long life is good only if the hoary individual retains his vitality and strength to an extent where he remains useful and capable of enjoying his days. The Jews are not only an "old" people. They are endowed with the grace of perennial youth and eternal creativeness. There is no other nation which for thirty-five centuries has remained steadily creative and virile.

Even in the last century and a half *hundreds* of Jews have

lastingly enriched world literature, the arts, science and philosophy. Yet we find that, despite the many Jews who chose to cultivate strange vineyards, there was still sufficient creative energy left within Jewry to bring forth a renaissance of Hebrew literature which in its choice fruits is not inferior to the "Golden Age of Hebrew Literature" in Spain, while quantitatively its output surpasses that of any previous period. Israel's Hebrew presses issue a book a day, on the average, besides daily papers, weekly journals, and monthly and quarterly magazines.

The birth of Israel and the achievements of the young Jewish state in its first trials-fraught year prove that the Jewish people is not only far from being tired and exhausted but, on the contrary, is just entering upon a new renaissance.

The Jew of the past, as the Jew of today whose life follows the traditional pattern, did not philosophize about "Jewish survival." He was certain of Israel's eternity and needed no theories to strengthen this conviction. Modern Jews rely on the *Wissenschaft des Judentums* and, especially, on "Jewish sociology" for tracing the elements of Jewish survival. Most sociologists, however, tend to emphasize the negative factors in the Jewish survival drama. They submit that the Jews survived largely because of the pressure from outside, i.e. anti-Semitism, the "social barrier" created by the Jewish law, and the "alien character" of the Jews, i.e. the "separatism" resulting from it.

No doubt, the "alien character" of the Jews, which was partly of their own making and partly forced upon them, contributed to keeping the group distinct and intact. Yet it is no satisfactory explanation of the "puzzle" of Jewish eternity. Negative factors are not sufficiently potent to keep a people alive and vigorously creative for over two thousand years, especially if all tangible vestiges of nationhood are absent. Moreover, the forces of hatred operating against the Jew in the past did not deny him the choice of ceasing to be a Jew. Until the rise of racial anti-Semitism, Jews could stop being Jews by embracing Christianity. The positions of honor some Jewish apostates attained in the medieval Church prove that baptism was indeed the key to equality for Jews who cared to use it. It is patently anachronistic, therefore, to assert that the Jews survived because they could not become extinct in the nations. Until the promulgation of the Nuremberg laws, Jews could stop being Jews—and multitudes did so.

The record proves that the Jews survived not because of negative reasons, but because they had something to live for. The negative factors, chief among them anti-Semitism, should be cited as a reason why many Jews deserted their people rather than as a prop of Jewish survival. Persecution and hatred were, after all, aimed at the "stubborn" Jews only, while those who yielded to persuasion were received with open arms. The Jewish masses made homeless by expulsions, of which the "Expulsion from Spain" was but one, could have kept their homes had they consented to baptism.

The notion that the Jews survived because of the force of hatred which held them together is a delusion of the philosophy of emancipation and assimilation, which argues that favorable conditions and relaxation of the outside pressure tend to wean Jews away from Judaism. But those Jews who wanted to escape from the ghetto did not have to wait for its official abolition; they could walk out triumphantly at the moment they stepped up to the baptismal font. The epidemic of baptism which gripped German Jewry in the first half of the nineteenth century was not a reaction to anti-Semitism; it was not an escape from a burden. It was little more than a nonchalant gesture. There is an answer to the question why the children and grandchildren of the Jewish martyrs deserted their people and its faith without compunction: Ignorance of Judaism and the concomitants, thereof—the loss of a Jewish *raison d'etre* and of the positive values of Jewish life, had made the emancipation-intoxicated and assimilation-dedicated Jews an easy prey for the negative forces tearing them away from their people.

It is not infrequently argued that conditions most favorable to the prosperity of the individual Jew are most injurious to the survival of the Jews as a religious community and as a nation. Here, too, confused thinking leads to mistaking the effect for the cause. Jewish history proves that the creative periods of Jewish self-assertion were times free from persecution. The Bible was created by a free people, living on its own soil. The Talmud and the Midrashim originated in a setting of relative freedom and toleration, only their codifications were hastened by the fear of impending disaster. Rashi's commentaries were written in a setting of freedom and tolerance, before the Crusaders made life unbearable for the Jews of the Franco-German territory. During the "Golden Age of Hebrew Literature" in Spain the Jews enjoyed liberty and security in the Islam dominated parts.

Virtually all the great Jewish classics, the works which in their sum total represent the Jewish heritage, originated in times of Jewish prosperity and freedom from persecution and oppression.

Jewish history and literature prove convincingly that it was for positive reasons that the Jews survived the most trying hardships. To aver that they survived because they were bitterly persecuted is about as logical as to state that Mr. X survived a severe illness because of the added complication of double-pneumonia. If Mr. X recovered from his sickness, aggravated by pneumonia, it was doubtless due to his physical fitness and the skill of his physician. Analogously, the Jews survived because of their almost miraculous fitness and their unique spiritual stamina.

Again, and over again, it must be stressed that the Jews survived because they had something to live for: the fostering and propagation of the national-religious-cultural heritage.

Many definitions of "Judaism" have been advanced. "Judaism as a religion," "Judaism as a nationality," "Judaism as a civilization," "Judaism as ethical monotheism" are just a few of the catch-phrases denoting varieties of Jewish introspection. As a matter of fact, Judaism warrants all of these and some additional definitions: It is "religion," "nationality," "civilization" and "ethics." Above all, however, it is a way of life and its constitution.

Judaism encompasses life as a totality. It supplies an all-comprehensive regimen and philosophy. It orders the most trivial as well as the most important events. It blends religion, national devotion, cultural aspirations, and the hope for a better future into an inseparable union of purposeful holiness. Judaism is a system of religious culture and cultural religion which most closely approximates the highest ideal of "humanism." It infuses its followers with the assurance of the meaningfulness of life by answering the questions "whence?", "whither?", "why?" Like philosophy on the highest plane, Judaism answers these eternal questions of mankind in a manner which stresses the *"whither"*—the goal and the purpose—thus identifying and aligning itself with the future. Through all the great books of Judaism there runs the conviction that the problems of the origin of the world, even of God, are less important than the challenges presented by the *purpose* of the world and the *meaning* of life.

## IV

We Jews have come a long way extending over close to thirty-five centuries, reckoning from the exodus. The bulk of these thirty-five centuries were spent in exile and beset by percution. Indeed, we could have ended the story and its agony centuries or millennia ago. Some of us, or rather the majority of us, at one time did take this counsel of despair, to wit, the Ten Tribes who, within a short time after the fall of Samaria (722 B.C.E.), submerged themselves in the populations of the Assyrian provinces where they had been deported. But the minority, the Judeans, refused to let their conquerors annihilate them as a nation. By the waters of Babylon, after the destruction of Jerusalem and the Temple (586 B.C.E.), they declined to sing the Lord's song on strange soil and vowed, "Let my right hand forget her cunning if I forget thee, O Jerusalem, if I set not Zion above my chiefest joy."

And to this oath we have remained faithful. To be sure, there were always some among us who decided to shed what they called "the burden" of Judaism, but those who gloried in this burden were in the majority. They followed their God "through fire and water," suffering agony and death, so that their people might retain its identity and integrity.

No precise figures are available on the Jewish martyrs who died for the "Sanctification of the Name" throughout the ages —but the number runs into many millions. All these men, women, and children laid down their lives so that our people might live. If the will to live is indeed the single strongest force motivating man's actions, the millions of Jews who readily and joyfully forfeited their lives were either abnormal and thwarted in their natural reactions—or they were possessed of an ideal and a purpose which meant more to them than the prolongation of their individual existence.

Why did these martyr-heroes want the Jewish people to live at all costs, even at the price of their own lives? They were deeply convinced that Judaism is a goodly portion and that to be a Jew imposes the obligation to defend this legacy to the last ounce of strength. They believed, in terms of the prophetic promise, that the world's salvation was up to Israel and its Torah of truth, justice and peace. In accordance with a pithy Midrash, they regarded themselves as "God's partners" in diffusing the light of ethics among those who were still walking in darkness. How, then, could they forsake the covenant of choice and chosenness?

But do not all peoples and religions regard themselves as "chosen" in one respect or other? Can it be that we have been deluded when regarding ourselves as "chosen"? Have we, then, something special to pursue and achieve besides the aims and ideals common to all men?

Of late the "Chosen People Idea" has been under attack in many quarters. Those who are familiar with the profusion of biblical, talmudic and rabbinic texts elaborating on Israel's chosenness know that, throughout the ages, it has never been interpreted otherwise than as the special burden *implicit* in the charge "to be a light unto the nations." No matter from what angle we look at Jewish history—and no matter how much we may strain to minimize the effects of the charge "to be a light unto the nations"—the fact looms large and irrepressible that what little of genuine humaneness there is in the Western world stems from the Jewish tradition.

Need we point to Christianity's and Islam's descent from

Judaism? Need we reiterate again that all the ideas and ideals of democracy were born and brought to fruition in ancient Israel, from where the seeds were carried to the four corners of the earth? Whatever there is today in the Western world of human fellowship and social awareness, of eagerness for peace and resolve to make this world a better place for all, stems from Israel's tradition.

The Jewish people—almost sterile in purely artistic realms and in speculative theoretic philosophy, fields where other nations are supremely "chosen"—has given the Western world its religion and its ethics, its real *raison d'etre*. And the Jews who would not bow to the Cross knew this all too well! They knew that the grandeur of the inexplicable and indefinable Oneness of God had been tampered with by Christianity and they were determined to uphold and safeguard this unique unity in all its majestic supremacy—and so they died with the words, "The Lord Our God is One!" on their lips.

"But all this is past history," it may be argued. Today all civilized nations and all monotheistic religions profess the ethical-humane program of Judaism. So may not the Jews now close the book of long suffering for the sake of the "Kingdom of God?"

Questions like these are often raised by Jews and non-Jews who feel that, as far as its "mission" goes, Judaism has run its course and should therefore retire from the world's stage. But in reality the "mission" of Judaism is today as little fulfilled as it was in the days of the Prophets. The Jewish ideas and ideals have hardly made a dent upon the conditions they mean to correct. The Jews therefore have a supremely good reason to go on teaching, preaching and fighting for the prophetic ideal "to do justice, love mercy and walk humbly with God." Indeed, for the last nineteen centuries this program has been part of Christianity's equipment as well—but are we Jews wrong in believing that we, who have wrested this program from God and from ourselves, suffering for it as no people has suffered, are uniquely fitted to bring it to fruition and lasting success?

"Jewish realists" not infrequently resent those who picture the Jewish past in favorable hues. They emphasize that Jews inclined to pacifism because they had no power to wage war, and that they adhered to higher standards of morality and practiced more "charity" to protect themselves against disintegration.

But this "factual" interpretation of the Jewish ethical climate cannot do away with the fact that throughout their history—even in its very earliest stages—the Jews were never quite as "bad" as their neighbors. From the very beginning the Jews felt themselves invested with a special responsibility. They sensed the impact of a "mission." The concept of the "Mission of Judaism" has been discredited and made light of by some Zionist ideologists, who failed to see that, as defined by the Prophets, it is a far cry from its interpretation by modern assimilationists. On the other hand, in their eagerness to prove the "universality of Judaism," the early leaders of Reform Judaism failed to note that the "Mission of Judaism" presupposes a healthy Jewish nation.

The Jews early discovered that their own prosperity and well-being were interrelated with and contingent upon the destiny of the rest of the world. This is why the Prophets postulated the "Mission of Judaism" as an implementation of Jewish nationalism rather than as a detraction from it. There is no doubt that the urge to be the idealists *par excellence* of history has also been one of the most powerful incentives of Jewish national survival.

## V

Ideals and ideas, no matter how sublime, are yet in need of tangible support. Jewish law—the thousand and one rules and regulations ordering every moment of private and communal life—fills that need admirably by furnishing a strong, concrete basis for the Jewish ethical program. Yet the complicated maze of ritual regulations was never felt to be the real purpose and essence of Judaism. The many laws the Jew observes are only the "fence," as it were, which safeguards the real treasure. The Rabbis of old who were eager to build more and more *seyagim*—"fences," to protect the inviolable purity of the essence of the *Torah,* were well aware of it that the ritual law is not an end in itself but only an instrument for the realization of ethics.

There were times when it was attempted to enthrone the ritual law supreme at the expense of its spiritual-ethical ends; and there were also periods when Jews experimented with living Jewish ethics without observing the Jewish rites. Such trials were always doomed to failure and spelled extinction, Jewishly speaking, for those who engaged in them, for the Law is the concrete, material basis of Jewish survival. If the Jews have continued to regard themselves as a nation, in the absence of a country and a government, it was because their religion was adapted by their leaders to serve as a portable fatherland that accompanied the exiles to wherever they carried the *Torah.*

The Talmud relates that when Jerusalem's fall was imminent, Rabbi Yohanan ben Zakkai left the city by a ruse and went to the Roman camp. Upon the offer of the Roman General to grant him the fulfillment of any wish, the Rabbi said: "Give me Jabneh and its scholars." And forthwith he proceeded to an obscure village, to set up the first academy dedicated to the interpretation of the *Torah* in the light of the changed conditions of Jewish life. Rabbi Yohanan ben Zakkai and his co-workers accomplished the feat of substituting for the tangible and concrete soil of Palestine and the Temple service of sacrifices and pontifical ritual the no less tangible and concrete medium of the "fences" of the Law and the no less stirring Divine service of prayer and personal devotion of the heart. The "fences" of the Law which were zealously built by Jewish teachers in the centuries after the Destruction of the Temple had the avowed purpose of safeguarding the biblical law against any possible infringement. Besides that, however, talmudic law also is an adaptation and reinterpretation of biblical law to make it serve as an adequate instrument under the new terms of uprooted homelessness.

The Law was meant to be the national norm of Jewish life. And it adequately served as such until the era of emancipation and assimilation when it was subjected to reform and change by Jews who maintained that there was neither need nor justification for the type of "fence" behind which the Law shut them up even more effectively than the ghetto walls. The experience of the last century and a half proves, however, that the reformers were wrong. The Jew who emancipated himself from the Law and thus was cut loose from the spiritual Jewish fatherland, eventually severed also his purely religious-ethical ties with a *Torah*-less "confession."

For those who stayed within the confines of the Law, it has served as a perfect substitute for the normal complements of nationhood, such as a country, a government, and a national discipline. To integrated Jews the Torah was their spiritual state, the rabbis its government, and the Hebrew language and its literature the language and culture they shared with all Jews the world over. Thanks to this uniform acceptance of the Law by Jews in all the corners of the globe, there is a remarkable harmony and uniformity of Jewish religious practice and cultural expression, uniting Jews of different countries and backgrounds into a strong fellowship cemented by common ideals and fired by identical hopes.

Thanks to the Law which regulates their every action and step, from the most important to the most trivial, Jews throughout the ages and in all countries, contrived to live in the realistic illusion that they were still settled on their national soil. This realistic illusion contributed much to Jewish survival strength, for, as Israel Zangwill put it so well, it made it possible "that Palestine should live in Israel, if not Israel in Palestine."

## VI

Jewish Law is not only an effective instrument of social isolation but also a potent means of safeguarding the biological survival capacity of the Jew. In view of the incessant drain on the Jewish community and its appalling losses in all ages, to say nothing of the unhealthy and abnormal conditions in which Jews have been living, it is truly remarkable that their physical resources have not become depleted. Despite the fact that medieval Jews lived crowded together in unsanitary ghettos, deprived of sun, light and air, and were incessantly subjected to persecution—they made a better showing in health and physical stamina than the general population. During epidemics of pestilence and other dread scourges the ghetto invariably had the lowest mortality, which not infrequently incited the Christians to kill the Jews as "well-poisoners" and spreaders of the murderous disease. When the "Black

Death" decimated the populations of all European countries, hundreds of thousands of Jews were slain by superstitious fanatics who charged them with having poisoned the wells from which the Christians drew their water, for how could it be otherwise explained that the ghettos were so little visited by the scourge?

The chief reason of the relatively greater immunity of medieval Jews to contagious diseases was not witchcraft but the hygienic laws of the Torah. These laws make it a serious religious transgression for the Jew to sit down at a meal without having first washed his hands. Judaism equates cleanliness with Godliness. Although the dietary laws are endowed with a sanctity which transcends their purely hygienic aspects, there is no doubting that they have immeasurably contributed to safeguarding the health of the Jews. If we reflect on the fact that trichinosis kills thousands of men, women, and children in this country every year, besides crippling tens of thousands without their being aware of the real cause of their infirmity, and all this despite the fact that the United States has the finest public health system and food supervision in the world, we can just about imagine what conditions prevailed in a time and age when there was no public health system whatsoever.

In the Middle Ages the poor seldom ate fresh and uncontaminated meat. If meat or fish was on their menu it was as a rule in a putrid condition. The inhabitants of the ghetto were kept from such dangerous foods, which were incidentally responsible for the widespread occurrence of leprosy, by the dietary laws which prohibit the consumption of any meat not strictly fresh and absolutely clean and healthy. Millennia before public meat inspection was introduced in the civilized countries, the Jews practiced a highly effective meat control by subjecting the vital organs of the ritually slaughtered animals to a minute examination in order to determine whether the animal was suffering from a disease which might have a harmful effect on those who eat its meat. It is interesting that in this country the verdict of the Jewish ritual meat examiners and those appointed by the boards of health are as a rule unanimous, although not infrequently meats that are passed by the examiners of the health boards are rejected by the rabbinical authorities.

Until recent times standards of bodily cleanliness were much higher among Jews than the general population. Since the earliest times the ritual bath has been esteemed of equal importance with the Synagogue, or if anything more important, for the rule is that if the communal funds do not suffice to finance both the building of a synagogue and a ritual bath, the latter takes unqualified precedence. In times when even the crowned heads and the nobility never took a bath, the dwellers of the ghetto repaired regularly to the ritual bath.

The ritual bath played, however, an even more important role in the laws of Jewish marriage hygiene, a set of rules singularly conducive to secure the fertility of the nation. Modern medicine has conclusively established that "the fertile period" of all but a fraction of women extends from about the twelfth day after the onset of menstruation to the eighteenth day, in other words the period which thanks to the laws of family purity is usually the time of the highest sexual activity of Jewish couples observing the Law. It is also an established fact that after a protracted period of rest and sexual inactivity the chances for conception are heightened considerably. Thus, for instance, Professor Van De Velde, one of the foremost authorities in this field, prescribes as a cure for sterility not due to organic causes a "rest period" to extend from the onset of menstruation to the eleventh or twelfth day. The remarkable fertility of the Jews may therefore be ascribed to a certain extent to a regimen of conjugal life making provisions which are eminently suited to stimulating fertility and producing a high birth-rate.

Thanks to the strict insistence of Jewish law on sexual continence of the unmarried and unconditional faithfulness of husband and wife, traditional Jewish communities have been virtually free from the plagues of degenerative veneral diseases. These scourges of mankind were unknown in the ghetto and are still unknown among Jews who observe the Law. Inevitably the immunity to veneral diseases had a large share in strengthening the biological survival capacity of the Jews.

It is significant that even contemporary Jews living under the same conditions as the general population make a better showing in vital statistics. Their mortality rate, especially the infant mortality rate, is appreciably lower which results, despite the fact that the Jewish birth rate in most countries is lower han the general birth rate, in a faster pro ratio growth of the Jewish population.

Another factor which favorably affects the vital statistics of the Jews is their traditional sobriety. Although Jews enjoy alcoholic beverages and utter special blessings over the fermented juice of the grape, they but rarely become alcoholic addicts. A drunkard was an anomaly in the tradition-bound Jewish community and is still a rare phenomenon even among those who have broken the bonds of restraining tradition. Thanks to these standards, crimes and sexual lapses committed in a state of intoxication do not sap the strength of the Jewish community.

The dietary regulations and the family purity laws inevitably conditioned their observers to higher standards of general cleanliness which, in turn, could not but result in better health. In tune with this appreciation of cleanliness we not infrequently find pious medieval Jewish fathers exhort their children in their wills to practice exemplary cleanliness. Thus, for example, Rabbi Eleazar the son of Isaac, an eleventh century scholar of Worms, Germany, left this will for his son:

"Keep your body clean, purify the abode of your soul. Do not befoul it lest you cause your own rejection. My son, be not impatient because of my insistence on this subject. Washing the hands is one of the sublime things that are of the utmost importance. Beware lest by its neglect you become as one excommunicated and forfeit of future bliss. For when you wash your hands you are bound to lift them up in adoration of your Creator; it would be unseemly to do so with dirty hands..."

Another medieval Jewish father bequeathed to his children these health rules:

"Be very particular about keeping your houses clean and tidy. I have always been scrupulous on this point, for every injurious condition, and sickness and poverty are to be found in foul dwellings."

The attitude of medieval Jews to bodily cleanliness is well summed up in this summary of a popular moral homily: "Cleanliness is a habit which is to be especially commended and to be zealously inculcated. Clothing, bed, table, table utensils, especially those used for food, indeed all and everything we take in our hands should be clean, sweet and pure; above all, however, the body should be immaculately clean, for we are made in the image of God that must never be defiled by dirt."

One more health factor conducive to developing physical stamina and survival power should be considered: the Sabbath rest. Modern medicine has emphasized the great importance of regular rest periods and relaxation. The Jews were benefitted by this discovery more than thirty-five centuries ago when they set aside the Sabbath as a day of complete rest and cessation of work of any kind. Inevitably these weekly rest periods, with their festive atmosphere and special delights, have contributed immeasurably to strengthen the body and spirit of the Jews, so that despite their harassed existence they could muster a greater equanimity of mind and a better balanced personality than those free from Jewish insecurity.

As a result of all these factors the Jewish people has grown steadily, except for temporary setbacks, although for two thousand years crisis has dodged its every move. Despite the loss of millions in pogroms and wholesale slaughter, to say nothing of the multitudes that broke away from the fold, the Jewish people has consistently and steadily grown. It is estimated that in the year 1000 the total Jewish world population was about 2,500,000. Five hundred years later, after the Expulsion from Spain and centuries of persecutions and massacres, this figure had shrunk to about 1,000,000. Three hundred years later, in 1800, when the first effects of a more enlightened and tolerant age were already felt in the ghetto, the Jews had repaired the losses sustained in the fatal five-hundred-year period from the year 1000 to 1500. The world Jewish population was again 2,500,000. In the next fifty years, from 1800 to 1850, the Jewish world population almost doubled. The next fifty years, from 1850 to 1900, again marked a more than 100 per cent increase of the Jewish people. The rate of this remarkable growth kept up undiminished, despite the rapid increase of defection by conversion and mixed marriages, so that in 1938, before Hitler's wholesale slaughter of millions of Jews started, the total Jewish world population was close to 17 millions.

This brief statistical survey shows that the vitality and virility of the Jews is still unimpaired and vigorous, despite the prophets of doom who aggravate the difficulties of the present Jewish world scene by painting the Jewish future in dark and utterly gloomy hues. Fortunately, the inventory of present Jewish assets reveals that there is no cause to despair of the Jewish future.

Taking stock of the large, though extremely young, Jewish center in America we find that there is little ground for pessimism, even here. The total Jewish population of America (United States, Canada, South America) is about six and a half million of whom more than five and a half million are concentrated in North America. This compact mass of Jews exhibits all signs of physical and spiritual growth and development. Disregarding the increase of American Jewry by immigration, the American Jewish population commands a considerable natural increase, despite the fact that about 90% of American Jews live in large urban centers with a low birth-rate.

Even more encouraging are the population statistics of Israel, which has one of the highest birth-rates among civilized nations, together with a very low infant mortality.

Although the staggering population losses in Europe are not nearly made up by the natural increase of American Jewry and Israel, still the upward trends of the Jewish population in the two countries which are the new rallying points of the Jewish people are extremely encouraging.

## VII

In consonance with the display of physical vitality in America and in Israel, there is a vital and significant spiritual renaissance of creative forces. Modern Hebrew literature, although still in its infancy, has yet already produced poets, writers, and scholars who are hardly inferior to the luminaries of the past.

With all its many shortcomings, the contemporary American Jewish scene yet holds the promise of a bright and fruitful future. Politically, American Jews enjoy complete equality under the Constitution; economically, they have achieved a fair measure of success and security. These favorable factors provide a most auspicious basis for physical expansion as well as for the deepening of cultural life. Jewish culture and the fostering of the religious legacy are stimulated, however, also by the American democratic conviction of the desirability of a happy blending of cultural and religious diversity in the body politic. There is consequently no need to feel apprehensive lest the progressive Americanization of American Jews must spell the death of Judaism.

Here, again, Jewish history provides evidence that sharing fully in the political and cultural life of their country does not blight or interfere with Jewish loyalty. Some of the most important classics of the "Golden Age" of Hebrew Literature were not written in Hebrew but in *Arabic,* the vernacular of Moslem Spain. Yehudah Halevi wrote his philosophical opus, the Kuzari, in Arabic, and Maimonides used the Arabic language for his "Guide for the Perplexed" and his Commentary on the Mishnah. These as well as numerous other examples prove that Jewish creativeness is not bound to a particular climate.

Physical and spiritual adaptability are among the most pronounced Jewish characteristics. If the Jews survived, despite all the many handicaps they were subjected to, it is not least due to their ability of getting acclimated to new surroundings. The complete integration of second and third generation Jews into the America scene to the extent of becoming leaders of American thought and literature, art and music, proves conclusively that this Jewish adaptability and faculty of cultural integration is far from a superficial mimicry. Yet his integration into the cultural scene of his country should be no cause of deterring the Jew to foster his own "minority culture." From the time of the very first beginnings of emancipation and assimilation it has been demonstrated that creative integration into the majority civilization in no wise precludes creative Jewish loyalty.

Moses Mendelssohn, who led German Jewry from their intellectual ghetto by teaching them the German language through translating the Bible into the vernacular, enriched German philosophy and literature no less than Jewish philosophy and literature. The same is true of numerous other writers who, thanks to their adaptive capacities, enriched the culture and civilization of mankind while simultaneously strengthening the resources of their own people.

The remarkable integrative capacity of the Jew is rooted in the universality of Judaism thanks to which the sacred books of the early Hebrews became the Bible of the Western world. Even as the Hebrew Bible supplied the incentive to innumerable works of art and thousands of poems, dramas and novels in all civilized tongues, without yet changing its character or losing its specific characteristics as the result of these adaptations to and interpretations by a variety of civilizations and languages, so the "People of the Book" too can share in many civilizations without yet losing its identity.

## VIII

There are older nations than Israel, but Israel is the only nation with an unbroken cultural tradition of uninterrupted creativeness for thirty-five centuries. The descendants of the ancient Babylonians and Egyptians, as well as those of the Greeks and the Romans can still be traced among the present-day populations of Mesopotamia, Egypt, Greece and Italy—however, these physical survivors have no connections whatsoever with their ancestors. They do not speak the languages they spoke, and their religion and cultural ideals are altogether different. There is lacking the "chain of tradition," the cultural continuity that makes the modern Jew not only the physical but also the spiritual descendant of his ancestors. The Hebrew language of today is still the same as that spoken in ancient Palestine and in which the Bible is written. While there is, for instance, a marked difference between Old English, Middle English and Modern English, no such distinctions, in either spelling, grammar, syntax or semantics, exist in Hebrew. Of course, the Hebrew language has grown and has been enriched in the course of millennia. Its basic structure, however, has not undergone any change whatsoever, a circumstance which enables the Jew whose mother tongue is Hebrew to read the Bible, or any other Hebrew classic, without any difficulty. An average Englishman will not be able to read "Beowulf" or the "Canterbury Tales," written only some centuries ago, without special philological training. To the uninitiated the language of these early English classics does not seem English at all. Nor will a contemporary Greek be able to read Homer with no greater difficulty than he would read a modern book or magazine—to say nothing of the populations of Mesopotamia and Egypt who were altogether unaware of the fact that their ancestors created a voluminous literature in picturesque cuneiform symbols and hieroglyphics, until modern archaeologists and scholars exhumed those treasures.

It is consequently not the eternity of the "Wandering Jew" that should puzzle the world but his retention of the continuity of Jewish culture and his remaining the heir, in all respects, of all the Jewish generations that lived and created before him. The remarkable thing is that the Jews who form less than one percent of the human race and should therefore hardly be heard of "have left and still are leaving," to quote Mark Twain, "their impress on the culture and civilization of mankind in a proportion altogether incommensurate with their small numbers. . . . The Egyptians, the Babylonians, the Persians rose, filled the planet with sound and splendor, then faded to dream stuff and passed away. The Greek and the Roman followed, and a vast noise, and they were gone; other people have sprung up and held the torch high for a time, but it burned out, and they sit in twilight now, or have vanished. The Jew saw them all, beat them all, and is now, what he always was, exhibiting no decadence, no infirmities of age, no weakening of parts, no slowing of his energies, no dulling of his alert and aggressive mind. All things are mortal but the Jew; all forces pass, but he remains."

CHAPTER 6

## *A Manifesto of Diaspora Survivalism*

I

"JEWISH SURVIVAL" and "Jewish survivalism" have become popular household words. The areas they connote are widely discussed in print and on the lecture platform. The concentration of our best minds on problems of Jewish survival is reassuring. On the other hand, however, it indicates that all is not well with Jewish vitality and confidence in the future. For, obviously, a hardy and vigorous person does not worry about his health. Survival worries only those whose state of health warrants a pessimistic outlook. The wide-spread anxiety over Jewish survival, therefore, seems to prove that something is wrong.

It is natural for a people to worry about the future after losing, in less than a decade, almost 40% of its members. At funerals even those in blooming health turn pensive, as they gaze into the open grave. We have buried fully six million of our most promising and Jewishly-dedicated sons and daughters. In our far-flung communities there is scarcely a family but has been placed into mourning by the harrowing catastrophe that destroyed their nearest and dearest, together with our most treasured cultural institutions and the most sanctified and authentic forms of traditional Jewish life. A holocaust of such dimensions is bound to make the survivors apprehensive about the future.

As a matter of fact and record, however, the worry about Jewish survival antedated the physical catastrophe represented by the almost complete annihilation of European Jewry. Even in this country, the problem of "Jewish Survival or Extinction?" was posed more than a quarter of a century ago by Elisha M. Friedman's book. Practically the entire Jewish ideological literature produced in this country over the past twenty-five years—there was little of this genre before—has been concerned primarily with problems of Jewish survival.

Elsewhere, too, the worry about the Jewish future has been the chief inspiration of scholars and thinkers. Thus the Science of Judaism (*Wissenschaft des Judentums*) was motivated by the need of an ideological-historical foundation for meaningful Jewish survival in the modern era. Zunz, Frankel, Graetz, Steinschneider, and the other pioneers of the Science of Judaism were fully cognizant of the survivalist significance of their philological, historical and bibliographic labors.

It is natural for a people to apportion strength and efforts to the entrenchment of its future. For that matter, all living organisms, from the primitive amoeba to man, "the crown of creation," are equipped and geared for the preservation and propagation of their species. While, on the upper rungs of the biological ladder, the preservation of the species becomes increasingly the domain of the brains, on the lower and middle rungs, the survival technique is instinctive and requires no conscious, deliberate effort. Mimicry, for protection and concealment, such as changes of coloring with changes of habitats and the seasons, reduction of the metabolism rate in hibernating animals, and similar phenomena, are devices with which "nature" bolsters the survival potential of the various species. The study of botany and zoology leads one to the inevitable conclusion that the purpose of life is—life and its perpetuation. The bright colors of the flowers and their sweet scent were not made for the poet's inspiration, but to attract the insects to the honey, so that while partaking of it they may carry the pollen to the ovule. Even the luscious fruit is only a by-product of the seed embedded in its core. Beauty, too, is no end in itself, but has its useful place in the economy of nature to further the ends of the species. The special beauty lures of voice, scent and coloring, with which animals blossom forth in the mating season, and the tender loveliness of the grown girl and boy are all part and parcel of nature's survival pattern and stratagem.

Human institutions and, especially, the colorful rituals and rites of primitive men likewise emphasize the focusing upon life and its perpetuation. There is, however, a profound difference between this natural, organic survivalist orientation and the efforts of Jewish survivalists, or, of survival engineers of any group attempting to preserve its identity through a carefully devised strategy. For while "nature," and "natural man," are instinctively, i.e. *unconsciously,* in the service of life, Jewish survivalism is *conscious,* deliberate and planned.

Contemporary Jewish survivalist efforts compare to the natural ease with which less troubled generations took their Jewishness in stride as the conduct of a healthy individual to the regimen of one who is ailing. To the healthy person diet and exercise are matters requiring little thought and planning. To the patient, on the other hand, every spoonful of nourishment and every step present problems. Thus, while the mind of the healthy person is free to concentrate on areas beyond the bodily functions, the patient's thoughts, and worries revolve around his physical condition and his doctor's orders.

At this juncture the Jewish people, outside of Israel's frontiers, resembles an ailing patient rather than a healthy, zestful man. There are many contributories to the precarious state of Jewish health in the Diaspora. The unspeakable tragedy of European Jewry was but the last link in a long chain of enervating events and situations. Significantly, the principal threat to Jewish survival in our time—as incidentally in previous periods too—lies not in the fatalities we suffered, despite their staggering dimensions. The real menace is the progressive weakening of Jewish survival determination in those who have emerged unscathed from the holocaust. If the Nazis slew millions, Jewish apathy and indifference have claimed hundreds of thousands in the most recent past.

Varying degrees of the weakening of Jewish survival determination are apparent everywhere. In some cases Jewish indifference has grown to disastrous proportions, and so there is imperative need for a regimen to arrest the disease and reverse the pernicious trend. Now a physician can do no more than diagnose and advise the patient to the best of his knowledge and experience.... The Jewish survivalist, too, must be satisfied with tracing and describing the healthy Jewish survival scheme, in the hope of moving and persuading those who have forsaken it to pick up its strands and weave them into an enduring Jewish pattern.

## II

There has arisen of late a school which views Jewish history as a series of crises. While one may disagree with the "crisis orientation" of some Jewish historians, there is no denying that crisis has been a perennially recurring *motif* in Jewish history. From the Destruction of the Temple to the cataclysmic Jewish tragedy of our day, periods of crisis and trial have marked in profusion our march across the centuries and continents. There is, however, a marked difference between the Jewish crises prior to the emancipation period and the crisis of our day. All major and minor crises of the pre-emancipation era were caused by outside forces and constellations over which the Jewish people had no control. The Hadrianic persecutions, the Crusades, the wave of medieval country-wide expulsions, starting with the expulsion from England (1290) and culminating in the expulsions from Spain and Portugal (1492 and 1497), the ghetto and the imposition of crippling discriminatory laws, the pogroms and persecutions without number, were inflictions against which Jews were powerless, as powerless and helpless as the millions who were exterminated by the Nazis.

The present Jewish spiritual crisis, however, has been brought on largely through our own omissions and commissions. Caught in the merciless vises of persecution and annihilation, the Jews were passive victims. Even the resistance some of them offered was frustrated by the handicap of insufficient numbers and equipment. There was no escape but *by a stroke of exceptional luck*. The Jewish spiritual crisis, on the other hand, although precipitated by extraneous conditions of emancipation and assimilation, can be cured by our own effort. If the masses of indifferent Jews were but to decide to close the ranks and identify themselves with the important and vital Jewish areas, the survival crisis of modern Jewry—and especially of the American Jewish community—could be turned into a triumphant assertion of Jewish strength and a blessed flowering of Jewish creativeness.

The challenges of the hour are too urgent to permit indulgence in wishful dreaming or reaching for the stars. . . . The present Jewish Diaspora scene warrants little optimism for a mass return on the part of the growing legion of apathetic, indifferent and alienated Jews. While in a very small and charmed circle of the intellectual elite there has been made much progress over the past two decades, or so, in making the American Jewish community spiritually-intellectually self-sufficient, the fact remains that, on the mass level, there has been a progressive decline in Jewish literacy and intelligent participation in Jewish life.

This decline is in direct ratio to the size of the American-born and American-educated group of American Jewry. For, unfortunately, over the past three generations, the law of diminishing returns has reaped an abundant harvest. Today, when the third generation descended of the immigrants of the eighties and nineties is about to enter upon adult responsibilities, it becomes apparent that there has been a terrifying decrease of Jewishness with each successive generation. The pattern traceable in most families corresponds in the main to this picture: grandparents were thoroughly integrated Jews who saw their lives' chief purpose in transmitting the tradition of the Jewish way of life to their children (grandparents of the Yiddishist radical persuasion were no less eager than the majority of the religiously orthodox to imbue their children with Yiddishist or Bundist ideals); children, who had absorbed sufficient Jewish inspiration to last them a lifetime, but who became "Americanized" and adapted their Jewishness to the tempo, convenience and alleged demands of the American scene; grandchildren, raised in "Americanized" Jewish homes, who identify Jewishness with *gefillte fish, Kaddish* and *Memorial Services*.

This is the overall pattern. In the light of the rapid decline and deterioration of Judaism in this country, over three generations, our anxiety about the future is amply warranted. For what Jewishness and what Jewish loyalties can the "grandchildren" be expected to transmit to *their* children?

The law of diminishing returns has operated, of course, among all emancipated Jewries. If not for a steady influx of Jews from Eastern Europe, the Jewish communities of the Western European countries would have become extinct, by defection and indifference, long before the Nazis annihilated them. In the first quarter of the 19th century, the bulk of Berlin's Jews had themselves baptized. Although the trend to baptism declined subsequently, the intermarriage rate of German Jewry, up to the Nazis' ascendancy, remained suicidally high. The same was true of the Jews of other Western European countries, who managed to survive only thanks to the steady influx of Jewish immigrants from the East.

In this country, too, the law of diminishing returns had been at work long before our time. There has remained almost no trace of the early Sefardic Jews and the subsequent German Jewish immigration, typified by the generation of Jacob H. Schiff. But while there was replacement available for the Sefardic and the German groups, there are no longer any reserves that could be called upon when the fourth and fifth generation descendants of the Eastern European Jews will have traversed the road of assimilation and Jewish indifference to its tragic and inevitable extremity. After the present insignificant trickle of Jewish DPs, there will not be another Jewish immigration to this country in the foreseeable future. Therefore, if we are in earnest about American Jewish survival, we must devise ways and means of arresting the trend which is sapping our strength and depleting our ranks. We must mobilize all our resources so as to rally all those who call themselves Jews, though they do not know why, for the urgent task of strengthening the Jewish survival potential.

To make Jewish survival a desirable and worth while goal for American Jews requires, first of all, the substitution of Jewish affirmations and satisfactions for the extensive negative area of frustrations under which too many are now chafing. Obviously, it is not in our power to uproot anti-Semitism and provide omnipotent physical protection against the many hurts devised by the Jew-hating mind. The most we can hope to accomplish is the winning of legal and constitutional safeguards. But this still leaves the extensive and painful region of social anti-Semitism and the "polite" discrimination and exclusion of which Laura Z. Hobson wrote in "Gentlemen's Agreement." To be a Jew in a non-Jewish world has always been and will continue to be a handicap in more ways than one. The positive side and worthwhileness of being a Jew will therefore have to be stressed and bolstered by props beyond the sullying reach of the Jew-hater.

Life is an end in itself. We do not require, therefore, the elaborate "Mission of Judaism" philosophy to justify our existence, although we *are* proud of our mission. Even if we had not contributed a thing to the welfare and progress of mankind, and were not endowed to make a future contribution likely, we still would have the right to live—because we are alive. Yet, although life is a end in itself, man does not live by bread alone. Merely to exist is a poor and unsatisfying prospect. On the civilized level, life must be purposive to be worth while. That vast numbers of Jews are without desire and zest for Jewish living, is due, in the final analysis, to the fact that Judaism is not worth while, as they see it. Neither the "difficulties" of being a Jew, nor the extraneous position of the Jew are at the root of Jewish indifference and desertion.

The real cause is—doubt in the worthwhileness of Judaism. This is why "the rationale of Judaism" must be taught, expounded and, if need be, "glamorized," so that it may become again the common and treasured possession of our people.

### III

"The rationale of Judaism" is the sum total of the great ideas and ideals that are the unique creation of the Jewish genius. There is a tragic and widespread misunderstanding of "the Jewish contribution to civilization" abroad. Virtually all students who have made this theme the object of their studies have defined "the Jewish contribution to civilization" as the achievements of individuals who happened to have been born or descended of Jews, even if they themselves were no longer identified with the Jewish community. Obviously, it is neither fair nor logical to claim the attainments of a Jewish (Jewish by "racial" definition) physicist, economist or chemist, who is in no way identified with Jewish areas of interest, for the credit ledger of the Jewish people. Moreover, what is there specifically Jewish, or French, or Russian about a mathematical formula?

"The Jewish contribution to civilization," as the distinctive contribution of any other people, is not the sum total of the achievements of individuals with doubtful and tenuous Jewish connections or sympathies, but the national contribution of our people, flowing from and informed by its unique national spirit. Even as the soil of various countries produces different plants, so national groups, too, are distinguished by special talents and inclinations. Jewish creativeness has celebrated its greatest triumphs in the discovery and proclamation of the eternity-orientated and eternity-guaranteeing ideas which we subsume under "the rationale of Judaism."

Jewish survival is the fruit of the union of "the rationale of Judaism," i.e. the sum total of the great ideas and ideals that are the unique creation of the Jewish genius, and "the technique of Jewish survival," i.e. the Jewish way of life. Among the contributories to "the rationale of Judaism," there is, first and foremost, *the Jewish God idea* which, in various modifications, has become the God concept of the Western world and large parts of Asia and Africa. According to the distinctive and singularly consistent Jewish definition, God is not merely *one* but *unique*. The articulation of God's uniqueness is the most distinctive feature of Judaism and its most significant contribution to "civilization." We Jews have "discovered" God and this *national* contribution is by far more important than the discoveries and feats of individuals of physical Jewish antecedents but without affirmative Jewish spiritual-intellectual identification.

The logical corollary of the Jewish God idea is the concept of *fellow man*. The hope for *the unity of mankind*, built upon *the fellowship of all men*, grows organically from the axiom of the *unique* oneness of God, which, in turn, implies the postulates of *human equality* and *brotherhood*. Despite their achievements in technical and abstract logical-philosophical areas, the ancient Greeks and Romans yet failed to perceive the first principle of genuine civilization, i.e. *human equality*. This was inevitable, of course, for human equality becomes a cogent necessity only when the uniqueness of God, as the basis of the unity of men, is acknowledged as axiomatic.

The Jewish ideas of God and fellow man are synthesized in the vision *of the Messianic age*. On its highest and purest plane of interpretation, "the Messianic age" connotes the realization in every-day life of *all* potentialities of the God and fellow man ideas. On the Jewish national level, *the Messianic age* is envisioned as the termination of Israel's sufferings and dispersion through the restoration of the people on its own soil and under its own government. On the international level, Jewish Messianism envisions peace for all amidst plenty, unity and understanding. Jewish Messianism is free from supernatural and miraculous expectations. Its orientation is thoroughly realistic—it strives for the ideal perfection of this world. The realistic (there is a vast difference between "realism" and "materialism") bend of the Jewish mind is especially pronounced in the emphasis placed on the need of the satisfaction of the physical needs as a prerequisite for the flowering of the spirit. Moreover, the orientation of Jewish Messianism is thoroughly democratic. While Plato and Aristotle submitted, in matter of fact fashion, that the common man lacks the intellectual endowment that sets the philosopher apart from the masses, the Prophets of Israel proclaimed that all men can become learned in the Law, if only they desire it.

The great triad—God, fellow man, Messianism—of the rationale of Judaism is supported by numerous ancillary ideas and ideals. Though not the exclusive discovery of the Jewish genius, these ideas and ideals have been indelibly stamped and uniquely fashioned by it. Chief among these ancillary ideas rank *Truth, Justice, Peace and Freedom*. Born and shaped in the Jewish national orbit and projected, first of all, for the welfare of the Jewish nation, "the rationale of Judaism" is yet thoroughly cosmopolitan. This is natural, for cosmopolitanism is the professed aim of the great triad of ideas upon which the rationale of Judaism is predicated. This, however, should not lead one to conclude that Judaism is intent upon levelling national differences. Far from it. The shallow quest for identity, which many mistake for democracy, had no followers among the great molders of Jewish thought. When envisioning the *one mankind*, the Prophets did not dream of the disappearance of all differences. They merely expressed the hope for a day when, above the differences—which are important and desirable because they lend color and variety to the human panorama—the all-significant common possessions of mankind would be recognized as sources of peace and harmony. Isaiah neither wished nor hoped that the lion would turn into a lamb; he hoped, however, that they would learn to lie down together. . . .

The *Chosen People Idea* occupies a very special niche in the rationale of Judaism. The Chosen People Idea, in its Jewish formulation, is not tainted with vaunted national pride and chauvinism of which it has been declared guilty. Jews believe that they hold a special place in the world because they submitted unconditionally to the service of God and His ethics. But—and this is of paramount importance—they never claimed to be the only chosen bearers of Divine truth. Chosenness, as defined by Judaism, is not a passive state, but the active espousal of the ideas and ideals that confer the mark of distinction. Jewish Messianism, which avows the advance of all mankind to ethical perfection, is as definitely a corollary of the Chosen People Idea as the ideal of fellow man complements the Jewish God concept. Messianism submits that all men are chosen if they choose to be chosen.

As the Jewish survivalist sees it, the Chosen People Idea has contributed abundantly to the fortification of the rationale of Judaism and of Jewish staying power. The comfort and reassurance that flow from the lovingly assumed burden of chosenness, compensate the Jew for the manifold hurts and humiliations of life in exile. Proud and satisfied with the rationale of Judaism, the Jew, who lives by it, is little concerned over the disadvantages of Jewishness, which seem to pose the main problem for the majority of alienated Jews. Obviously, persecution and discrimination are bound to hurt also the integrated Jew—but the wounds are only skin-deep. The Jew who knows that his people is *still* the Chosen People will not develop a neurosis because of the pin-pricks and dagger-thrusts of anti-Semitism. He will take them in his stride.

Suffering is intolerable only when it is not suffused with a purpose. To large sections of contemporary Jews, Jewishness has neither rhyme nor reason—and so, quite naturally, they chafe under the disabilities this "accident of birth" entails. Also the integrated Jew, imbued with the sense of the worthwhileness of the rationale of Judaism, is discriminated against, at best, and persecuted and hunted, at worst. However, and this is decisive, he knows *why* he suffers. He knows that all that is inflicted upon him is the dark and lesser side of his great fortune of being a Jew. The tragedy of modern Jewish life is not anti-Semitism, but the loss of the sense of the worthwhileness of being a Jew. Not suffering *per se,* but its seeming meaninglessness breaks the morale of the modern Jew and gives rise to his many psychological difficulties.

The history of anti-Semitism and the record of the Jewish fight against it prove soberingly that Jew-hatred is the inevitably recurring reaction of the majority to the Jewish minority. All serious students of the psychology of anti-Semitism know that, with the given factors of human nature, the chances for the eradication of anti-Semitism are infinitesimal. Obviously, in the democracies the physical security of the Jewish minority is well assured. We need fear no pogroms in this country, but there are large, painful and, probably, incurable areas that cannot, and dare not, be ignored. As the Jewish survivalist sees it, anti-Semitism can neither be wholly cured nor dare it be left to the devices of its progenitors. We do need organizations defending our civil rights guaranteed by the Constitution. As for the rest, i.e. social discrimination, overt and disguised anti-Semitic expression in private areas, there is not much that can be done. Even yesterday's panacea of "education" has failed, for recent statistical surveys prove that anti-Jewish prejudice is more widespread among the upper classes, with high school and college backgrounds, than among those on the lower rungs of the social ladder and of education.

Jewish historical experience for over two millenia and in virtually all lands, drives home the point that *there is only one real defense against anti-Semitism: the strengthening of Jewish survival determination by means of the rationale of Judaism.* The fate of German Jewry, that boasted the most efficient Jewish defense organizations and techniques, should cause even the most sanguine and trustful to be wary of relying too firmly upon our defense organizations. They are needed, of course, especially in a democracy—but what point is there in "defending" Judaism when many of its own "alienated" sons and daughters are even more vociferous than strangers in attacking and defaming it?

At this juncture of history, the first line of Jewish defense must be erected in the areas where doubt in the rationale of Judaism has wrought fatal havoc. It thus becomes imperative for Jewish survivalists to bolster the Jewish national will to live by giving the individual Jew a satisfying sense of worthwhileness, i.e. the certainty of a purpose and mission, through the rationale of Judaism. This calls, first of all, for an all-out campaign of enlightenment on the rationale of Judaism. On the level of school children, this campaign must concentrate on raising the scholastic levels of existing schools, extending the network of Jewish Day Schools and recruiting *every* Jewish child for attendance at a Jewish school. On the adult level, we must be done with paying lip-service to "Jewish education" and do something in earnest about teaching our men and women the facts of Judaism. While Jewish adult education has progressed in some areas, the total picture is somber and discouraging. Notwithstanding the paeans to education by leaders of our large Jewish organizations, education remains the proverbial step-child.

A people's hold on life is only as strong as the bonds that tie it to its culture and make for creative expansion of the values of the nation. The Sages of the Talmud knew what they were about in stipulating that education has unqualified precedence —even over the building of the Temple.

The time has come to enlist for "Jewish culture" all age- and-interest groups of American Jewry. There is no time to lose, for every day of delay adds new recruits to the camp of alienated, frustrated Jews that jeopardize our survival. Our tragic mistake in the past has been that we concentrated virtually exclusively on the needs of the body, while either ignoring the equally pressing needs of the spirit, or assigning to them the remnants and leavings.... This policy has proved disastrous, for we have raised a generation of Jews (we now refer to those who still desire to be identified with their people's community) to whom Jewishness is an affirmation of protest, and not a positive avowal of values. We have bred a lachrymose Judaism of charitable relief and a frightened Judaism of the fight against anti-Semitism. Even Zionism is to the preponderant majority of dues-paying Zionists largely a synthesis of lachrymose motives.

A wide diffusion of authentic knowledge about Jewish values requires, first of all, the emancipation of Jewish education. Despite the praises sung to Jewish education, the educational budgets of practically all large American Jewish organizations consist of crumbs that remain after all other organizational departments have been lavishly provided for. "There is no money for education," is the perennial and ubiquitous complaint. Already there are indications that the stinting on educational budgets will have serious repercussions on *all* phases of Jewish identification. For, after all, the men and women who are today actively identified with Jewish endeavors have had, almost without exception, the stimulating experience of intimate childhood contact with Jewish values. Because they are not ignorant of the rationale of Judaism they are found in the forefront of varied Jewish activities. But is it likely that indifferent, i.e. ignorant, and therefore frustrated and alienated, Jews will exert themselves to raise funds for Jewish causes, or fight for Jewish rights?

The emphasis upon the values that add up to *the rationale of Judaism* is therefore a sine qua non of organizational welfare as well as of the entrenchment of the spiritual survival potential of our people. The ancient formula, "Without bread there is no Torah," is incomplete without its second part: "Without Torah there is no bread." The physical and spiritual areas must be synthesized. There must not be an overemphasis on one area to the neglect of the other. Up till now American Jewry has concentrated its resources almost exclusively on the "bread area"—but the needs of the hour require that the "Torah area" come into its own. Unless we provide for the spiritual needs, in keeping with their imperativeness at this juncture, we shall discover, before long, that "without Torah there is no bread."

## IV

Disembodied ideas are not lifeworthy. The spirit becomes manifest only through the medium of matter. It requires the prop of the tangible, the concrete.... The ideas of the rationale of Judaism, too, need forms and props to become tangible and tactile realities of life. This is where "the Jewish way of life" comes in. It is *the technique of Jewish survival,* which provides the requisite forms of expression for the *rationale of Judaism.*

By way of general characterization we might say that *the technique of Jewish survival* aims at emphasizing and accentuating Jewish distinctiveness. The commandments regulating the diet, the weekday, Sabbath and festival deportment of the Jew, thus charting for him a definitive mode of life, clearly aim at setting him apart as "a people dwelling alone." Yet this concentration on the factors making for Jewish distinctiveness should not be confused with a regimen of separatism. Jewish distinctiveness does not aspire to aloofness from the rest of mankind. It merely aims at preserving the things characteristically and peculiarly Jewish.

The Jewish Utopia embraces all mankind. But those who projected this vision of the ideal future, also realized that its attainment imposes upon the Jewish people, from whose yearning this Utopia sprang, the inescapable duty of retaining the unique frame of soul that birthed the Messianic ideal. For the sake of the enduring World Sabbath, the Jews must pioneer in the Sabbath observance charted to its minutest details by the Law. To make all mankind conscious of the omnipresent, omnipotent and unique God, the Jew must conform with the complicated ritual of the thrice-daily prayer order. Lest the unique flavor of his genius be diluted, he must cling to his Hebrew language and set aside regular periods for learning and contemplation in "The House of Study." Lest the bond of loyalty and proud identification with his people weaken, he must make Eretz Israel a living reality.

For all this and more, *the technique of Jewish survival* provides amply. Moreover, by its unqualified and unconditional emphasis on life, it gives rise to a spirit of vigorous affirmation. The Jewish zest for life, unbroken and undoubting even after the most harrowing tragedies, is a variety of optimism which is as unique as the Jewish destiny. This zest for life, fed by the disvowal of asceticism and the joyous affirmation of the disciplined flesh, has time and again enabled us to make a new beginning when seemingly there was nothing left to live for. All of Jewish law is in the service of physical life as the presupposition of the life of the spirit. For the sake of the preservation of life, all commandments, except those designed to preserve life and its dignity, must yield. Life *per se* is the primary objective of Judaism, for "only the living can praise God."

In the wake of the ignorance of the great ideas and ideals of Judaism, there has developed a wide-spread aversion to the *rationale of Jewish survival*. On the other hand, there are not a few who pay lip-service to the *rationale of Judaism,* while denouncing the regimen, practices and concrete Jewish national aims that add up to *the technique of Jewish survival*. But the rationale and the technique of Jewish survival are interdependent and indivisible! They are soul and body, respectively, and so are lifeworthy only when united. A narrow and short-sighted emphasis on *the technique of Jewish survival* is as sterile as the vapuous sermonizing on "the ethics of Judaism." A Jewish orthodoxy that exhausts its strength in the letter of the technique of Judaism and is negligent in tending the areas of its rationale, is as untraditional and as alien to the indigenous

Jewish genius as the Jewish reform movement that flaunts the cardinal rules of the technique of Jewish survival in order to concentrate more completely on the rationale of Jewish survival.

Until the modern era of Jewish disintegration and degeneration, the impregnable fortress of Jewish survival strength was defended by *the technique of Jewish survival,* which proceeded according to the blueprint charted by *the rationale of Jewish survival.* There is no other way to entrench the Jewish survival potential in any generation and so we, too, must create a lifeworthy amalgam of *the rationale* and *the technique of Jewish survival.*

To achieve this goal, our schools must add courses in the art and technique of living as a Jew to the background courses of language and history. Furthermore, *the rationale of Judaism* must be restored to its rightfully important place in the thinking and creative expression (in writing and on the platform) of our people in this country. Even our few serious Anglo-Jewish periodicals allot much too little space to the important area of the idea-contents of Judaism. The exposition of contemporary problems must be implemented by the delineation of the vast realm of the eternity-begetting rationale of Judaism and Jewish survival.

It is significant that, in all periods of Jewish crisis, the day for Jewish survival was saved by those who—ignored the crisis and concentrated on refining the rationale and on fashioning the technique of Jewish survival. From Rabbi Yohanan ben Zakkai, who asked for "Yabneh and its scholars" to the DP's who, on the morrow of their deliverance from the Nazis, proceeded to organize schools and libraries, the unerring survival instinct of our people has invariably impelled the best of us to concentrate upon the rationale and the technique of Jewish survival in the crucial, decisive moments when *all* was in the balance and at stake.

There is no other alternative for our Diaspora but to do what other crisis-bedevilled generations of Jews did: *To proclaim and entrench the rationale of Jewish survival as the meaning of our Jewish existence, and uphold and support this conviction with the variegated props of the technique of Jewish survival.*

CHAPTER 7

*Zest for Life*

I

GRAETZ, THE MASTER chronicler of the Jews, characterized their history as *Leidens und Gelehrtengeschichte,* the record of martyrdom and scholarship. But another important strand is woven into this record: optimism, manifest in unbounded zest for life.

The student of Jewish history cannot but marvel at how this persecuted and afflicted group managed to survive under the most staggering odds. How can a people so excruciatingly broken on the wheel of life not despair of existence and seek relief in extinction? Yet in all the many thousands of Hebrew tomes, up to the era of emancipation, there was no utterance expressing doubt in the worthwhileness of life under the aegis of Judaism. The chronicles of Jewish martyrdom are soaked in blood and tears; they echo the sighs of death's agony; they erupt in desperate prayer for Divine assistance; they call down the punishment of heaven upon "the wolves" that attack Israel, the defenseless lamb—but they question neither the desirability of life nor the worthwhileness of Judaism.

There is no need to resort to the past for proof of the

unshakable Jewish trust in the worthwhileness of life. The history of the Nazi dark ages attests that, regardless of how well the Nazis succeeded in destroying the *bodies* of six million Jews, they failed in breaking their spirits and the courage of the pitifully few survivors of the carnage.

Even when hunger, disease and death stalked the Nazi-made ghettos of Poland and mass deportations to extermination centers were already in full progress, the doomed Jews—and they knew they were doomed—affirmed life in the most definitive manner. In the ghettos Jewish cultural activities were carried on until the very last moment. The schools were in session, although the class rooms were unheated and teachers and pupils were weakened by hunger. Lectures and concerts were popular. And while the Nazi henchmen tightened the noose to throttle the last remaining inhabitants of the ghettos, symphony orchestras were giving concerts and young artists of talent and promise made their debuts. There was infernal suffering and unimaginable tragedy in the ghettos and in the many death traps the Nazis operated all too efficiently, but there was no despair. Torture and death lost some of their stings for the sufferers because, as a report of two of their leaders who likewise were murdered put it, "They remained true to the ideals of our culture. Until death, they held aloft the banner of culture in the struggle against barbarism."

In Oswiencim, Buchenwald, Dachau, Sachsenhausen, Bergen-Belsen, and other Nazi torture and death camps where hundred thousands of Jews were foully put to death, after having been worked to their last ounce of strength, the sick, emaciated and tired Jewish "slaves" met clandestinely at night to study Hebrew and impart Jewish instruction to the small number of children in their midst. They knew that soon they would have to die, but they never forgot that Israel is eternal. They knew that the Nazis would go down before long and that life would go on, and that, in the better world of tomorrow, their people, the Jewish people would play an important role. This is why the Jews in the Nazi death camps did not despair; this is why at the threshold of doom they defied the finality of death by nurturing the living tree of the Jewish cultural heritage, committing its care to the children who *might* escape.

The Talmud records that during the Hadrianic persecutions, when the study of Torah was punishable by death, the Sages nevertheless continued to teach and ordain disciples. To many a modern reader the narratives describing the heroism of Rabbi Akiba and Rabbi Hanina ben Traydon, who found solace and relief in the eternal treasures of Jewish wisdom, while being flayed and burned alive, may seem incredible. But now, alas, there is the testimony of men and women of our time—men and women who were tortured more horribly than the Ten Martyrs of the Hadrianic persecutions—confirming that the indomitable spirit and unyielding zest for life which emboldened Rabbi Akiba and Rabbi Hanina also filled an Emanuel Ringelblum and the many thousands of devoted teachers and the writers who verily and truly *"sanctified the Name of God"* in our generation by affirming life and the eternity of Israel until their last breath was spent.

## II

The first Yiddish book printed in Europe after the downfall of the Nazis was a volume of poetry. But even in the ghettos and death camps Jewish creativeness was alive under the embers. While awaiting death, Yiddish and Hebrew writers who knew that they were doomed continued to write—and as there were no facilities for printing, they read their works to their fellow-captives in the dark hours of the night when their torturers were off on drinking bouts and debauched orgies.

Many of the great Jewish masterworks were written under the shadow of persecution. Rashi's last ten years were poisoned by the tragedy of the massacres of the First Crusade; Maimonides wrote voluminously while fleeing from Almohade persecution; Abarbanel records in his Bible commentaries that, first after his expulsion from Portugal and later after his expulsion from Spain—together with 300,000 men, women and children—he found solace in Jewish scholarship. And so it has been throughout the ages, *Leidens and Gelehrtengeschichte* not consecutively but simultaneously; death joined to the affirmation of life.

The type of zest for life displayed by our people does not grow in a vacuum. It is an attitude born of the studied and consistent cultivation of the will to live. Judaism is predicated on the conviction that life is good since God is its source. Indeed, all monotheistic faiths share this view, but Judaism is alone in infusing the daily routine wth zest and flavor by reminding its followers at every turn and corner of the sheer goodness of life.

When the Jew partakes of food and drink he is enjoined to pronounce a benediction—and a different benediction it is for the various kinds of foods. The psychological result of such a regimen cannot be anything else but that those who pause before an enjoyment to define its nature with a benediction, become more keenly aware of savoring it.

The fact that thanks to the benedictions virtually all Jews of yesterday lived on a more "conscious level" has immeasurably added to the tenacity with which they clung to life amidst the most appalling sufferings. The benedictions reminded them that, even under the knout of persecution and in the shadow of death, there remains much that is worth while, much that can be enjoyed; a crust of bread, perhaps; a cup of water; a tree in bloom which one may espy through barred windows, or a word of wisdom from the mouth of a fellow-sufferer.

Thanks to this positive attitude to life, the mood and tenor of the traditional Jewish community were never gloomy, not even in the most tragic periods. As in our own sorrow-fraught days, the victims of barbarism stood up bravely by holding fast to the imperishable things of the spirit. This is why the Jews of the Middle Ages, persecuted, shunted about and shut away in ghettos, were yet far from despair and dejection. To be sure, one cannot remain unconcernedly stoical when massacres destroy one's brethren and when the evil is knocking persistently on one's door. But if one's spirit is strong and the belief in the worthwhileness of life is undaunted, one can face the evil more composedly and continue to savor life as long as there is breath in one's nostrils.

Jewish life in the Middle Ages was joyful despite its corporate and individual hopelessness and frustrations. There was joy and happiness, too, in the ghettos for, in the words of the Sages, "there is no gloom in the presence of the Holy One, blessed be He," and the Jew of yesterday did live in the presence of God. There was first of all, the great boon of the commandments. The outsider cannot but consider the hundreds of regulations which hedge in the life of the Jew as an obstacle to enjoyment, but to the Jew the commandments are joy incarnate. *Simchah shel Mitzvah*—the joy bound up with the commandments is a source of unbounded bliss and, consequently, a stimulant for the love of life and the will to live; it is a joy which Israel's enemies cannot blunt, for it is beyond their reach.

A cursory examination of the vocabulary of Jewish life reveals the emphasis placed on "the joy of the commandments." To the Jew the Sabbath is synonymous with *oneg*—delight, while at the festivals he thanks God for having given Israel "festivals for joy and festive seasons for pleasure."

That the Jews have survived and emerged victorious from so many crises is not least due to their genius for the art of living, that is to say, the faculty to get more joy than sorrow out of life. Although the cup of Jewish sufferings was virtually always running over, the cup of Jewish joys was yet fuller.

There is, first of all, the Sabbath, the day which is all joy, a day out of the ordinary, when everything is and must be *different*. Modern psychologists have emphasized that many neuroses are caused by *ennui* with the dull and consequently enervating routine most moderns follow day in day out, year in year out without break and change. Medieval Jews, although their insecurity was more than merely conducive to the development of neuroses, were almost free from this affliction so wide-spread among modern Jews. That they kept their mental health and balance was largely due to the Sabbath, when the cares and worries of the weekday world were forgotten, because the Law ordains that sorrow must be erased from the mind on the Sabbath, which is a day all joyous and delightful. One day in every seven the traditional Jew has a vacation, as it were, from drab reality. Everything on this day *must* be different, so the Law decrees. A different bread—the *Sabbath* bread; different *dishes*—Sabbath dishes; *different* clothes—Sabbath clothes; *different* lights—Sabbat lights; *different* prayers—Sabbath prayers; everything *different*, nothing reminiscent of everyday routine, a complete vacation one day in every seven!

Heine, the baptized Jew who in later life consumed himself

in yearning for the faith which he had bartered away for the "entrance ticket to modern society," understood well the magic power of Princess Sabbath. He, the renegade Jew, knew the Sabbath's blessing and its contribution to Jewish survival, for "Princess Sabbath" gives the Jew strength to endure his "dog's life" during the rest of the week.

The Sabbath gave joy to an otherwise dreary and drab existence, thus enabling the Sabbath observer to consider life worth while. Six days the Jew may be dejected and cast down, but on the seventh day—the Sabbath of Delight—he is a sovereign prince, as Heine put it so aptly, drinking strength and joy from the very fountain of life.

In other realms, too, Jews have a flair for making the most of the happy moments of life. Thus they do not join the celebration of one joyous occasion with that of another, as, for instance, solemnizing a marriage on the Sabbath or on a holiday. Each joy is important and so a special day must be assigned to it. They are blessed with the faculty of being able to drain the cup of joy to the dregs. No matter how gloomy the week may be, it culminates in the Sabbath. No matter how wearily the seasons may drag on in a world of persecution and hatred, there are always holidays of delight and rejoicing, when all worries are forgotten in the exultation over Israel's eternal treasures which are beyond the reach of even the most powerful and vindictive enemy.

Besides the holidays, the joyous occasions of family life added much color and zest to the Jewish community scene of yesterday. Today, when men are born in hospitals and are married in hotels, happy events are observed at "functions" of a few hours' duration at most. In the traditional Jewish community of yesterday, however, a wedding provided joy and festivity for almost a month, what with preliminary celebrations at the homes of bride and groom, the festive "calling up" of the groom to the Torah, and the "Seven Blessings" (*Sheva Brochos*) recited at festive boards during the week following the wedding.

## III

The Sages called attention to the fact that the Hebrew language boasts ten synonyms for "joy." In point of fact, Jews are singularly sensitive to joy, which is to them both a Divine gift and a Divinely ordained attitude to the bounties of the world. This significant interpretation of joy finds pithy expression in the benediction offering thanks for the happiness of bride and groom. "Thou didst create joy and happiness," this prayer addresses itself to God. "Bride and bridegroom, mirth and exultation, pleasure and delight, love and comradeship, peace and fellowship. Soon may there be heard, in the cities of Judah and in the streets of Jerusalem, the voice of joy and gladness, the voice of the bridegroom and the voice of the bride, the jubilant notes of bridegrooms from their canopies, and of youths from their feasts of song. Blessed art Thou, O Lord, Who makest the bridegroom to rejoice with the bride."

The origins of the Jewish affirmation of life can be traced to early biblical times. To the ancient Hebrew the universe was a symphony of joy in which even inanimate nature joins delightedly. "The statutes of the Lord" are a delight, too, for they are "rejoicing the heart." Accordingly, one must not serve God in gloom and fear, but with joy and gladness. The call to joyful Divine service is sounded insistently. "Thou shalt rejoice before the Lord thy God" is the Pentateuchal injunction, and Isaiah demands, "Thou shalt rejoice in the Lord and shalt glory in the Holy One of Israel." The identical call to joyousness is sounded in the Psalms: "Serve the Lord with gladness; come before His presence with singing," and "Let the heart of them rejoice that seek the Lord."

Rabbi Israel Baal Shem-Tov, the founder of Hasidism, the movement which restored to Jewish life much of its indigenous joyousness, advised his family and his disciples to avoid worrying about their conduct. "For such an attitude is produced by the evil instinct's plot to overawe one, to cause one to despair of doing one's duty. Despair is a sure impediment to Divine service. If one has really stumbled, let him not yield overmuch to paralyzing grief. Indeed, he should sigh for his sin, but then let him turn again in joy to the Creator, blessed be He."

One of the most beautiful tributes to joy comes from Yehudah Halevi, whose mystical-poetic soul was alert to the creative potentialities of pure spiritual joy. In his *Kuzari* Halevi explains that, in Divine service, Judaism assigns equal importantce to fear, love and joy. "By each of them one can draw near to God. Yet, your contrition on a fast does not please God more than your joy on the Sabbath and the holidays, provided it flows from a devout heart.... And if joy impels you to sing and dance, it becomes worship and a bond of union between you and God." Jews ardently uphold the belief that the joy accompanying the good deed is even more acceptable to God than that deed itself. Even so pronounced a rationalist as Maimonides extolled cheerfulness as the ideal disposition.

The most potent stimulant of the Jew's zest for life, however, is the conviction that Judaism is worth while. Judaism in its wholeness, and not merely one or several of its parts, fills the Jew rooted in the tradition of his people with the certainty of significant self-fulfillment before which even the harshest sufferings pale. To be a Jew—to read the Bible and know that it is the book of his people; to study the Talmud and be awed and thrilled by its scope and profundity; to wander among the flower beds of Midrashic folklore and to delight in Hebrew poetry; to know and see on every turn and corner that Israel is, indeed, a holy and a chosen people, by the grace of God, it is true, but also by its choice of living on a higher plane of ethics, is rich compensation for the fate the world metes out to the children of Israel. The Jew steeped in this tradition keeps his zest for life strong and vigorous, for no matter what the enemy may impose upon him, he will never be able to touch the core of his being or make him doubt the worthwhileness of Jewishness.

Up to the modern era of emancipation and assimilation, there were no Jews who committed suicide because of Jewish despair engendered by feelings of Jewish inferiority. To be sure, during the period of the Crusades, many Jews took their own lives because they knew they were doomed. They saw the enemy waiting at the door to slay them and they preferred to die by their own hands and to kill their children, lest they be baptized. Men and women of our generation, and some of that preceding ours, were the first really to despair of Judaism; to feel inadequate, inferior and handicapped on account of being Jews. The most tragic sector of the modern Jewish scene is that which is held by Jews who have no zest for Jewish living. As they see it, Judaism is nothing else but a burden. The root of this evil, of course, is that vast numbers of contemporary Jews no longer *enjoy* Jewish life. They do not delight in Jewish culture (for reasons of ignorance) and so can feel neither soul-stirring experiences nor satisfactions of quests and needs in the affirmative Jewish areas.

The many remedies tried for making Judaism more palatable to the jaded Jew have proved unsuccessful. The virtual elimination of Hebrew from Reform Jewish practice has not stimulated zest and enthusiasm—on the contrary. The emphasis on "Jewish art" and "Jewish music" in congregations of Reconstructionist sympathies has been equally unsuccessful in engendering the Jewish enthusiasm and fervor by which our grandparents and some of their sons and daughters were possessed. Something more basic is lacking: the conviction that to be a Jew is a piece of good fortune of which one must prove himself worthy.

Is there a possibility of imbuing young Jews in the Diaspora with a semblance, at least, of the traditional zest for life? The chances are slim and the outlook is not favorable. To appreciate art one must have an opportunity to see great paintings and sculptures; love of music springs from intimate association with music, and the love of books thrives on the absorption in great literature. The zest for Jewish living, too, cannot grow in a vacuum and out of seeds that were never planted. A positive Jewish atmosphere—first in the home, then in the school and in extra-curricular associations—is the only soil from which can grow the certainty that Judaism is worth while.

It would be fool-hardy to shut our eyes to the fact that in this country there are not many Jewish homes left where the parents are sufficiently well integrated into Judaism to inspire their children with its worthwhileness, and only an infinitesimally small fraction of American Jewish children attend the kind of Jewish schools that provide the intensive training indispensable for the appreciation of the great treasures of Judaism.

We Jews have survived because, throughout the ages, there have always been a sufficiently large number of us who considered Judaism worth while. The rationale and technique of Jewish survival were found adequate because there was the basic conviction that to be a Jew is such a boon that it even calls for a special benediction.

The real danger besetting Jewish survival in the Diaspora is not anti-Semitism, but loss of the zest for life in the Jewish orbit. It may be too late radically to change the attitude of hundreds of thousands of young Jews who, through the guilt of their elders, have grown up to be indifferent and, often, antagonistic to Judaism. It may be too late, but try we must. Our future in the Diaspora is contingent upon stimulating zest and creating enthusiasm for the things that *make* the Jew: *Torah* (understood in the widest sense), *Mitzvoth* (that is to say, forms of tangible Jewish expression), and *Eretz Israel*— the return to Jewish national normalcy.

CHAPTER 8

*Distinctiveness*

I

DISTINCTIVE ORIGINALITY is the most highly prized asset of the creative personality—the artist, the thinker and the writer. The great geniuses of mankind, in literature, the arts, philosophy and science—share one characteristic: they all were innovators and trail-blazers. They introduced an altogether new note expressive of their unique selves.

Rembrandt's light effects, Van Gogh's colors, Wagner's crashing themes, Mozart's lilting, playful variations and Gershwin's staccatos with the tempo of New York pulsating in them are readily identified even by those who do not specialize in art and music. A Rembrandt canvas or a Van Gogh still life is unmistakable. The style of the artist and his characteristic originality are so thoroughly fused with his creation that it appears, as in fact it is, as an extension of the master's self.

Distinctiveness, however, is not only prized and cultivated by the creative personality and the genius. All normal men and women crave individual self-expression. In every day life this quest for distinctiveness may show itself in a woman's desire to furnish her home "different" from the homes of her friends, or to wear a "different" dress or hat.

In keeping with our culture's high valuation of original distinctiveness, we reward most lavishly those who contribute the original note. The virtuoso's prominence is least due to his technical mastery of the violin strings or the piano keyboard. There are musicians who can match the technique of an Elman, a Heifetz, or a Horowitz, but they lack the flash of originality that lifts a musician from the orchestra pit to the concert stage.

Although our economic system is geared to mass production and standardization, we respect highly and reward prodigally those who express "originality" in their chosen fields of endeavor. Nor is the quest for distinctiveness necessarily an expression of the desire for greater functional efficiency. It is not only the man who makes a better mouse-trap who attracts the crowd — the dress designer who launches a *new* style, the architect who draws plans for a *different* house, the hair-dresser who thinks up a *distinctive* hair-do, the writer who inaugurates a *novel* trend, the artist who paints horses as nobody else does, the composer who handles harmonies altogether autocratically, the violinist who commands a tone no other virtuoso can elicit from his instrument, the crooner who sings as nobody else does—they are the idols of our standardized society.

National civilizations and cultures, as the cumulative expression of creative personalities, are original and distinct. *Typically French, typically British, typically South-American, typically Russian* are household words. We admire the "typically what-we-are-not" because it is different, original and distinct. Nations are jealously guarding their typical civilizations, analogous to the creative personality who stands watch over his distinctiveness. To renounce his originality spells artistic and spiritual death for the creative personality. To relinquish national distinctiveness is tantamount to the extinction of the nation that takes this path.

Only Babbits and Fascists dread distinctiveness. Babbits feel secure only on Main Street, in the crowd where everybody drives the same car, tunes in on the same program, builds the same standardized house filled with the same pieces of furniture and bric-a-brac. The frustrated Fascist feels safe against the pricks of inferiority-consciousness only when noisily goose-stepping in a mass of other frustrated, inferiority-conscious people.

The totalitarian regimes' insistence on *Gleichschaltung* is as unmistakable a symptom of a disturbed equilibrium and a lopsided scale of values as the democracies' encouragement of distinctiveness bespeaks self-assurance and spiritual vigor. Only those who know that their own contributions are without value imitate others. While the creative artist dreads nothing more than the loss of his distinctive style, the hack is always casting about for models to imitate.

## II

A highly creative people, the Jews have consistently nurtured and guarded their national distinctiveness. From their debut on the stage of history to this day, they have been conscious of the blessing of Balaam who acclaimed them as "a people dwelling alone." This fact should be stressed in these times when Jews aspire "to be like the rest." The trend to unworthy assimilation—unworthy because it is predicated on the divestation of personality and distinctiveness—is the major disability resulting from emancipation and assimilation. In point of fact, it is not really true that the Jew was emancipated by the granting of equal rights. This boon was not bestowed upon *the Jew,* but solely upon a caricature of Jew who had pledged himself to renounce his Jewish distinctiveness in return for the promise of equality. The slogan of the 18th and 19th century emancipators, all worthy gentlemen and fighters for human equality, was: "To the Jews as human beings everything—to the Jews as Jews nothing."

Here is the crux of the problem—and this is the real sin the world committed against the Jew: its refusal to accept him as a Jew and thereby compelling him to cease being himself in order to qualify for "human rights."

Inevitably, the refusal of the modern Western states to accept the Jew as a Jew had a blighting effect on Jewish self-respect. The wave of mass-baptism which followed upon the legal emancipation of the Jews in Western Europe was one symptom of the great unhappiness of large groups of emancipated Jews. They craved to be accepted as "human beings" and, upon realizing that this was denied them, they bartered their Judaism for the entrance ticket to European society.

When large sections of American Jewry today object to certain types of Jewish cultural expression—the Jewish Day School, the fostering of Hebrew and its literature, the creative espousal of distinctive Jewishness—their opposition is not really directed against Jewish culture as such. It is primarily the expression of fear lest "the others" may deduce from intense and positive Jewishness that Jews *are* Jews.

The average modern Jew has a pathological aversion, caused by a fear complex, for everything "typically Jewish." While he, together with other Americans, may admire a French accent as "quaint"—he will abhor a Jewish accent. While he will consider serving South-American dishes sophisticated, he will deride typically Jewish food. While he may proudly buy a Spanish or a Russian paper, he would blush to be seen walking into the elevator of his Central Park West home with a Yiddish paper.

The average modern Jew is ashamed of his Jewishness. There is no denying this fact. Jewishly illiterate, he evaluates Judaism and the Jewish people with the perverse measurements of a hostile world. All this "abashed Jew" knows is that Jews are being persecuted, vilified and discriminated against; all he hears is that Judaism is "obsolete" and "outdated." And so he is ashamed of being a Jew. To him Jewish distinctiveness is not a badge of honor but a stigma—a misfortune from which he attempts frantically to escape. He is mortally afraid of Jews who insist on being Jews and thus remind the world of "the Jewish problem." What the embarrassed and abashed Jew desires most is to be inconspicuous. He wants the world to forget about him.

Judaism has always been alert to the fact that survival is contingent upon distinctiveness. All of Jewish law, from the Pentateuch to the latest Rabbinic enactment, is, besides all else, an attempt to entrench Jewish distinctiveness. This tendency became especially pronounced when, after the Destruction and Exile, a spiritual substitute for the homeland had to be provided. This substitute, and a highly efficacious and perfect one it has been throughout, was found in the Jewish way of life as charted by Jewish law.

Some Jews argue that the ritual laws should be abrogated, as they segregate the Jew by making it impossible for him to break bread with his Gentile neighbors at their homes. These critics of the Jewish way of life forget, however, that the fostering of Jewish distinctiveness is precisely the aim of Jewish law. The architects of Judaism knew that national and religious syncretism must prove fatal because they level distinctive originality. There are numerous Jewish prohibitions declaring certain actions and customs out of bound for the Jew for no other reason than that they are part and parcel of the Gentile way of life. *Mipnei hukos hagoyim*—"Because these are Gentile laws" is a phrase which one frequently encounters in talmudic and rabbinic literature.

The Rabbis zealously entrenched Jewish distinctiveness by prohibiting Jews to dress in Gentile fashion, wear their hair as the Gentiles did, and imposing upon them numerous similar restrictions. Long before the Church marked the Jew with the yellow badge, Jews could be recognized by their distinctive clothes and hats. And long before the ghetto restriction was legally enacted, Jews tended to flock together in certain sections of the cities they inhabited—even as they are still inclined to do today.

Jewish survival is impossible without a certain amount of Jewish segregation. Most modern Jews are unwilling to face this fact which is borne out by a historical experience extending over centuries and millennia. From the Jewish survivalist's point of view, the ghetto was no curse but a blessing. It engendered a homogeneous, proud and creative Jewish community, whose members fulfilled themselves in Judaism.

Modern Jews are pathetic sufferers of the affliction known as split personality. They ache to be "citizens of the world," but the world will have none of them. They loathe being Jews, while mouthing the platitude, "I am proud of being a Jew." And yet, no matter how hard they may try and strain at the leash, they will find it impossible to be anything but Jews—unwilling Jews, to be sure, but Jews nevertheless because "the world" won't admit them into its precincts.

The effects of this split personality tragedy are that not a few Jews are turning upon themselves in masochistic self-flagellation. The young American Jewish writers who write about

Jewish life in what they term realistic, but what is in fact a hostile, defamatory, manner, are thwarted neurotics whose exit from the Jewish camp is barred by a concatenation of circumstances and who therefore spent their disappointment and resentment in effusions of Jewish self-hatred.

## III

Any program that aims at securing Jewish survival must give due consideration to the role Jewish distinctiveness has played in preserving our people. Assimilation, which really stands for relinquishing of distinctiveness, has always spelled the doom of those Jewish groups who delivered themselves without reservations to this treacherous and hollow ideal. In order to survive, the Jew dare not assimilate himself to the world. What he must do is assimilate the world to himself. Even as the creative artist does not renounce his distinctive style and approach while studying—and perhaps enjoying, too—the creations of other artists, so the Jew must view the world through Jewish spectacles, as it were, and interpret it in terms of Jewish categories of thought.

The fruitful creative Jewish minds of the past did precisely this. Maimonides did not assimilate the Bible to Aristotle; he analyzed and assimilated Aristotelianism with the Jewish catalyst. Hermann Cohen did not make Jewish ethics subservient to Kant's "Ethik der Reinen Vernunft"; he assimilated the latter to the former, so that both Hillel and Kant contributed independently to his system of thought.

With all creative Jewish personalities, and with the large multitudes of our people anchored in Jewishness, Judaism has been the catalyst, with which they assimilated the world. The failure of modern Judaism is largely due to the loss of confidence in its own catalytic powers.

A Jew must approach the world and all that fills it from the Jewish point of view—otherwise he ceases to be a Jew. Certainly, "nothing human is strange" to Judaism, but the common human elements, as well as alien national possessions, must be brought into the Jewish orbit, not vice versa. Judaism is outgoing certainly, but it is even more pronouncedly in-gathering. It is expansive and expanding—in the manner and best tradition of the creative personality and the creative group.

What is required, then, is more emphasis on Jewish distinctiveness. Everything that strengthens Jewish distinctiveness is to be fostered and encouraged. On the other hand, all trends aiming at levelling Jewish distinctiveness must be fought as attacks upon the Jewish survival potential. Jewish segregation is not to be feared and shunned; on the contrary, it is desirable and should be encouraged within reason. Even as the creative personality requires solitude and concentration, so the creative collective of a people, too, needs a measure of aloneness. Again, this does not mean that we should withdraw from "the world" —it implies, however, bringing the world under our own roof, instead of treking about homeless and roofless.

Jewish segregation is a small price to pay for Jewish survival through creative distinctiveness. Our ancestors knew this because their lives were illumined by the reality of the worthwhileness of Jewishness. We must recapture the sense of the worthwhileness of Judaism—then Jewish distinctiveness will be a blessing for us too.

CHAPTER 9

## *The Chosen People Idea*

### I

WHEN THE millions of hapless Jews whom the Nazis had marked for extermination were marched to the gas chambers and death factories, many of the victims intoned Maimonides' article of faith, "I believe with perfect faith in the Messiah's coming—and though he tarry, I shall wait for him!"

Throughout two millennia of unmatched sufferings, Jews have believed and waited. They waited patiently because they were utterly certain that ultimately the powers of evil would be defeated; wrong would be righted and Israel's wounds would be bound up.

During this long vigil, we have been sustained by many fortifying ideals and, above all, by the Messianic promise. More than all other props of the spirit, however, the chosen people idea, has contributed to strengthening the Jew to go on, clinging to life and affirming life triumphantly in tribulation and adversity.

The belief in their special role implicit in chosenness has been the strongest and most efficacious Jewish survival incentive. Our people could not have endured two thousand years of homelessness, persecutions and pogroms unless there had been the comforting assurance that all these tribulations, far from being a stigma of Divine rejection, were the seal of God's choice of the people—for God's elect are tried in the crucible of pain to purge them from the dross of sin and imperfection.

In view of the singular contribution of the chosen people idea to Jewish survival, it is short of hazardous folly to make light of this doctrine as some in our midst have attempted. There can be no Jewish continuity without belief in Jewish chosenness as interpreted by the Jewish genius.

Few concepts have been so fatally misinterpreted as the idea of Jewish chosenness. While most non-Jews see in the Jewish claim to the title of "The Chosen People" an obnoxious affront of arrogance, Jews who are ignorant of the real meaning of the chosen people idea rest satisfied in the smug and complacent delusion of being the Lord's elect.

Nor is it only the man in the street who distorts the meaning of Jewish chosenness. Intellectuals and writers, from the early Roman historians and satirists to such contemporary literati as G. B. Shaw and H. G. Wells, have proved themselves to be equally uninformed. Shaw and Wells have taken special glee in pointing to alleged similarities of the Teutonic dogma of "Aryan chosenness" and the Jewish belief in Divine election. Yet the idea of Jewish chosenness has as little in common with the Aryan racial fancy as the God of Israel with Wotan, the warrior idol of the Teutons.

In the first place, the doctrine of Israel's Divine election has no racial basis whatsoever. It is not a claim of those of "Jewish blood" to be "racially superior" to the rest of mankind. Jewish chosenness rests solely on Israel's spiritual-religious treasure. And as the Torah is accessible to all men, all are potentially chosen. It does no matter whether one is born into a family of the Torah's people, i.e. Jews, or whether he be a convert. Judaism does not discriminate against the proselyte. Except in the time of Ezra and Nehemiah, when those who had returned to the Land of Israel, from the "Babylonian Captivity" were threatened with complete assimilation as the result of intermarrying with the Canaanites that outnumbered them, Judaism has never opposed "intermarriage" following upon the conversion of the non-Jewish partner to the union.

"Jewish chosenness" is not racially delimited. All who desire may enter the Jewish fold and thus be chosen. The Nuremberg laws, on the other hand, excluded even those with a mere trickle of "non-Aryan" blood from the community of the German people. No matter what a "non-Aryan" might do, he could not become a German, for according to the Aryan racial theories character is contingent upon the blood. This is why the Nazis proclaimed: *"Was der Jude tut ist einerlei—in der Rasse liegt die Schweinerei."* (It does not matter what the Jew does—he belongs to a swinish race.)

Judaism never endorsed the fatalistic view that a man's soul is the concomitant of his physical-racial traits. For this would be tantamount to the denial of freedom of the will, one of the cardinal Jewish convictions. Judaism emphasizes that a wicked father may sire a pious and righteous son. It is man's ethical choice and not his "blood" or genes that make him good or bad.

The idea of Jewish chosenness is altogether free from notions of racial exclusiveness. All authoritative Jewish teachers stress that ethical-religious choice, and not racial heritage, makes the Jew. Judaism emphasizes that *all* mankind are descended from the same Adam and that, as a result, there are no chosen "races."

Realizing that claims to superiority are too often based on

quack biological "facts," the Rabbis guarded the idea of Jewish chosenness from racial-biological justifications by stoutly asserting that Jews and Gentiles alike are decended from Adam. The same universalizing tendency motivated Rabbi Meir's statement, "Adam was created from dust collected from all corners of the earth," which precludes the possibility of any nation claiming the distinction of having cradled mankind.

From the declaration of mankind's biological equality, the Sages proceeded to aver that God desires all mankind, and not merely Israel, to worship Him. Thus the Midrash comments on Isaiah's, *All flesh shall come to worship before Me, saith the Lord,* "it does not say, *all Israel* shall come, but *all flesh* shall come." With the same exegetical method another Rabbi deduced from the Pentateuchal promise "*a man* who keeps the Divine statutes will live by them," that "A Gentile who keeps the Law is equal to the High Priest." The identical lesson is deduced from such biblical passages, as, "Open ye the gates that the righteous nation that keepeth faithfulness may enter," "This is the gate of the Lord; the righteous shall enter into it," "Rejoice in the Lord, O ye righteous; Praise is comely for the upright in their hearts."

The fact that none of these passages restricts piety and its reward to Israel is, according to the Sages, proof that if "a Gentile practices the Law he is equal to the High Priest." All men can attain chosenness by accepting the Law. The "election" of one nation does not imply the "rejection" of the rest of mankind. Judaism emphasizes that God "does not reject anybody; He receives them all. The doors are always open, and everyone who so desires may enter."

Although proud of its role, Israel does not exclude the rest of mankind from serving in God's vanguard. All men are potentially eligible to serve God. Israel's ancestor, Jacob, and

Esau, the progenitor of the Gentiles, were twin brothers, sons of the same father and mother, born in the same hour and brought up in identical surroundings. It was not "race" that made Jacob serve the Lord and Esau serve his instincts. Jacob's free choice and Esau's equally free decision determined their paths. Jacob's chosenness was within the grasp of Esau as well, even as it is still accessible to his descendants.

Judaism, however, does not rest satisfied with merely emphasizing that Esau had the chance of chosenness but failed to make the grade. Judaism is ethical optimism. It avows that all mankind will ultimately see the truth and so it cannot acquiesce in the status quo that "the nations," who did not avail themselves of chosenness, are "rejected." All Jewish generations are under the obligation of leading "the nations" to chosenness, for, as Isaiah put it, "It is too light a thing that thou shouldest be My servant to raise up the tribes of Jacob, and to restore the offspring of Israel; I will also give thee for a light of the nations, that My salvation may be unto the end of the earth."

Jeremiah was not merely a prophet sent to Israel but "a prophet unto the nations," while Jonah's mission was altogether and exclusively to Gentiles, the people of Nineveh. Divine solicitude extends to *all* nations, for "the Lord is the God of all the inhabitants of the world." He therefore "asks the nations to repent, so that He might bring them under His wings."

Far from jealously guarding the crown of chosenness, Israel is eager to share it by serving,

As a light of the nations;
To open the blind eyes,
To bring out the prisoners from the dungeon,
And them that sit in darkness out of the prison-house.

Talmudic and rabbinic literature abounds in statements

that the Torah is not the exclusive property of Israel, but belongs to all who are ready to accept it. The Rabbis emphasized that the Torah was revealed in the desert—"no man's land"—to emphasize that it may belong to all who want it.

The Sages delighted in stressing the universality of the Torah. They suggested that God revealed it in the third month, in the Zodiacal sign of the Twins, to teach that Esau, Jacob's twin brother, is welcome to study the Torah and become a proselyte. The same universalizing tendency is at the root of the statements that at the Sinaitic revelation every word that proceeded from the Lord divided itself into seventy languages, while Moses, too, expounded the Law in seventy tongues, so that all the nations might be swayed to its truth.

Israel emerges not as the only chosen one of the Lord but merely as pioneering in chosenness. It is "the first-born" of the Lord, as it were. The Gentiles, too, are His children. In the words of Solomon Schechter: "This doctrine of election was not quite of so exclusive a nature as is commonly imagined. For it is only the privilege of the first-born which the Rabbis claim for Israel, that they are the first-born in God's kingdom, not to the exclusion of other nations."

## II

The Prophets stressed in many contexts that Israel was in no way especially favored. Thus Amos flung the challenge at his contemporaries, "Are ye not as the children of the Ethiopians unto Me, O children of Israel, saith the Lord. Have I not brought up Israel out of the land of Egypt, and the Philistines from Caphtor, and Aram from Kir?" In other words, Israel's exodus from Egypt is no different from the

Philistines' and the Arameans' migrations from the countries of their origin.

Amos was the most outspoken opponent of interpreting chosenness as superiority. He asserted that Israel is being judged according to the same standards as its neighbors. If anything, it is subjected to severer penalties for, as he put it, "Only you have I known from all the nations, therefore, I shall visit upon you *all* your iniquities." Chosenness implies the duty of intense ethical effort. *Noblesse oblige.*

As the result of this exacting interpretation of chosenness and the Prophets' tirades against their people, the Hebrew Bible is, to quote a Zangwill witticism, almost an "an anti-Semitic book." Obviously, the ancient Hebrews were no worse and certainly in many respects they were considerably better than their neighbors. But the conduct of the Canaanites and Arameans, the Babylonians and the Egyptians was not good enough for Israel, the "Servant of the Lord." It was upbraided not for being worse but for not being better than the nations. God is very exacting with Israel.

Divine mercy embraces all of mankind. The Prophets represented God as grieving not only for the inevitable destruction of the kingdoms of Israel and Judah, inevitable because of their transgressions, but also for the calamities of other nations. Isaiah represents God as sorrowing for Moab's misfortune: "My heart crieth out for Moab'" And in his vision of Israel's restoration, he also anticipates the return of Israel's despoilers, Egypt and Assyria, to their erstwhile strength and power. "In that day shall *Israel* be third with *Egypt* and *Assyria*, a blessing in the midst of the earth; for the Lord of hosts hath blessed him, saying: 'Blessed be Egypt, My people, and Assyria, the work of My hand, and Israel, Mine inheritance.'"

In the ideal future-to-come all nations will be blessed and chosen. Universalism has never triumphed more gloriously than in Isaiah's reference to his nation's foes as God's people and handiwork. It was this kind of universalism that led the Sages to believe that God objected to the angels' jubilation when the Egyptians were drowning in the Red Sea, "You rejoice while My handiwork is drowning!" Jews believe that God mourns even while he punishes the sinners.

The same universalizing tendencies kept Israel from considering only its own country a "Promised Land." In pointing to the similarities of Israel's conquest of Canaan and the settlement of the Philistines and Arameans in their territories, Amos reiterated the Pentateuchal conviction that God "gave to the nations their inheritance ... He set the borders of peoples." Territorial boundaries must therefore be respected. The Israelites dare not encroach upon the children of Esau that dwell in Seir, because, says the Lord, "I have given Mount Seir unto Esau for a possession." Nor dare they covet the land of Moab: "Be not at enmity with Moab, neither contend with them in battle: for I will not give thee of his land for a possession. ... The Enim dwelt therein aforetime, a people great and many, and tall as the Anakim. ... And in Seir dwelt the Horites aforetime, but the children of Esau succeeded them; and they destroyed them before them, and dwelt in their stead; as Israel did unto the land of his possession which the Lord gave unto them."

The purpose of the archaeological inquiry into the antecedents of Moab and the children of Esau is clear; it is to prove that Israel's conquest of its land was in no wise different from the manner in which its neighbors entered upon the possession of *their* Divinely assigned countries. *They did as Israel did unto the land of its possession which the Lord gave unto them.* And thus Israel's inheritance of the Promised Land is no sign of special Divine favor above that shown to other peoples, who received *their* lands from God.

### III

Judaism never identified the entering into the precincts of God as synonymous with conversion to Judaism. The Synagogue lays no claim to being the sole guardian of salvation. As Jews see it, "the righteous of *all* nations have a share in the world-to-come." Salvation is not reserved for the confessors of one creed; it is the reward of all who adhere to the fundamentals of humaneness. King Solomon, at the dedication of the Temple, prayed also for the stranger who might seek God's mercy in Israel's sanctuary. To be sure, the expectation of the eventual conversion of the stranger may have partly inspired this prayer. However, the Jewish desire to make the House of the Lord "a house of prayer for all peoples" never gave rise to the intolerant view that only Israel, and those converted to its faith, will be saved. It was he consensus of the Sages that "just as the sin-offering atones for Israel, so righteousness atones for the peoples of the world."

The Jewish God idea is too sweeping to leave room for the narrow notion that He is only the Lord of Israel. He is the Creator and Ruler of the universe and as a sovereign does not expect the same tribute from all his subjects, God, too, requires different modes of worship and service from different men and peoples. Those who accept the Torah are obliged to keep its 613 commandments. But the Gentiles need only observe the seven Noahidic laws, general humane principles all, to secure a share in the future bliss. God does not narrowly restrict His blessings to the confessors of one faith; many roads lead to Heaven. This broad tolerance also informs most Jewish prayers. They address themselves not to the "God of Israel" but to the "God of the Universe," in accordance with the Rabbinic dictum that "a benediction that lacks a reference to the Divine Kingship is no benediction." Accordingly, all Jewish benedictions open with the formula, "Blessed art Thou, O Lord, Our God, *King of the Universe.*"

As the Jewish people do not engage in missionary efforts, it is taken for granted that Judaism is not a "Missionary Religion." This, however, is only correct if "Missionary Religion" is meant to connote a religion which resorts to the fire and sword in carrying afield its banner. Judaism is innately tolerant; it concedes that salvation is reserved not only for Jews but also for the righteous Gentiles. Why, then, go to extremes for gaining converts? Yet Judaism is always ready to welcome sincere proselytes. Moreover, in some respects the proselyte is judged as superior to the born Jew, for he voluntarily joins the community of Israel.

Some Rabbis did not hesitate to assert that "God loves the proselyte who has become converted to Judaism more than the Israelites who stood at Mount Sinai. For if they had not witnessed the thunder and lightening, the quaking mountains and sounding trumpets, they would not have accepted the Torah. But the proselyte, who saw none of these things, came and joined himself to the Holy One, blessed be He, and accepted the Kingship of Heaven. Can anyone be dearer than He?" This is why "the names of the proselytes are as precious to God as the sacrificial wine poured out upon the altar."

Thanks to this attitude to proselytes on the part of most talmudic Sages (only a few pessimists distrusted the proselytes), authoritative Rabbinic endorsements of proselytism are not lacking. "Every Jew should endeavor to bring men under the wings of the Divine Presence, even as Abraham did." Some Sages even held that "God scattered Israel among the nations for the sole purpose of making proselytes."

The Sages made much of the exemplary proselytes that figure in the Bible, holding them up as examples to would-be proselytes. They comforted the pagan who despaired of the possibility of becoming a true Jew, "Were you worse than Rahab, the harlot, or Jethro the idolatrous priest?" They pointed out that old age was no valid reason for persisting in religious errors, for was not Abraham ninety-nine years old when he entered into the Covenant?

The proselyte is in all respects the equal of the born Jew. If anything, he enjoys greater respect. Rabbinic literature abounds in exhortations to honor him more than a born Jew and to spare his sensibilities by not referring to his origin or the sins of his erstwhile coreligionists. The proselyte is unconditionally accepted into the community of Israel and thus he is obliged to regard Israel's history as his own, although, obviously, the Jewish patriarchs are not his "fathers," biologically speaking. To the proselyte Obadiah's question, whether he could call upon the Lord as the God of "*our* fathers" Who has separated *us* from the nations; and has brought *us* out of Egypt," Maimonides replied:

"Pronounce all the prayers as they are written and do not change anything. Your prayers and benedictions should be the same as those of any other Israelite, regardless of whether you pray in private or conduct the service.... The proselyte, no less than he who confesses the Unity of God as taught in the Torah, is a disciple of Abraham our father. Such persons are of his household....

"You should therefore pray: 'Our God and God of *our* fathers,' for Abraham is also *your* father. In no respect is there a difference between us and you. And certainly you should say, 'Who has given unto *us* the Law,' because the Law was given to us and the proselytes alike.... Remember, most of our ancestors who went out from Egypt were idol-worshippers; they mingled with the Egyptian idolators and imitated their ways; until God sent Moses our teacher, the master of the Prophets. He separated us from the nations, initiated us into the belief in God, us and all the proselytes, and gave us one Law.

"Do not think little of your origin: We are descended from Abraham, Isaac and Jacob, but your descent is from the Creator, for, in the words of Isaiah: 'One shall say, I am the Lord's; and another shall call himself by the name of Jacob.' " Maimonides even concedes the faculty of prophecy, the highest human perfection, to proselytes.

The complete acceptance of the proselyte into the Jewish community *eo ipso* implies the sanctioning of intermarriage with proselytes. Opposition to intermarriage in the period of reconstruction following upon the return from the Babylonian Captivity and in our time, is not due to racial prejudices but is motivated by the fear lest the proselytes are not in earnest about the obligations they assume when pledging fealty to Judaism. As only a fraction of the men and women who now embrace Judaism for matrimonial reasons do so out of religious convictions, Jews concerned over Jewish continuity are naturally apprehensive. It is not objection to a son-in-law or a daughter-in-law born outside the fold that causes Jewish parents to oppose intermarriage, but the almost universal experience that those converted to Judaism for matrimonial reasons rarely take their change of religion seriously, especially since, as a rule, the Jewish partner to such a union is indifferent to

Jewish values and probably only insisted on the conversion in order not to give offense to his parents.

These reservations, however, do not extend to the sincere proselyte. There is no reluctance to take him into the fold of a Jewish family. This is perhaps most compellingly attested by the biblical Scroll of Ruth which records that King David was descended from Ruth the Moabite who chose to worship the God of Israel. Tradition also has it that the eminent Sages Shemaya and Abtalyon were converts to Judaism and that Hillel, Rabbi Akiba and Rabbi Meir were descendants of proselytes. Judaism's disdain for "race" and "blood" speaks eloquently from the tradition tracing Rabbi Akiba's origin to the villain Sisera. If anything, the handicap of unworthy ancestors adds to the prestige of the proselyte by emphasizing his merit and ethical achievement.

The Sages of the Talmud rigorously legislated against the few relics of racial prejudice in biblical law, as respecting the rules pertaining to the Amonites and Moabites. According to biblical law, "an Amonite or a Moabite shall not come into the assembly of the Lord forever." To be sure, they could confess the Jewish religious truths, but they were not accepted as members of the Jewish community and Jews were forbidden to intermarry with them. The Sages of Jabneh, irked by this emphasis on racial and hereditary factors, declared this law had become obsolete "when Sanherib marched against the nations mixing up all the peoples." In other words, the Rabbis declared that there were no "pure races" and thus, as there were no pure Moabites or Amonites, logic required that the legislation which excluded them from the Jewish community be revised.

Obviously, once any and every outsider is admitted into a "chosen" community, its concept of election is not synonymous with exclusiveness. Nothing, therefore, would be more erroneous than to charge Judaism with tendencies of racial snobbishness. Throughout the ages Jewish teachers and thinkers have stressed that our people is only spiritually conditioned and delimited. Not family descent but acceptance of the Torah and the Jewish way of life make the Jew. "For," in the words of Saadia Gaon, "our nation is only a nation by virtue of the Torah." In point of fact, Judaism is neither more nor less exclusive than the modern democracies which restrict certain privileges to their citizens but do not exclude from citizenship those who pledge allegiance to the flag.

## IV

Naturally, the patriot—like the ardent religionist—believes that *his* people is the best. It is natural for a man to consider his own people, his own country and his own culture most perfect. Patriotism becomes a menace only when it advances claims of *a priori* superiority. The Aryan racial theories are of this kind. Of the same class was the ancient Greek claim that only Hellenes are true human beings, while all others are "barbarians" destined to be slaves to the superior master nation of the Greeks. The confidence in their racial-national superiority was so deeply rooted in the Greeks that even philosophers of Plato's and Aristotle's standing endorsed it as indisputable. They were firmly convinced that mankind was divided into two groups: Greeks and "barbarians," the former chosen to rule and the latter condemned to be ruled. A "barbarian" was forever excluded from the Greek community. No matter what he contributed to Greece or its culture, his "blood" and "race" disqualified him.

When the Jew renders thanks to God for having been born a Jew and not a Gentile, he does not therewith aver that a Jew is by destiny superior to a Gentile. He merely rejoices in the fact that he is enjoined to observe 613 Divine commandments, while a "righteous Gentile," in order to qualify for the future bliss, need observe only seven laws. As the Jew considers "the yoke of the commandments," as the minutiae of the Law are fittingly designated, not oppressive but a burden of love, he praises God for having placed this precious load upon him. There is no trace of supercilious and smug overbearing in the Jew's benediction for not having been born a Gentile.

Socrates and Plato, too, are said to have rendered thanks unto the gods for having been born Greeks and not barbarians. Their benediction, however, was not motivated by gratitude for added obligations, but by the proud joy in being members of the ruling nation and the caste of the privileged few for whom other men must toil. In the final analysis, there is no difference between the Greek attitude to non-Greeks, later adopted by the Romans as well, and the frame of mind that gave rise to the perversion of the Nuremberg laws. Both spring from the vaunted and stubborn delusion of pre-ordained national and racial superiority. No matter how low a Greek stooped, he remained a "destined" ruler over the "barbarian," even if the latter was his superior on all counts. Analogously, there was only one crime that disqualified an "Aryan": racial pollution, for the Nazis axiomatically held that an "Aryan" moron was "by birth" superior to a Jewish Einstein.

As the result of such fallacious misconceptions broadcast with conviction by peoples of high cultural attainments, many students have failed to see that the idea of Jewish chosenness is free from perverted claims of predestined superiority. It has been the perennial tragedy of the Jews and Judaism to be interpreted in terms of fiction rather than of fact. When men of letters like Shaw and Wells profess to see in the doctrine of Jewish chosenness nothing else but arrogance, it is perhaps not least due to the circumstance that English patriotism, too, expresses itself as the claim of British superiority over the "colonials." If mankind were not steeped in the mistake of interpreting chosenness as a prerogative rather than as a stern duty, its articulate spokesmen could never have denounced the doctrine of Jewish chosenness as a manifestation of arrogance.

Jewish chosenness has never been interpreted otherwise than as a regimen of sacrifice and service. The law and ethics of the sea ordain that the captain of a sinking vessel be the last to abandon ship. As the highest ranking officer—"the chosen one"—he must excel his crew in sacrificial courage and self-discipline. Israel, too, conceived of its role as stewardship to the nations who, as yet, have not advanced to the full knowledge of the Lord, as revealed in the Torah. As guardians of the Torah, the Jews are keenly cognizant of their obligation to the rest of mankind. This is why all Jewish sacred writings stress Israel's obligation wherever there is reference made to its Divine election.

Thus the Pentateuch makes chosenness contingent upon the keeping of the Law. Israel is only chosen if it chooses to abide by God's commandments. "Now, therefore, if ye will hearken unto My voice indeed, and keep My covenant, then ye shall be Mine own treasure from among all peoples." Israel's election is largely of its own making; it is the reward for the acceptance of the Torah.

The prayers and benedictions which refer to Jewish chosenness anchor Israel's election in faithfulness to the Law which confers the distinction: "Blessed art Thou, O Lord our God, King of the Universe, Who hast chosen us from all peoples and hast given us Thy Torah. Blessed art Thou, O Lord, Who givest the Law." The benediction praises God both as the One Who gives *us* His Torah as well as the One Who gives the Torah, *without any specification to whom*. Thus the very assertion and affirmation of Jewish election leaves room for others besides Jews to partake of chosenness through their choice of the Law, that is given to Israel *and* to those not of Israel who desire to make it their own.

A Midrashic exegesis forcefully stresses this point. Commenting on why the Psalmist represents God as addressing Israel as *My people,* the Rabbis observe that this is "because of the Torah." For previous to the revelation at Sinai and the acceptance of the Torah "Israel was just called 'Israel,' as other nations are called by their names.... But after they accepted the Torah, God refers to them as My People."

Jewish ethics requires that man strive toward emulating the perfection of God: "And ye shall be holy, for I the Lord am holy." It is noteworthy that the passage which stresses the duty of *imitatio dei* also strongly affirms Israel's election, supplying additional evidence that chosenness is a task and a challenge. In the picturesque language of the Midrash, "Israel is the retinue of the King, and its duty is to emulate the King."

The interpretation of chosenness as purposive choice implies the correlation of God and Israel through their espousal of Him and His choice of them. The Rabbis were intensely imbued with the certainty of this reciprocity between the choosing and chosen God and the chosen and choosing Jewish people. "One God through Israel, and one Israel through God," they asserted. "They are his chosen people and He is their chosen portion." But if Israel does not choose God, by observing His commandments, they are not chosen. In the words of Jeremiah: "Hearken upon My voice, and I will be your God, and ye shall be My people."

The reciprocation of the God-Israel relationship is thoroughly equalitarian. God and Israel are co-partners in the "covenant," for He requires Israel's homage no less than they need His law: "Israel professes God's unity in the words, 'Hear O Israel, the Lord our God, the Lord is one,' and the Spirit of Holiness proclaims their election, 'And who is like unto thy people Israel, a nation that is one in the earth'"

To the Rabbis Israel's Divine election and their choice of the Eternal One was essentially a love truce. They figuratively represented God as addressing himself to Israel: "You have made Me the only object of your love in the world." God's love of Israel, however, is not uncritical, as it were. According to the Sages, God chooses only those who espouse goodness. Rabbi Jose ben Halafta, in replying to a Roman lady who accused God of making arbitrary choices, said: "God draws to Him only the one in whom he sees good deeds."

## V

Israel Zangwill aptly observed that "a chosen people is really a choosing people." The Sages of the Talmud, too, shared this view, stressing that Israel was chosen because they chose God. This emphasis on "the choosing people" aspect rather than on "the chosen people" accentuation is a natural corollary of the Jewish esteem for freedom. Moral responsibility is predicated on freedom of the will, as only the free can be held accountable for his deeds. If the Jews had been merely passively elevated to the role of "the chosen people," the distinction would be all but meaningless. Moreover, it would be infused with predestination, which is unacceptable to Judaism. To avoid these pitfalls, the Rabbis resorted to various allegories in order to prove that Israel was chosen because of their choice of God and the Torah. "Why did the Holy One, blessed be He, choose Israel? Because all the nations rejected and refused the Torah, while Israel agreed and chose the Holy One, blessed be He, and his Torah." The Midrash has it that God first offered the Torah to the nations. Only after it had been rejected by them did He propose to give it to Israel, who were so eager to have it that they declared themselves ready to observe it even before they knew what it demands.

Despite this emphasis on the choosing aspect, however, some of Sages were beset by doubts whether a certain preference was not shown to Israel. They resolved these doubts by averring that even as the Prophets were compelled to prophesy, frequently against their will, by the message that was searing their hearts, so Israel was impelled to be the "servant of the Lord." The Aggadah ventures that the Israelites did not wish to accept the Torah, and so God had to force them, as it were. He held them captive under Mount Sinai, threatening: "If you will accept the Torah, well and good; if you won't, this will be your grave."

Obviously, the Aggadah does not intend to dispute Israel's freedom of choice, rather it strains to explain why Israel accepted the Torah when all other nations rejected it. This apologetic tendency, evident in many texts dealing with Israel's election, goes to show that the doctrine of Jewish chosenness is free from vaunted claims to superiority. In the words of the Bible, "The Lord did not set His love upon you, nor choose you, because you were more in number than any people—for ye were the fewest of all peoples." In the same spirit the Jerusalemian Talmud submits that God chose Israel because it was so insignificant that otherwise it would have been lost among the nations.

While other nations laying claims to chosenness interpret it as the right to dominate, in the Jewish realm it has invariably been defined as the duty of stern and unremitting sacrificial service. In this connection it is instructive to compare the British anthem "Rule, Britannia," the avowal of Anglo-Saxon chosenness, with Isaiah's strophes on the Servant of the Lord, the avowal of Jewish chosenness. The British define their "election" as being called upon to rule the world:

> When Britain first at Heaven's command
>    Arose from out the azure main,
> This was the charter of the land,
>    And guardian angels swing the strain:
> Rule Britannia, rule the waves;
>    Britons never will be slaves.
>
> The nations not so blest as thee
>    Must in their turn to tyrants fall;
> While thou shalt flourish, great and free,
>    The dread and envy of them all.
>
> To thee belongs the rural reign,
>    The cities shall with commerce shine:
> All thine shall be the subject main,
>    And every shore it circles, thine.

Contrast this with Isaiah's vision of Israel, the Servant of the Lord:

> Who would have believed our report?
> And to whom hath the arm of the Lord been revealed.
> For he shot up right forth as a sapling,

And as a root out of a dry ground;
He had no form nor comeliness that we should look
 upon him,
Nor beauty that we should delight in him.
He was despised and forsaken of men,
A man of pains, and acquainted with disease,
As one from whom men hide their face:
He was despised, and we esteemed him not.
Surely our diseases he did bear, and our pains he carried;
Whereas we did esteem him stricken,
Smitten of God, and afflicted.
But he was wounded because of our transgressions,
He was crushed because of our iniquities.
The chastisement of our welfare was upon him,
And with his stripes we were healed . . .
He was oppressed, though he humbled himself
And opened not his mouth . . .
Yet it pleased the Lord to crush him by disease,
To see if his soul would offer itself in restitution,
That he might see his seed prolong his days,
And that the purpose of the Lord might prosper by his
 hand:
Of the travail of his soul he shall see to the full, even My
 servant,
Who by his knowledge did justify the Righteous One
 to the many,
And their inquities did he bear . . .

This, then, is the meaning of Jewish chosenness: to be the *servant* of the Lord and the *servant* of mankind; to bear crushing hardship and suffering in order to lead mankind to God. Not might and strength, but wounds and stripes are the marks of Jewish chosenness. The "Servant of the Lord" must suffer so as to teach mankind that the ways and measures of God are not those of men; that might is not the mark of His favor nor pain the stigma of His wrath. True chosenness means service—not domination. Israel therefore does not conceive of its role as that of a *master* but as that of the servant of God—and men.

Thanks to this interpretation of what might be termed worldly failure, Jews would never regard their afflictions as proof of Divine rejection. On the contrary, they took them as a mark of Divine love. "Because God loves Israel he multiplies their sufferings." The Aggadah therefore interprets the sigh of the Shulamith, "I am love-sick," as follows: "Israel says to God: 'Lord of the Universe, all the sufferings you inflict upon me only make me love you more."

Obviously, such a definition of chosenness is contrary to the accepted view. But, then, the Prophets precipitated a revolution in ethics when they proclaimed that not the triumphant, conquering hero but the humbled, oppressed sufferer is the chosen one of God.

Christianity adopted the Jewish ideal of the "Suffering Servant" and therewith rejected the worship of force and might. Regrettably, however Christianity was not consistent in applying this new criterion of true nobility. While pointing to Jesus' passion as proof of his election, the Church maintains that the exile of the Jews and their perennial afflictions attest that they are rejected by God.

The refusal to accept that success testifies to the truth of an idea or the ethical quality of an ideal has immeasurably buoyed Jewish survival strength. Even as God accepts as offerings of the altar only animals that are preyed upon but do not prey upon others, the Rabbis reasoned, so He chooses Israel as His favorite because it is the innocent prey of the peoples. Once, however, exile, persecution and torture are accepted as marks of chosenness rather than as stigmas of rejection, they lose their sting and hurt. Israel could—and can —bear its afflictions without despairing because it knows that worth while possessions must be acquired by painful sacrifices. "The Holy One, blessed be He, gave Israel the three precious gifts—the Torah, the Land of Israel and the world-to-come— only by suffering." This is the ultimate rationale of Jewish survival amidst suffering and tribulation.

Our inquiry into the meaning of the Jewish idea of Jewish chosenness has carried us rather far afield. But the "excursion" has proved illuminating by enabling us to see that to the Jews chosenness connotes not privileges of nobility and ease but obligations of a stern code of ethics. Jews have never regarded Divine election otherwise than as a crown, splendid, it is true, but also thorny and pressing. There is no trace of overbearing arrogance in the many liturgical references to Jewish chosenness. They constitute the acknowledgment, proud, to be sure, but humble, of a certainty, of being weighed down by the heavy and yet sweet burden of serving as a light unto the nations, of being singled out for service and suffering, so that a better day may dawn:

> You only have I known of all the families of the earth;
> Therefore I will visit upon you all your iniquities.

CHAPTER 10

*Study of the Torah*

I

WHEN THE medieval ghetto restrictions were raised in the Western European countries, in the first half of the nineteenth century, Jewish youths flocked to the universities which had previously denied them admission. Today, more than a century and a half after the incipient stages of emancipation, Jewish boys and girls are still crowding the colleges and universities in disproportionately large numbers. It would be difficult to find an American Jewish family that could not boast one college or university graduate, at least.

The predilection for the learned professions is not a recently acquired Jewish trait. It is one of the most solidly rooted Jewish characteristics. Jew are, indeed, "The People of the Book" and thus, inevitably, they are also a people of scholars and students. The very constitution of Judaism, as revealed in the Written Torah and interpreted and elaborated by the Sages of the Talmud, makes it obligatory for *every* Jew to devote himself to the study of the Torah, which represents the sum total of Jewish law and lore amassed by a hundred generations of scholars, thinkers, philosophers and poets.

245

If the modern Jew is so strongly attracted to intellectual pursuits it is not least due to the fact that his ancestors, for so many generations, did not consider a day well spent which was not partly, at least, devoted to study and meditation. Even today, Jews anchored in the tradition of their people will not let a day pass without study of the Torah. This intellectual pursuit, tinged with pious motives, has been our glory and delight, our refuge and our staff in suffering—the sanctuary of the spirit where invariably we found solace for the tribulations of our tragedy-fraught pariah existence.

Judaism does not leave the dedication to things of the spirit to the discretion of the individual. It has laid down the rule that "every Jew is obligated to study Torah, whether he be rich or poor, healthy or sick, in the bloom of youth, or aged and weak. Even the pauper, who is supported by charity or goes begging from door to door, and the man who has a wife and children to support must set aside fixed periods by day and night for the study of Torah, in accordance with the commandment: 'You shall meditate therein day and night.'" According to Maimonides' authoritative decision, a Jew must study Torah all the days of his life—until death freezes its words on his lips. This exacting regimen has been diligently complied with by Jews in all countries and in all periods.

As keen psychologists, the ancient Sages were cognizant of the weakness of the flesh which seduces one to sigh, perhaps with some justification, "As soon as I shall have leisure I'll study." But "what if you will never have leisure?" the gentle Hillel censored those inclined to put matters off. In the same vein Maimonides warned those who habitually look to the next day for solving today's problems: "Perhaps you will say: I shall study after having earned some money and provided for my necessities.... Should such a thought enter your mind, you will never be worthy of the crown of the Torah."

General education and universal dedication to the study of Torah have flourished in Israel since very early times. Jews know of no privileged class or caste where study is concerned. The duty of Torah study is incumbent upon all. Moreover, there is no set limit to the course of studies, as even a lifetime does not suffice for mastering all that should be known.

The Bible is the text-book of democracy which has basically influenced all modern states. Jewish democracy flourishes on the fruitful soil of general universal education, for all Jews alike are privileged and obligated to study. Thus the Pentateuchal law emphatically stresses that *all* Israel received the Torah. Consequently, the Rabbis taught that he who withholds Torah instruction from a Jew robs him of his rightful inheritance, for the Torah is the legacy of the *entire congregation* of Jacob, and not the prerogative of the priests and scholars. Jewish educational democracy at is best is reflected in the parable of "The Three Crowns," the crown of the Torah, the crown of Priesthood and the crown of Royalty. While the latter two are reserved for descendants of certain families, the most exalted of "The Three Crowns" can be attained by all those who strive for it. Accordingly, the Sages stressed that Torah scholarship is not inherited and that great scholars not infrequently come from very poor families. Consequently, one must bestow special care on the instruction of the poor and the children of "ignoramuses," for Torah proceeds from them.

Excellence in scholarship is the kind of success traditional Jews worship and crave more fervently than all else, with the result that study and learning are idealized as the very meaning and purpose of the good life; the badge of nobility and honor. There is no greater bliss and satisfaction for a traditional Jew than to excel in Jewish scholarship. And there is no greater shame and degradation than to be known as an *Am Ha-Aretz*—unlettered and ignorant.

Jews have many "firsts" to their credit. Among the numerous innovations they have introduced, general adult education is especially noteworthy. The vast expanse and the intricacy of the Torah, the written and the oral Law, make its full mastery impossible during the years of childhood and youth normally allotted to study. This is why Jews are bidden never to lay aside the book for any length of time, for "if one does not increase one's knowledge, it decreases." He who abandons his studies for a day, forgets the lessons of two days. Every Jew therefore is expected to devote a definite period daily to the study of Torah, for it is not meet that one should let pass even one day unhallowed by dedication to the things of the spirit which endure forever.

## II

Jewish literature of all periods touchingly attests the devotion of average Jews to study. The best way to observe how medieval Jews discharged this sacred duty is probably afforded by their last wills and testaments. These personal documents prove, even more convincingly than the Law codes, to what extent study dominated the life of average Jews. Thus, for instance, one father bequeathed to his sons toiling for a livelihood this set of rules for pursuing learning:

"There are two appropriate times for the regular daily study of Torah: (1) In the morning, before breakfast, immediately after the morning prayers. Nothing must be permitted to interfere with this habit.... At any rate, never leave home, not even on pressing business, before studying a passage, or at least a single rule or sentence if the matter is very urgent. (2) At night, immediately after supper, and again before retiring. It is advisable to study early in the evening, before supper, either the whole or the better part of the set portion, for eating makes one sleepy and then one cannot study effectively. Don't depend on rising before dawn to study your set portion. In all likelihood you will be too sleepy. Night, our Sages stressed, was made for no other purpose than study."

Another father enjoined his son always to keep a Talmud tome or two, or a Rabbinical work, within easy reach, so that he should be able to study at any time. "He should read as much as possible and consider it a duty to study in any text he likes at least four lines before eating. Also, let him not neglect to study every week the Biblical Portion, twice in the Hebrew original and once in the Aramaic." This fourteenth century parent religiously practiced what he preached by laying down an even stricter rule for his own discipline: "As long as I am healthy, free from coercion, and think of it, I shall not taste a morsel on any day before having studied one page of the Talmud, or of one of its commentaries. Should I transgress this rule intentionally, I must not drink wine on that day, or I shall pay half a ducat to charity."

Study is so all-important to the Jew because the religious truths of his faith are not so much to be believed as to be comprehended. Although Judaism does not minimize the importance of the religious emotion and of belief, it yet emphasizes the significance and desirability of the rational understanding of the religious teachings. The Sages deduced this from the fact that the Pentateuch places the "study" of the commandments before their "practice" in the passage, "Hear, O Israel, the statutes and the ordinances which I speak in your ears this day, that ye may *learn* them and *observe them to do."* Commenting on this text, the Rabbis emphasized that "doing depends upon study, not vice versa." Consequently, according to one opinion, the punishment for the neglect of study is severer than that for laxity in religious practice. Maimonides admirably summed up the accepted view by stating that "study unconditionally takes precedence over practice, for study leads to practice, but practice does not lead to study." To be sure, there were always Jews who would not subscribe to this glorification of study and assigned to belief, although blind, more importance than to faith built on intellectual premises. Although, at times, such emotional-mystical tendencies scored significant triumphs, the progress of Judaism and the evolution of its rationale have been charted almost exclusively by those who subscribed to the principle that "of all precepts none equals in importance that of the study of Torah," and who believed that, at the final judgment in the world-to-come, "one will first be called to account regarding one's compliance with the duty of study, and only afterwards for his other deeds."

This triumph of "the rule of the intellect," to borrow a term coined by Ahad Ha'Am, had some very remarkable consequences, among others that the sanctity of the synagogue was subordinated to that of the academy. In their zeal to enthrone the academy as the holy of holies the Sages of the Talmud even had it that God addressed Himself to David, "a single day which you devote to the study of the Torah is dearer to me than a thousand burnt-offerings which your son, Solomon, will sacrifice to Me upon the altar." Even more revolutionary from the formal, pietistic viewpoint was Raba's comment on one of his colleagues, who was in the habit of prolonging his prayers. "Such men neglect life eternal to occupy themselves with transitory things," he said. Another Sage, Rabbi Jeremiah, was so indignant when a colleague interrupted his studies for the sake of prayer, that he almost insulted him by quoting the passage, "If one turns his ear from hearing the Torah, his prayer, too, is an abomination."

In keeping with this high esteem for study, even above prayer, Rabbi Moses Hasid, a 17th century pietist, counselled less prayer in favor of study. And in order to lend more force to this exhortation, he confessed in his will: "Even at the midnight services I prefer to pray less in order to be able to study more."

The study of the "Written Torah" and its numerous commentaries, of which the Talmud is but one gigantic specimen, which represent the "Oral Torah," is the most pleasing Divine service Judaism knows. Thanks to the conviction that "the soul without knowledge is not good," the ritual of the Synagogue emphasizes study no less than prayer. Major portions of the Sabbath and holy day services, as well as of the weekday devotions, are devoted to the reading of the Portion of the Week, consisting of Pentateuchal chapters, and of the Prophetic Portion, i. e., biblical chapters which are either reminiscent or otherwise connected with the respective Portion of the Week. In this manner the Pentateuch and the five Scrolls (Song of Songs, Ruth, Lamentations, Ecclesiastes and Esther), as well as large sections of the Prophets, are religiously studied as part of the Synagogue services year after year, for no sooner is one reading cycle concluded, on the Festival of the Rejoicing of the Law, then the same cycle is started all over again, study being of the things to which Judaism refuses to assign a limitation.

Jewish liturgy, too, is primarily of a didactic character. The prayerbook contains a large number of biblical selections, talmudic teachings and maxims, historical reflections and accounts, besides special petitions for the granting of understanding and knowledge.

## III

Unlike some faiths, which fear that knowledge may prove a stumbling block to the piety of lay persons, Judaism holds that "the ignoramus (in religious lore) cannot be pious." Only the increase of knowledge stimulates piety, for, as Maimonides put it, "one loves God only in accordance with one's knowledge, the degree of his love corresponding to that of his knowledge." Here, too, Maimonides only voiced a conviction which was entrenched in Jewish tradition, for in as early a source as the Jerusalemian Talmud God is represented as exclaiming concerning the sinners, "I would not mind if they had forsaken Me and clung to My Torah, for its light would bring them back to Me."

The Rabbis knew that the intellectual effort tends to lessen the temptation of the "evil inclination," but they also were aware of the fact that scholarship and virtue do not always go hand in hand. Being more than partial to the scholar, they decided that "sin does not cancel the merit of knowledge of the Torah," although it blots out the merit of pious deeds. This type of spirited tolerance made the pious and saintly Rabbi Meir hold fast to his friendship for Rabbi Elisha ben Abuya, even after he had been placed under ban for heresy as *Aher*—misbeliever. Although Jews are averse to overlooking ethical transgressions because of intellectual achievements, they are yet sufficiently biased toward the scholar to make special allowances. On the other hand, the attitude to the spurner of knowledge is almost cruel, for "it is forbidden to pity him."

The mad struggle for worldly possessions in excess of the necessary has invariably been decried by Jewish teachers. This does not imply a predilection for asceticism. Judaism appreciates the good and beautiful things of life, so much so that certain Sages held that, in the world-to-come, we shall have to answer for those legitimate pleasures we denied ourselves. The Jewish genius decries, however, the folly of devoting one's strength to provide for the cravings of the physical appetites while neglecting the spiritual needs. The Sages, therefore, counselled: "Lessen your toil for material goods, and occupy yourself with the Torah." Since Torah study is the favorite recreation and diversion of the well integrated Jew, this advice is really tantamount to advice on how to get worth while enjoyment out of life.

It would be mistaken to conclude that pious Jews pursue the study of Torah solely for the sake of the "future reward." No doubt with the simpler souls the "reward" held in store for diligent Torah students will act as a spur—but they, too, are studying largely for the sheer enjoyment of this keen intellectual pursuit. I recall a poor, sickly, emaciated Jewish laundryman in a summer resort near New York, on whose shelves, side by side with the laundry packages, I saw Talmud foliants and the important codes of Jewish law over which he would be poring a good many hours a day, hours that were spent by his competitors in soliciting new customers, with the result that our learned laundryman was barely making a living. "What good is Talmud study to you?" I asked him one day. And he, with a glance of infinite contempt commingled with limitless pity, replied (in Yiddish, of course): "You wouldn't understand—and then, perhaps, you will. Study is what I am really living for. The store and all the rest is mere regrading drudgery—but study, that is the real thing. Here a man is a man and not merely an automaton rushing about to make a few dollars for rent and food."

Fortunately there are still some Jews left who follow the advice of the Sages "to lessen the toil for worldly goods," not for the ulterior hope of a heavenly reward, but because this study is their real life, its meaning and its consummation.

As all ideals, Torah study not infrequently calls for personal sacrifices. The Sages well understood that possessions, material and even more so spiritual ones, are appreciated in accordance with the effort spent on their acquisition. This truth is rather touchingly expressed in the talmudic tale which represents Moses addressing Israel as follows: "Don't you know with what travail I obtained the Torah! What toil, what labor I endured for its sake! Forty days and forty nights I stayed with God.... My life, my blood I gave for the Torah. As I learned it in travail, so do you teach it in travail." The same intimate knowledge of the birth-pangs that bring forth the scholar is evident from such matter-of-fact statements as that "the words of the Torah endure only with him who would suffer death for their sake," and that "God gives Torah only to him who submits to pain for its sake."

Jews have endured the very agonies of hell to study Torah. They have suffered martyrdom on the burning stake, in the waters of icy rivers and in the seven seas because they would not forsake their books. They left behind good and solid houses, security for themselves and their loved ones, in order to retain the freedom to study Torah and observe its commandments. They have voluntarily submitted to an exacting regimen of eighteen and more hours a day of intensive study, more often than not on an empty stomach, in order to acquire ever more of the precious knowledge which represents the real glory and dignity of the Jew.

And not only those who studied were willing and ready to stake on it their very lives, but their families — and the community at large — were under the sway of this ideal. Jewish wives would assume the task of providers, so that their husbands might give all their time to the study of Torah. Not a few critics have denounced the *batlanim* (idlers) who passed their days and nights in the House of Study, while their wives grew old and wasted before their time by being both mothers and fathers, homemakers and breadwinners. But, in fact, these men were not idlers, nor were the women to be pitied—they were idealists who pooled their resources to attain their most cherished ideal: Torah— the acquisition of learning—the victory of the Jewish spirit over the corroding forces of a hostile world. These women, who were most of the time either bearing or nursing a child, cheerfully faced the heat of the summer and the cold of the winter in their market stands, happy in the knowledge that their husbands and sons were studying, studying and thus realizing the purpose of life which they instinctively felt, yet would not have been able to express in words—for they were simple women, untutored and weighed down by the material cares of life from which they freed their men, so that they might devote themselves to the sacred tasks of the spirit.

Now this world has been eclipsed, but it will live on in the memory of our people. It was a world where money counted for little and was only esteemed useful because it enabled one to get a learned husband for his daughter. It mattered little whether the young man had a shirt on his back, if only he had rabbinic testimonials praising his scholarship. In that enchanted world where Torah learning was "the best merchandise," fathers would journey hundreds of miles to the famous academies to secure for their daughters some budding Talmud genius as a husband. Astute businessmen would regard it as a privilege and honor to support a scholarly son-in-law for years and bask in his reflected glory.

Naturally, the ideal of every Jewish mother and father was to see their sons grow up to be learned rabbis and scholars and train their daughters to appreciate scholarship. Already

Josephus, some two thousand years ago, boasted in his pamphlet against Apion that "we apply the greatest zeal to the education of the young." Throughout the centuries, Jews have never relaxed this zealous devotion to learning and education. There is a touching Yiddish lullaby which answers the question as to what is "the best merchandise" with the confident assertion: Torah. Torah was to Jewish parents of yesterday "the only profit in sons," as the Gaon Elijah of Vilna put it. Consequently, parents would stake and sacrifice their all on the education of their children. Father and mother would gladly subsist on a piece of herring and dry bread, washed down with bitter tea, in order to raise the tuition fee for their children. Years of skimping and deprivation were light in their eyes, if they were crowned by the scholarly achievements of those for whom these sacrifices were made.

It was in this wise that the Jewish eternity was entrenched and fortified.

## IV

One of the passages which is most characteristic of Judaism reads "The world exists only thanks to the merit of the school children." There is no other pronouncement which summarizes so perfectly and succinctly the dedication to the eternal things of the spirit which, in turn, has endowed us with eternity.

About the turn of the century pedagogues and progressive parents proclaimed, "The Century of the Child" (see Ellen Key's famous book). To us Jews this slogan is rather an understatement—for to us, children, trained to carry on the tradition of our people, are eternity itself.

In keeping with the supreme valuation of the "school children," the people of the Torah introduced general compulsory education some two thousand years ago. The Talmud categorically avers that "a town without a school deserves to be destroyed." Moreover, a Jew may not dwell in a town where the Jewish community does not provide for the education of the children. Under the stress of war and other emergencies, our modern school facilities are not infrequently curtailed. Jewish law does not authorize the suspension of instruction to use school buildings for the registration of soldiers and similar purposes unrelated to study. As a matter of fact, "The instruction of school children must not be interrupted even for the sake of the building of the Temple." Nothing is permitted to interfere with Jewish education!

Jewish civil law interdicts the operating of business establishments that would disturb residential quiet and privacy. Yet if a teacher opens a school in his apartment, the neighbors cannot object that the noise disturbs them. And a teacher with an established class may not object to the opening of a school next door to him by another pedagogue. All usual amenities and claims are set aside by the principle of the primacy of study. Accordingly, a pithy Midrash has it that the Glory of God stayed on in the Holy Land after the Ten Tribes and, later, Judah and Benjamin had been exiled. Even when the Sanhedrin and the Priests were carried away, the Divine Glory abided. However, when the school children were taken captives, the Glory of God, too, departed.

Those who know little about Jewish scholarship not infrequently tend to judge it as being narrow and of limited scope. Although traditional Jewish learning is centered in the Talmud and its biblical foundation, it is yet infinitely larger in scope than most "secular" disciplines. Jews are fond of referring to the "Sea of the Talmud" and, indeed, the Talmud has the vastness of the ocean, but it also has its depth and the rich variety of the flora and fauna of the seas. According to the Sages, "everything" is in the Talmud, and this is far from an idle boast. The Talmud is not merely a book or a series of books, a commentary or a code of law, it is the literary repository and epitomy of Jewish life of a thousand years, in all its many-sided, multi-hued and contradictory totality. Like life, the Talmud is not orderly and systematic, but a series of ascents and descents; it is a transcript of actual life and therefore difficult to fathom.

In the Talmud one finds, side by side with penetrating, trenchant and logical discussions of fine points of law, exotic and fantastic tales and legends. Here one encounters, on the same folio, the most spiritual and sublime definitions of God and very naive descriptions of the Divine Being. It contains acute psychological observations and thoroughly modern medical opinions on vitamins ("green vegetables"), for instance. Unequivocal condemnations of superstition are listed side by side with the most weird superstitious notions, and exquisite spiritual interpretations of the hereafter are found side by side with luridly materialistic descriptions of the world-to-come.

When Ben Bag Bag counselled: "Turn it, and turn it over again for everything is in it—and contemplate it, and wax gray and old over it," he did not impose upon the students of Torah a limitation of interests. Of the Talmud it may truly be said that "nothing human is foreign to it." Nothing, therefore, could be more erroneous than to judge Jews who are students of this one work and its commentaries as being limited in scope and outlook. Their terminology may be different and their aims and programs of study may vary from those of the modern colleges and universities, but in acuteness of thought, philosophical and human understanding, the disciplining of the mind and the sharpening of the memory, to say nothing of the broad, integrated, humanistic-ideational outlook acquired through this study, they are often superior to those who pity the *Yeshiva Bachur's* "backwardness."

That the peculiar discipline of Torah study develops the faculties of the mind is conclusively demonstrated by the record of the Jewish youths, who, after a preliminary Yeshiva training, enter the universities to win fame in all fields of intellectual pursuits. The alleged "coldness" of Talmudic logic does not stifle the creative instinct, as is attested by the host of creative poets and writers, in Yiddish, Hebrew, and the vernaculars, who have made their marks since the beginning of the nineteenth century. If Jews lived until modern times, and modern times did not dawn for Jewry until the nineteenth century was well under way, almost exclusively by the Bible and the Talmud, they were not worse off on account of it.

## V

Once we grasp the scope and nature of what the Jew groups under the heading of Torah, we also begin to understand why its study is so dear to him. It is the "light," the joy and the real meaning of his life. It is his companion in loneliness and the balm to all his ills.

Generations upon generations of plain, everyday Jews considered poor only him who had no Torah knowledge. In the ancient Palestinian academies they used to say: "He who has knowledge has everything; but what has he who lacks knowledge? On the other hand, what does he who possesses knowledge lack?" The result of such teachings was that Jews were inclined to recognize only one type of aristocracy, the nobility of the intellect. It was only recently, due to the influence of a set of values created by more materialistic philosophies of life, that captains of business and industry rather than scholars became the spokesmen and leaders of the Jewish communities.

Jews also discovered early the intimate bond between knowledge and freedom. They regard "knowledge" not as "power," but as the instrument of liberation from narrow prejudice. As to the traditional Jew knowledge is almost synonymous with Torah, the Rabbis postulated that "nobody is free except he who labors in the Torah." The Torah, therefore, is the herald and the instrument of liberation, for with it "freedom came into the world." One need but study a page of the Talmud to see that its makers placed freedom of expression above all else. Jew-haters not infrequently argue that one can prove practically everything, and its opposite, with a talmudic quotation. There is much truth in this. The Sages who edited the final version of the Talmud were so thoroughly imbued with the spirit of freedom that they would not suppress minority opinions differing from the decisions of the majority. Even such a heretical view as that Israel has no prospects for another Messiah, since King Hezekiah was this Messiah, was incorporated into the text of the Talmud, although only one Sage seems to have adhered to this opinion.

The study of Torah bestows not only the spiritual acumen that grows from knowledge, but also teaches how freedom should operate in the intellectual sphere. "Academic freedom," spurned by the dictatorships and occasionally even by the democracies, has been tacitly taken for granted in the Jewish academies since millennia, with the result that freedom, in the best sense of the word, has become the very presupposition and the medium of Jewish intellectual expression.

There are few peoples who assign to knowledge such an important place in the scheme of things as Jews do. Torah is to them one of the three foundations of the world. Sociologists know that among the Jews "the poorest mechanics and small traders are more apt to send their children to high schools and universities than the Christians of the same social and economic status." This is not only true of the United States, but of all countries where Jews have access to institutions of higher learning. The disproportionately large representation of Jews on the campuses of colleges and universities often adds impetus to the fiction of the wealth of the Children of Israel, for few Gentiles know that, as Max Nordau put it, "among the Jews alone exists the delusion that a man can study without having money. Only among us does one think of being able to penetrate into institutions of higher learning, and of working with the head without filling the stomach."

Modern Jews not infrequently have substituted other disciplines for the study of Torah, but the love of learning has remained essentially unchanged and unimpaired. Inevitably, centuries upon centuries of intellectual pre-occupation are bound to condition a group in the same way physical specialization results in special bodily aptitudes and skills. Jews as a group usually rate a higher I. Q. than the majority population. It would be mistaken to conclude from this that Jews are *per se* possessed of greater intellectual gifts. Their keener intelligence is solely due to the circumstance that for centuries they have been forced to rely on their brains rather than on their brawns for survival in a hostile world, and that their community has ceaselessly stressed Torah study. As a result, the average contemporary Jew is somewhat keener in matters of the intellect than the average member of the majority group. Thus, for instance, Lewis M. Terman, the foremost American authority on intelligence tests, found that among the thousand most gifted pupils in Californian schools, twice as many were Jewish than the proportion of Jews in the general population. And according to figures collected by

Lewis Browne in India, the children of the native Bene-Israel, although strongly intermarried, still show a definite superiority over comparable groups of Hindu children.

As a survival factor, Torah study cannot be overestimated. The rigid regimen of the Jewish law, which raises a protective fence about the community, is largely predicated on study. Moreover, the all-inclusive nature of the Torah afforded a rather satisfying substitute for the concrete possessions of nationhood, such as territory and an independent government. The Torah became the Jews' "portable fatherland," which enabled them to live and survive wherever they build a shrine for its study. For "although Israel be in exile among the nations, if they occupy themselves with Torah, it is as if they were not in exile." Were the Torah merely religious law and guidance, it might have proved impotent to stay and sustain Jewish vitality. Being, however, vast, vigorous, profound and multi-hued like the ocean, the Torah supplied the inexhaustible strength which has preserved our people in creative and virile strength.

The ancient Sages were fully cognizant of the preservative powers of the Torah. They knew that "if you want to destroy the Jews, you must first destroy their synagogues and schools, for as long as the voices of their children continue to ring out in the schools, and they are taught the word of God, the world will not prevail against them."

The Torah is the "life elixir" by the grace of which we have survived. This is why Jews throughout the ages have been willing to die rather than forsake it. To renounce the Torah is tantamount to Jewish extinction, a fact which has been tragically demonstrated, especially in the last hundred and fifty years of Jewish emancipation and assimilation. Precisely because "Israel is a nation solely by virtue of the

Torah," it ceases to be a people when it neglects this nationalizing element.

Perhaps this truth is better recognized if we substitute for Torah the term "Jewish Culture" (and what else is Torah, if not *also* "Jewish Culture" in its totality and unbroken continuity?) Consequently, what the Sages really meant to say by pointing to the Torah as the "life elixir" of the Jew was that, in the absence of a physical fatherland, the cultural fatherland of the Torah must be built into a strong and enduring refuge and fortress.

This aspect of the Torah was keenly appreciated by the makers of Judaism in the centuries of transition following upon the destruction of the Temple. "God foresaw," they taught with one eye on the masses of the people, "that the Temple would be destroyed, and so He said: 'While the Temple stands and you bring sacrifices, the Temple atones for you. When the Temple will be no more . . . occupy yourselves with the Torah, for it is equivalent to sacrifices and will atone for you." The same thought is expressed in the statement, that "since the day when the Temple was destroyed the Holy One, blessed be He, has only left to Him the four ells of the *Halacha*," that is to say, the realm of the Torah.

## VI

It is natural that a people which respects learning the way the Jews do, should hold the scholar in special respect. He is the pivot of the community, the "guardian of the city," and the true hero who is held up for emulation. Jewish literature of all centuries abounds in praises of the scholar. So greatly was the keeper and guardian of knowledge honored in medieval Jewish communities, that a seventeenth century Polish rabbi could ask with perfect ease, "And who if not the rabbinical students are to be regarded as royalty?" For that matter, already the talmudic Sages had proved, by means of an ingenious piece of exegesis, that the scholar is superior to the prophet.

Jewish law places scholars in an especially privileged class, the rights reserved for them being not so much personal prerogatives as means for the fostering of learning. Thus scholars are exempt from community levies. "They do not go out to participate with the rest of the people in building, digging or similar work for the government . . . nor are they assessed for the cost of building the walls, repairing the gates, paying the watchman's wages, etc., or for tribute to the king. Nor are they obliged to pay a tax, collectively or individually levied upon the inhabitants of the city. . . . Also, if a scholar has goods for sale, he is to be given the opportunity of disposing of them first; and no one else in the market should be permitted to sell, till the scholar has first sold his stock. Similarly, if he has a trial pending and he is waiting among a large number of litigants, his case is to be heard first." Obviously, these privileges are not so much conferred upon the individual scholar as upon the Torah, which is to be honored in his person.

According to the Talmud, "a scholar of illegitimate birth takes precedence over an unlettered High Priest, and every one who excels his fellow in learning takes precedence over him." By and large, Jews have abided by this principle through the ages. Until almost our day, the scholars were the uncontested rulers of Jewish life, the royalty to whom respect and veneration was offered and whose circle to join was the ambition of every Jew. If money counted for aught, it was but to finance scholarly projects and institutions; to maintain schools and students, to enable scholars to pore over their books, without worry for their daily bread.

Jewish ethics is predicated on the principle of unselfish motivation. The good deed must be performed for its own sake—and not for reward. The Jew must not serve God in the manner of slaves looking for recompense. Study of the Torah, the crown of ethical endeavor, must likewise be pursued for its own sake and not for worldly advantages. "Do the words of the Torah for the doing's sake; speak of them for their own sake. Perhaps you will say, 'I shall study Torah to be called master, or sit in the academy or gain life in the world-to-come.' Lest you fall into this error, it says: 'Thou shalt love the Lord thy God'."

By divorcing Torah study from any ulterior motivation, the makers of Judaism laid the foundation for universal general dedication to the things of the spirit. In more recent times this idealistic orientation of Jewish scholarship has all but been eclipsed. The office of the rabbi, formerly primarily an honorary appointment, is now a paid profession. Moreover, the rabbi is no longer primarily a scholar, closeted with his books and addressing the community only a few times a year. Instead he has been compelled to turn into sort of a ministerial social worker and twice-weekly orator.

Among the character traits of the Jewish scholar cast in the traditional mold, humility ranks prominent. Not an artificial and posed humility, to be sure, but the meekness of the man who has absorbed much knowledge and knows that there is so much more he will never be able to master. Although the Jewish scholar is respected as a "prince," he is yet warned against the idiosyncracies and the conceit of a spoiled favorite. It is impressed upon him that scholarship, although the noblest endeavor from the Jewish point of view, is yet only a cog in the wheel of the world. The Talmud preserves the touching soliloquy of a Sage who, lest he become overbearing, would say: "I am a creature of God, as is my neighbor. My work is in the city and his in the field. I rise early to my work and he rises early to his. As he cannot excel in my work, so I cannot excel in his task. But should you say that I achieve great things while he does small things—we have learned that it does not matter whether one does much or little, if one only concentrates his heart upon Heaven."

The ideal occupation for the Jewish scholar is, of course, teaching, for thus he benefits the community at large. Judaism is very explicit in stressing the scholar's obligation of transmitting his knowledge.

While elementary school teachers were paid for their labors, the Sage imparting instruction in the Talmud Academy, corresponding to a modern Graduate School, was expected to donate his services. There are numerous admonitions not to derive financial benefits from teaching the "Oral Law." One rather compelling argument adduced is that "God gave the Torah gratis," and consequently the teacher should do likewise. The Sages even warned that "he who takes a fee for teaching the Law destroys the world." The practice of free tuition in the Graduate Schools of Torah-learning has persisted. Moreover, in most of these schools, the students are provided with free board and other necessities, the cost being borne by patrons or by the Jewish community at large.

The teacher holds a place of unique love and respect in the Jewish community. With characteristic emphasis on the superior importance of the things of the spirit, the Sages taught that "the true father is not he who begets the child, but he who educates him." For "if one teaches the son of his fellow the Torah, it is accounted to him as if he had begotten him," or, as Rabbi Eleazar maintained, "as if he had created the Torah proper." Disrespect toward the teacher is decried as a serious crime—more heinous even than disrespect to parents. The law provides that if one sees an article that his father has lost and another that his teacher has lost—the teacher's property should be restored first and then the father's. If his father and his teacher are carrying burdens, he should first relieve the teacher and then his father. If his father and his teacher are in captivity, he should first ransom his teacher and then his father. If, however, his father is a scholar, though not of the same rank as his teacher, he shall ransom him first. "There is no honor above that due to the teacher; no respect greater than that which should be paid to him."

The Talmudic Sages were well deserving of this tribute for they took a genuine paternal interest in their students. Even so eminent a Sage as Rabbi Akiba thought nothing of it to nurse a student who had no one else to care for him.

## VII

The Jews were the first nation in the Western orbit to introduce universal education with the organization of a far-flung net-work of schools in the first century (B.C.E.). The significance of this fact cannot be overestimated, for it made knowledge the possession of all and established democracy upon the firm foundation of the democratization of education. Autocratic and dictatorial regimes invariably restricted education to the select few, afraid lest knowledge give power to "the mob." The leaders of Judaism, on the other hand, were eager to share the power which resides in knowledge. During the time of the Second Temple, Palestine was dotted with elementary schools where children from five years of age and up were taught the Torah. The course of studies was adapted to the capacity of the children: "At the age of five they began the study of the Bible, at ten, the study of *Mishnah,* and at fifteen, *Gemara.*"

The ancient Jewish schools were not inferior to modern schools. Jewish law provides that no more than twenty-five pupils must be placed in charge of one teacher, lest their progress be jeopardized. If there are more pupils in a class, an assistant teacher is to be appointed, and if the number exceeds forty, three teachers must take charge. To discipline communities that would skimp on their educational budget, Jewish law permits to place a community under ban if it fails to provide adequate educational facilities for the youth. The extent to which Jews would tax themselves to endow educational institutions is demonstrated by the statutes of Moravian Jewry imposing upon communities of thirty or more taxpayers, the maintenance of a *Yeshiva* with at least six advanced and six elementary students—a truly staggering burden for a small community.

It remained for twentieth century educators to demand classes for gifted children, a demand which is more often than not disregarded by school boards. In view of this, it is truly amazing to note the progressiveness of medieval Jewish education. From "The Book of the Pious" (13th century), it appears that classes for especially gifted children were a regular feature of the Jewish educational system, at a time when universal education was unknown among the general population. "When one instructs children, some of whom are more gifted than the others," Rabbi Judah Hasid summed up the consensus on this problem, "and it is inadvisable for all of them to study together, inasmuch as the brilliant children need a special instructor, the teacher should not keep quiet. He ought to say to the parents, even if he loses money by making the division, 'These children need a special teacher; and these a special teacher'."

The contributions of the Jews of Mohammedan Spain to science, philology and philosophy prove that the Jewish educational program can be expanded to include other than Torah studies. The education of the intelligent Spanish Jew during the "Golden Age" embraced all disciplines of secular knowledge. We get a rather good picture of what the young thirteenth century Jew of the Moorish countries was expected to study from Joseph Ibn Kaspi's program for his twelve-year-old son. "My son!" the father admonished him, "Obey my words! Today you are twelve years of age. For another two years keep on diligently studying Bible and Talmud. When you reach the age of fourteen, fix regular hours for continuing the previous studies, and give also a good part of your time to mathematics; first Ibn Ezra's Arithmetic, then Euclid, and the astronomical treatise of Al-Fergani and Abraham Ben Hiyya. Besides, appoint for yourself definite periods for reading more treatises which will introduce you to all good qualities, such as the Book of Proverbs and Ecclesiastes, the Mishnah tractate 'Fathers,' with the commentary and introductory chapters to the 'Code.' Also read Aristotle's 'Ethics,' of which I have made a digest. There is also available a collection of the 'Maxims of the Philosophers.' This course of studies should occupy you about two years. Then, when you are sixteen, appoint study periods for the Scriptures, the writings of Alfasi, Moses of Coucy, and the Code of the Perfect Teacher (Maimonides). Also give some time to the study of logic. With the help of God, I will compile for you a satisfying compendium on this subject, as I did with the 'Ethics'."

Persecutions and ghetto conditions eventually restricted this broad educational program. Yet, whenever Jews were free to participate in the cultural life of the majority group, they shared in it with zest and enthusiasm, enriching the cultural scene with important contributions. The disproportionately large number of Jews who have lastingly and creatively contributed to all fields of science and the arts, in the last two centuries, attest that the modern Jew, too, has lost none of the elasticity and creativity of mind that made his fathers the teachers of Scholastic philosophers and the gifted map and instrument makers, who enabled the great discoverers, Columbus, Magellan, Vasco Da Gama and others to sail their ships to unknown continents. There is no contradiction in combining traditional Jewish studies with the mastery of secular disciplines.

In postulating Torah as the most sacred ideal, Judaism does not isolate its follower from secular interests and knowledge; it only asks him to view the world through "Jewish" spectacles, not colored or distorting lenses by any means, but glasses that enable one to see the world, man and God with the healthy common sense and the tender humaneness of the written and the oral Torah.

## VIII

Anything and everything connected with the sacred pursuit of study has been invested with special love and sanctity by the Jewish genius. This love extends to the houses where learning is imparted as well as to the books from which it is drawn and to the teachers who open up these fountains of the true life for the eager disciple. Jews are book lovers par excellence. Ezekiel who when eating "the scroll of the book," upon the command of the Lord, found it "like honey for sweetness" expressed his people's general attitude to permanent records of wisdom and literature. Throughout the ages, books have been sweet to the children of Israel beyond all else. This love dates back to hoary antiquity and was fostered by Jewish law. It is significant that, in the course of time, the obligation of owning a copy of the Torah was extended to every Jew, while originally it applied only to the King, in accordance with the biblical commandment: "He shall write himself a copy of this law in a book." While the Talmud emphasizes that every Jewish king must have his own copy of the Torah written, and not use that of his ancestors, the *Shulchan Aruch* provides that "every Jew must either write a Scroll of the Torah himself or, if he does not do so, he must have it written for him." Moreover, the *Sefer Torah* is an inalienable possession which must not be sold, except for the purpose of getting married, pursuing the study of the Torah, or ransoming captives. Already in the days of the Talmud many Jews owned Torah Scrolls, for the Sages warned against selling Torah Scrolls which one has inherited from his parents, as a Torah Scroll fills the house with "splendor and riches." The owners of Torah Scrolls seem to have taken much pride in them, for on the Day of Atonement "each and every one brought his Torah Scroll from his house and read in it to display its beauty to the congregation."

Medieval Jewish literature is replete with attestations of the love of books. Parents regarded books a necessary provision for their children. Rabbi Judah Asher, therefore, in reproaching his son for not duly appreciating the facilities provided for his intellectual advancement, reminds him, "regularly were your meals provided, and all your wants. You own many books." The eminent translator of Arabic works into Hebrew, Rabbi Judah Ibn Tibbon, exemplified the Jewish love of books at its best, although due to his scholarly calling this love and interest were rather those of the scholar than of the average person. Still, it is instructive to follow Rabbi Judah's lengthy admonitions to his son of how to appreciate and care for his books. "My son," he wrote in his last will and testament, "make your books your companions, and let your cases and shelves be your pleasure grounds and gardens.

Bask in their paradise, gather their fruits, pluck their roses, take their spices and their myrrh. If you get perchance tired and weary, change from garden to garden, from furrow to furrow, from prospect to prospect. Then will your desire renew itself, and your soul be filled with delight."

Rabbi Judah also knew how to preserve books and employ them to best advantage. "Examine your Hebrew books at every new moon," he instructed his son Samuel, "and the Arabic volumes once in two months, and the bound codices once every three months. Arrange your library in good order so as to avoid wearying yourself in locating a book which you need. Always know the case and chest where the book should be. It would be a good idea to place in each chest a written list of the books it contains.... I have favored you by providing for your use a large library, thus relieving you of the necessity to borrow books. Most students must scurry about to get books, often without finding them. But you, thanked be God, need not borrow. Many books, indeed, you own in two or three copies."

That average persons and women, too, craved to own books, especially in order to be able to perform the meritorious deed of lending them to poor scholars is attested by two rather quaint stories illustrating how a husband's attitude to spending money on books could make or break happy marriages in the Jewish setting of the Middle Ages. "The Book of the Pious" relates that a pious woman who was married to a stingy man who did not want to buy books and contribute to charity, one day decided to deny herself to him until he would mend his ways. "I shall not immerse myself in the ritual bath unless you buy books and contribute to charity," she told her niggardly husband. Since he refused and she remained adamant, they finally consulted "a wise man" who, after duly censuring the tight-fisted husband, advised the wife to find some other way of bringing him to terms than making herself inaccessible to him. The same volume records the story of the wife who used the money which her husband had given her for a luxurious cloak to have a book written "to lend it to students so that they may study therein."

The lending of books is a virtue Jews have zealously practiced. Before the age of printing presses this was especially important and an act of true generosity, for manuscripts represented a veritable fortune. The Talmud already interpreted the Psalmist's references to those whose "righteousness endureth forever" as referring to persons who buy books and lend them to those who need them. The codes and moral guides are very explicit in laying down rules for owners of books. They are admonished to lend them to deserving students, although the manuscripts might become tattered and spoiled, for "it is better that one's books should be used and the script be erased than that they should be hidden away without anybody studying in them." A special incentive to providing scholars with books was no doubt the promise that "those who lend books to students share in their reward."

When medieval Jews commissioned a scribe to copy for them a certain book, they apparently did so with the thought in mind of making it available to other students as well. Consequently, the Book of the Pious advises to bind every chapter separately rather than all of them in one volume, "for if he binds them all together, how can he lend the chapters to the individuals who need them one at the time?" The lending of books is of those meritorious *Mitzvoth* with which nothing must interfere. Even if one's enemies are in need of certain books which one owns, he must lend them the sources of Torah knowledge they require, for the spreading of Torah silences all considerations of personal pride. Naturally, it is more meritorious to lend books "to those who study for study's sake and to the poor rather than to the wealthy." He who owns a collection of books is enjoined by the "Book of the Pious" to make provisions so as to enable the community to benefit by it also after his death. Therefore, "if one has sons one of whom does not lend books, while the other lends them readily, it is advisable to bequeath them to the one who shares his books." Moreover, "a private book collection which was placed by its owner at the free use of the public must not be sold after his death to persons who will not let the public use them."

The written word has always been surrounded with a special halo by Jews. Tattered and torn Hebrew books of a religious character are not discarded, but are carefully and respectfully stored in some corner or the garret of the synagogue. Thanks to this pious custom the most important collection of ancient Hebrew manuscripts was discovered by Solomon Schechter in the *Genizah* (hide-away chamber) of a Cairo synagogue, where for many centuries stray leaves and manuscripts were stored away. "One must honor books" is a principle to which Jews have invariably been faithful, so much so that not only the books (written or printed), but even the pens and the ink with which they are written bask in reflected glory and sanctity.

The honor of a book requires that in a company of several persons he takes precedence who carries a book. Of course, a book must always be carried in the right hand, even if one has to carry his money in his left. Also in handing someone a book and receiving it out of his hand, it should only be handled with the right hand. One must not touch books with unclean hands as this would be disrespectful. If one is loaded down with books he must not complain that they are heavy, as he would do in the case of another burden, for the blessing of books is such that any toil incurred for them is a privilege. The honor of books also precludes the hunting of bargains. The pious book buyer, who happens to chance upon a bargain, should warn the book dealer: "The price is too low. Don't say I deceived you, for I told you so."

Books are "heavenly objects," consequently they must be salvaged first in an emergency. If there is a fire, they must be carried out before any other objects. If "one has both gold and books in his hand and they drop, he should first pick up the book and only afterwards the gold." Similarly, if one's clothes and the book one happens to be holding get spattered with ink or something else, the book should be cleaned first. If one falls on evil days and faces the choice of either selling his house and other valuable possessions or his books, he should dispose of all other things and keep the books as long as possible. And if he owns duplicate copies which he was in the habit of lending out, in an emergency he should still sell all his belongings first and only then the books.

The honor of books also rules out their being used for any undignified purpose. For example, one must not use a book to shade oneself against the sun, or to protect oneself against smoke, or hide behind it from people one does not want to see. One must not scribble memoranda, or anything else, in a book, nor put a pen or sheets of paper or parchment in it for straightening them out.

Books must be kept in a fitting place, they should neither be put on the floor nor on the bed. If one has to keep a book case in a bed-room, one should place it at the head of the bed.

CHAPTER 11

## *The Joyful Burden of the Law*

### I

JEWISH HISTORY impresses upon the student that Jewish Law, as patterned by the multitude of commandments which regulate the life of the conforming Jew, has been the single strongest force making for Jewish survival. As the Jewish survivalist sees it, objections raised against "the yoke of the commandments" represent a frontal attack upon the survival stamina of our people, for the argument that "the commandments of two thousand years ago" cannot be binding for modern Jews is a deadly shaft aimed at the Jewish life nerve.

If Jewish history proves anything beyond peradventure of doubt, it is that Jewish survival is contingent upon the preservation of the way of life charted by the Law to its smallest and most trivial details. Experience attests that whenever Jews shed "the yoke of the commandments," they thereby cut themselves off the living tree of their people. "Our nation is a nation solely by virtue of the Torah." This statement by Saadia Gaon is neither wishful thinking nor an unrealistic chimera; it is the voice of factual and collective experience extending over three thousand years. It has never been demonstrated—neither in Antiquity, nor in the Middle Ages and certainly not in our own time—that Jews can survive as Jews after disposing of "the yoke of the commandments."

Whenever and wherever Jews forsook the Torah's way of life, they went under. This fact is writ large upon all pages of Jewish history. Jewish continuity is contingent upon faithfulness to the Torah. This statement is borne out by incontrovertible evidence.

It is significant that the appreciation of the survivalist potential of Jewish Law has of late gained even among Jewish groups that not so long ago were antagonistic to religious tradition. Characteristic of many contemporary Jewish secularists' despair and yearning for definite Jewish forms is the late Menachem Boraisha's description of the mood at a social gathering of leading Yiddish writers and educators in 1946. Boraisha wrote: "In the evening a few *minyanim* friends gathered at his home (of Joseph Feder, the late Yiddish editor and writer) to talk over matters which were uppermost in our minds. One of the group related that his children had attended a Yiddish school and had learned some Yiddish—but they never speak it. Another colleague confessed that he had taken his child to Synagogue on Yom Kippur—but he himself couldn't muster the will-power to stay for the whole day. One of those present said that when he urged his daughter to study Yiddish literature, she argued: If Mendele, Peretz and Sholem Aleichem are all there is to your Jewishness, why should I read their books when Shakespeare's, Byron's and Dickens' works are unquestionably superior? Some of those present tried to console themselves with the thought that although their children did not know Yiddish they would nevertheless remain Jews—that is to say, there would be no other alternative, as the world would not let them be anything else but Jews."

To be sure, children of orthodox parents do not always remain in the traditional fold, nor do all sons and daughters of religiously indifferent Yiddish and Hebrew writers grow up to be indifferent Jews. Experience, however, shows that a Jewish religious home atmosphere, implemented by intensive Jewish schooling, is conducive to the breeding of Jewish loyalty and survivalist determination in the young. As far as the creative genius is concerned, the abstract idea and the transcendental ideal may suffice for him. For the average man and woman, however, the idea and the ideal become real only when translated into concrete forms of everyday living. Bialik, the Poet Laureate of the modern Hebrew renaissance, was thoroughly cognizant of this fact, when he concluded his essay "Law and Legend" (*Halacha Ve-Aggada*) with these profound and accute observations:

"People talk of a renaissance, literature, creation, Hebrew education and Hebrew thought—and all these are suspended on the hairbreadth thread of love: the love of the land, the love of literature, the love of the language. What is the value of these airy infatuations? Love, you say? But where is duty?... Ambition, goodwill, enthusiasm and love are all excellent and admirable qualities when they are consummated through action; iron-strong, determined action and cruel duty.

"Do you indeed wish to build? Then 'make a covenant and subscribe to it; and let our priests and Levites set their seal unto it.' Also, 'set up ordinances for yourselves,' for so did your ancestors begin to rebuild their home.

"The lofty visions of Isaiah enthused the heart, but when the hour of reconstruction came, the two Prophets, who were among the builders, Haggai and Zechariah, were the last of the Prophets and the first of the men of Law, while those who followed them, Ezra and his party, were purely and solely men of the Law.

"Come now, let us set up ordinances for ourselves! Give us moulds wherein our soft fluid may be minted and given definite and enduring form. We are thirsting for actual deeds. In life—give us a stronger disposition for performance than for talk, and in literature, a stronger proclivity for Law than for Legend. We bend our neck: where is the iron yoke? The strong hand and the outstretched arm—why don't they come?"

Bialik was not an "orthodox" Jew in the accepted sense of the word. He was cognizant, however, of the barrenness of "the love of the land, the love of literature and the love of the language." That is to say, he knew the emptiness of sentiment not wedded to "iron-strong, determined action and cruel duty." Bialik fully realized the pernicious threat of subjective, individualistic interpretations of Judaism keyed primarily to personal convenience. This is why he called for "the iron yoke." He knew the unlimited creative potential of "the strong hand and the outstretched arm" of the *Halacha*. He knew that Jewish survival is inextricably bound to faithfulness to the Law. Poesy and esthetics have their assigned roles, but they lack the strength required for entrenching Jewish eternity.

In various Jewish quarters it is now being suggested that "Jewish art, Jewish music and the centrality of Eretz Israel" are "sancta" sufficiently potent to assure Jewish survival. Bialik, who created great Hebrew literature which inspired Jewish music, and who lived in Eretz Israel, knew that all these are but "airy" infatuations and that only "iron-strong, determined action and cruel duty..." can save us from going under.

"The impetus of dogma," as Hermann Cohen termed what

Bialik called "iron-strong determined action and cruel duty," has been the strongest cohesive force making for Jewish identity, unity and survival. Neither the "airy theories," nor Jewish scholarship of the "Science of Judaism" type and couched in the vernacular, have succeeded in engendering enthusiasm for and loyalty to Judaism.

Bialik was the first modern creative Hebrew writer who demanded the return to the *Halacha* for the sake of Jewish survival. In recent years, numerouse Hebrew and Yiddish writers and intellectuals have followed his lead by extolling a *"naie Yiddishkeit,"* which stands for Sabbath and festival observance and appreciative respect for traditional forms of Jewish living. Like Bialik, the proponents of the *"naie Yiddishkeit"* are not concerned with theology—they approach Jewish religious forms from a mere pragmatic point of view. Recognizing that the divestation from traditional Jewishness has impoverished their lives and stunted their creativeness, these intellectuals attempt a studied return to tradition in the hope that it will imbue them with creative Jewish survivalist vigor.

Obviously, this is a far cry from the traditional approach to the ways of the Torah. Still, it is not wholly irreconcilable with Judaism, for the Sages taught: "One should keep the commandments even if not for their own sake, because practice not for its own sake leads to doing for its own sake." Our Sages knew that "doing" the commandments is important, regardless of the motives, for thus the primary and principal condition for the flowering of the higher aspects of Judaism and, especially, for the continuity of our people is fufilled. And this is what matters, above all else: the survival of our people.

It is significant that even such a contemporary spokesman of Jewish orthodoxy as Isaac Breuer maintained that, for the modern Jew, faithfulness to the Torah is not so much a religious as a national choice. "Not religious conviction," he wrote, "but the binding national force of the Law must be sufficient reason for the individual Jew to observe the commandments."

The great weakness of all Jewish Reform movements is that they consider only the convenience of the individual, while disregarding completely the welfare of the Jewish people of which he is a member. No doubt, abrogations and relaxations of Torah commandments considerably easen the burden of "the yoke of the commandments" for the individual—but they undermine the strength of our community. Of course, "it is difficult to be a Jew." It is much more convenient to observe Sunday as the day of rest and to eat an unrestricted diet than to be limited by the dietary laws. Reform Judaism certainly has made being a Jew more convenient, but by providing for the comforts and conveniences of the individual, it has permanently injured Jewish survival strength. For if, after the destruction of the Temple, there was nothing left for God but "the four ells of the Law," for Galuth Jewry, deprived of all normal vestiges of nationhood, the Law provides security and survival stamina by supplying a Jewish climate and environment.

## II

Notwithstanding the talmudic principle, "the (civil) law of the land is binding for the Jew," life in the ghettos of yesterday was such that, from the cradle to the grave, the Jew moved in the orbit of the Torah. Life and religion were inseparably intertwined; they overlapped and were co-extensive. The Jew expressed himself not only in Synagogue but also in the market-place, where he conducted his business in accordance with the law of the Torah. Whether he bought or sold a house, whether he entered into or dissolved a business partnership, it was all done according to Jewish Law, which raised an air-tight, protective "fence" about the landless, and yet not homeless, Jews, for the Law was their homeland in a very real and concrete sense.

As the centuries of the Jewish dispersion dragged on, the Rabbis put layer upon layer on the rather simple foundation of the biblical law. In part, of course, this elaboration was necessitated by the "progress" of life. For example, our own technological age has necessitated hundreds of additional decisions which were not needed half a century ago when there were neither radios, nor electric refrigerators—to say nothing of dish-washing machines.

Not all post-biblical laws, however, came into being in this manner. The early architects of Judaism *deliberately* elaborated and complicated simple laws and rules for they held that, after the loss of their country and religious center, Jewry had to be "fenced in" to be guarded against disintegration.

For the American at home the transmission of the American way of life to his children presents no problem. For the American abroad, however, this is an almost insuperable task. And so virtually all Americans whose business compels them to live abroad attempt to sent their children "home" to attend American schools.

The exiled Jews could not send their children "home." But the architects of Judaism successfully solved this most crucial of problems: they made Jewish law *the* home of the Jew and, in order to fortify and secure it, they surrounded it with a "fence," to whose height and depth each generation added in accordance with the intensity of the attack from outside.

This is how the Written Law of the Pentateuch grew into

the vast expanse of the Oral Law, the hundreds of major and minor, formidable and minute laws, rules and regulations, all equally sacred because equally important for Jewish survival.

The men of the Great Synagogue, who ordained: "Make a fence around the Written Law" knew well what they were aiming at. They wanted, above all, to secure the survival of their people and so they clad them into the impenetrable armor of the Oral and the Written Torah. They knew that "when the fence of the vineyard falls, the vineyard is bound for destruction" and so they fortified the fence. Those who stayed within its confines were sheltered almost as by a real, earthly fatherland. It made the Jew "different," to be sure, but this was how he retained his identity.

The exponents of Reform Judaism are right in charging that the Law segregates the Jew and deprives him of the possibility of entering fully and without reservations into social relations with Gentiles. Indeed, the Law is "guilty" of this—and more. It decrees for the Jew a special diet, thus making it impossible for him to eat at the houses of Gentiles; it institutes for him a day of rest when the vast majority of people work, and it prescribes a regimen for this day of rest altogether different from that of the Christian Sunday. No doubt, the Law does set the Jew apart—but, then, this is its purpose! For a homeless people there is no chance of survival without a national discipline that substitutes for the regular vestiges of nationhood.

As far as the *individual* Jew goes, the Law is certainly both an encumbrance and a barrier. But as the collective Jewish conscience sees it, opportunism must not be the criterion for evaluating the Law, the cornerstone of Jewish survival.

The Sages, who deliberately and systematically raised

fence after fence around the Written Law, were thoroughly cognizant of the consequences of their enactments. They were well aware of it that the commandments add up to a heavy and pressing "yoke," as it were. "Israel assumes the yoke of the commandments and is weighed down by them," they said. But there is a meaning to this burden: "As long as you will cling to the commandments, you will live."

Although the Jew regards the commandments and their "fences" as divinely revealed, he yet does not shrink from searching for their meanings. Many of the pious Sages and thinkers of our people reached the conclusion—and a daring conclusion it was—that *per se* the ritual law has no meaning; it is a pedagogic regimen and an instrument of Jewish differentiation and, consequently, of preservation. "If not for the Law, Israel would not have differed from the nations of the world."

The Sages candidly admitted that to God, it cannot really matter how an animal is slaughtered. As they saw it, the ceremonial laws—unlike the ethical commandments, do not touch the core of God's Being. "What does God care," they asked diffidently, "whether a man ritually slaughters an animal and eats it, or whether he strangles it and eats it? Will the one benefit Him, or the other injure Him?" As the eminent Rab saw it, "the commandments were only given to Israel so that they should be purified by them."

The points raised by the exponents of Reform Judaism also agitated the minds of those who built "the fence." However, while Reform Judaism, viewing the Law from the vantage point of the individualist, decided for its abrogation, the builders of the "fence," and with it of Jewish eternity, taught that although God is too exalted to be concerned with the minutiae of the laws, these commandments are of paramount importance as they make Israel "different" and thus preserve them in the dispersion. It was because the Sages regarded the Law as a national discipline and survival prop, that Rabbi Hanina could go on record as follows: "It is better to do what is commanded, than to do the same thing when it is not commanded." That the Sages regarded the raising of "the fence" as an emergency measure is also proven by the talmudic statement that the ceremonial laws will be rescinded in the Messianic era, for then their purpose will have been fulfilled. The medieval philosophers and thinkers frequently compared the regimen of the Law to a physician's orders. The physician does not benefit from the patient's compliance, yet a sensible man will follow his doctor's advice. While Israel is in exile, the ceremonial Law must be faithfully guarded—for does a physician dismiss a patient before he is restored to health?

The "practical" objections usually raised against the Law have their points. But "practicality" fitting the individual is not the rod of measure to be applied in this case. History has demonstrated, over and over again, that Jewish survival is predicated on faithfulness to the Jewish way of life as charted by the Torah. The Law, therefore, cannot and must not be judged from the narrow viewpoint of the individual. This neither implies nor necessitates that the individual sacrifices his personal happiness. It means, however, that the Jew should submit to the national discipline of the Law in order to help preserve his people. Those who say that there is no logical justification today for observing the dietary laws, should ponder the talmudic statement that our ritual compliances or omissions cannot possibly matter to God. *Observing the Jewish laws is not only a test of belief!* Jewish teachers throughout the ages candidly admitted that the "motives of the laws" (*ta'amei hamitzvoth*) are in many instances totally obscure. Yet there is a rationale of Jewish adherence to the

Law: the conviction, tested by a two thousand years' history, that only this Law, with all its devious complicated rules and regulations, can preserve our people from extinction in the Diaspora.

### III

Talmudic and rabbinic literature affords many glimpses into the psychology of the men who entrenched Jewish survival by means of building the fence about the Law. The ancient Rabbis were anything but dry legalists. They knew, however, that their people was facing an emergency and that authority would have to step into the breach. They realized that only a strong national discipline, and the cohesiveness born of it, can keep the Jewish people from going under. This was why discipline (not blind obedience and subordination) was so insistently stressed by the Sages.

How the Rabbis conceived of the individual's duty of obedience to the Law is strikingly—and touchingly, too—illustrated by the example of the illustrious Rabbi Meir. He held that it was permissible to mix a potion of wine and oil for a patient suffering an attack of acute indigestion on the Sabbath, although his colleagues considered it a violation of the Sabbath law. "Once," related Rabbi Simeon ben Eleazar, "Rabbi Meir suffered an attack of acute indigestion on the Sabbath. We wanted to give him wine mixed with oil; he, however, refused. 'But this is contrary to your own teachings!' we told him. Whereupon he replied, 'Yes, I permit it—but my colleagues don't and I could never bring myself to act contrary to the decisions of my colleagues.' "

The contemporary leaders of Reform Judaism, who enthrone the discretion of the individual as the criterion of acceptance or rejection of the Law, have thoroughly misunderstood the perennial Jewish approach to the Law. It has never been a matter of whether "one could believe," or whether "one found it feasible" to observe the laws and regulations. The acid test for adherence to the Law was whether the majority of the people, who had not bartered their Jewish strength for easy conveniences (only this majority counted!), were convinced that these laws represented the survival strength of their people.

The extent to which the concern over Jewish survival agitated the Sages of the Talmud and their successors may be gauged from the fact that talmudic law authorizes the infliction of penalties severer than those decreed by the Torah in order to safeguard "the fence." This should not be interpreted as proof that the Sages, by adding to the height of the fence, lost sight of what it guarded. Far from it—they regarded, however, "the fence" as the first line of fortification. When the onslaught of a hostile world grew more menacing to Jewish survival, they strengthened these fortifications, adding ever new forts so as to render the Law proper invulnerable. To be sure, the Rabbis were almost exclusively concerned with mending "the fence"—but, then, where does an army defending a city do its fighting? On the outskirts or in the center which is to be shielded from invasion by the enemy forces?

"When our love was strong, we could sleep on a bed no wider than a sword's edge; now that our love has waned, a bed sixty ells wide is too narrow for us." This talmudic adage applies not only to the love of men and women, but to other spheres as well. So long as we are interested in our work, nothing connected with it seems too hard. But as soon as ennui or discouragement enter, even slight efforts are found too taxing. Psychologists know that a very large percentage of "breakdowns," ascribed to acute cases of fatigue and exhaustion, are not warranted by physiological causes, but are due to psychological maladjustment.

The modern Jew's straining at the leash of the Law is not satisfactorily explained by the alleged difficulties of the Law. It is, first and last, occasioned by the loss of the belief in the worthwhileness of Judaism. All but Jewishly ignorant, "the rebellious Jew" no longer finds fulfillment and satisfaction in Judaism and so he chafes under Judaism, "the pressing burden," regardless of how many relaxations of the Law are offered him. It is not the Law but the psychological attitude of the modern Jew to the Law which presents the real problem.

To the well adjusted Jew the Law is neither a theological nor a behaviorist problem. It is the means whereby he identifies himself with his people; it is the link which binds him to all Jewish generations of the past and of the interminable tomorrow.

A favorite stock-in-trade argument against the ritual of the Synagogue and the Law is that their monotonous sameness blunt the zest of the worshipper. At first impact this argument seems valid and convincing — but life does not always conform to theories. The services of most Reform Temples are geared to "worshippers' interests," yet the conclaves of Reform rabbis resound with melancholy complaints about the ineffectiveness of "worshippers' interest."

Well integrated Jews are not troubled by the problem of "monotony." As Solomon Schechter put it so well, "When every Jew prayed, one prayer-book was satisfactory for all; today, when hardly anybody prays, we need a hundred different ones." Far from seeming monotonous, the same beloved practice of the commandments becomes ever more beloved to the well integrated Jew—it grows on him with time. "A thing of beauty is a joy forever." This truth was not hidden from the ancient Rabbis either. "Words of the Torah," they said, "resemble golden vessels. The more diligently you rub and polish them, the brighter they shine when reflecting the face of him who peers at them. And thus it is also with the words of the Torah, whenever you rehearse them, they shine and brighten the face."

What modern ideologists term the relevance, the worthwhileness and the actuality of Judaism was duly considered also by the builders of "the fence." But they were keen students of human nature. They knew that one's attachment to a person or a cause grows in proportion to one's efforts on their behalf. The integrated Jew lives with and for the *Torah* and its "fences" and so, in accordance with the ideal laid down by the Sages, the commandments never seem old or obsolete to him. For this type of Jew, life under the Law is an ever new and exciting adventure; it is an eternal and challenging giving and taking.

## IV

But what about "the modern Jew?" The ideologists of Reform Judaism, Conservative Judaism and Reconstructionism argue that "modern man" is not inclined to submit to group discipline. The modern Jew, we are told, is thoroughly individualistic and realistic, he will only practice what he considers rational and reasonable.

But is "modern man" really so rebellious an individualist? On the surface it might seem so, but then there is to be considered the readiness with which so many moderns have bowed to dictatorships of either rightist or leftist tendencies. Can it be that "modern man" has tired of his freedom? The sweeping success of Fascism in some parts of the Western world and the enthusiasm for the dictatorship of the proletariat in others provide a rather embarrassing commentary on modern man's capacity to make the most of freedom.

Among modern young Jews, too, there is abroad a yearning for some kind of duly constituted authority. Bialik's plea for "the iron-yoke" and the Yiddishist intellectuals' quest for definitive forms and rituals of Jewish living are straws in the wind. Already there are young, assimilated American Jews who are timidly but persistently endeavoring to introduce authority into their anarchic lives. Jo Sinclair's novel "Wasteland," which won the 1946 Harper Prize, proves this point rather forcefully. Jake Brown, the hero of the novel, is a self-hating, frustrated Jew. He received no Jewish education and there was nothing in his Jewish home atmosphere of which he could be proud. As a result, he developed an inferiority complex, with added complications. Yet, in this "Wasteland" of fear, shame and frustration, there was one stable thing: Friday Night. "Through the years, there had always been Friday, with its candles and Sabbath food. A custom, a landmark in the undirected week, a stable thing in a world that was insecure and perilous."

While unburdening himself to the psychoanalyst, Jake reverts over and over again to "Friday Night." Jake cannot read Hebrew; he never goes to Synagogue; all his friends and associates are Gentiles, who do not know that he is a Jew.... But Jake, who changed his name to John, never misses a Friday at his parents' house. The psychoanalyst concludes that "the Friday night which he stressed so much seems a matter of identification, one of his very few possessions of security, stability."

The author of "Wasteland," a young American Jewish woman speaks for her entire generation when she depicts Jake's feelings at the Seder table—his pathetic yearning for belonging which can yet not be consummated because Jewish identification calls for more than mere sentimentality.

Even as Bialik looked to the Law as a bond of strength and identification, so Jo Sinclair, the young American Jewess, voices her yearning for some kind of definitive bond, some expression of assuring and comforting authority.

What Jake Brown felt, inarticulate at the Seder, when he read the Haggadah in English (he knew no Hebrew), is a feeling experienced by multitudes of young Jews who have freed themselves of "the yoke" of Judaism and thus have cut themselves off the safe moorings.

At the Seder table, Jake Brown, who could only make love to Christian girls that called him John, "felt part of something universal, something strong and ageless. The emancipation of the Jewish people from Egypt. How long ago, before Ma and Pa were born, and before their parents were born; and yet here they all were, sitting around the table the same way as those Jewish people. And all over the world Jewish people were ready to sip the wine and to take a bite of matzoh. All over the world families were together, waiting for a father to start praying. All over the world the youngest son present (just like him!) was getting ready to ask the questions. . . .

"Behind you, in the shadow of history, in the thousands of years of Jews, stand other boys, like you; ahead of you, in the future, in the tomorrow of the world, stand other boys, not even born yet, not alive yet, but you know they will sit at tables like this some day, they will ask the meaningful, historical questions."

Do modern Jews really crave new rituals? Do they, indeed, feel that the ancient, time-hallowed prayers are out-worn and that the age-old customs and ways of our people call for change?

A sorely confused and atomic-energy-frightened mankind has broken with the *laissez faire laissez aller* philosophies of the 19th century. If a little technology has removed modern man from what is loosely termed "religion," the spectacular advance in technology is leading him back to the imponderables of ethics and faith. Since the explosion of the first atomic bomb, all leaders of thought and philosophy have sounded the call for moral rearmament. There is a universal yearning abroad for ethical authority and spiritual reorientation.

The breaking of the bonds of Jewish law by emancipated and assimilated Jewry was a reaction typical of the 19th century. The groping back to some sort of duly constituted authority and regulated forms of living is a reaction typical of the insecurity of the physical and spiritual climate of the 20th century.

For survivalist Jews there is chiefly one criterion for judging the Law and its "fences": their unique power to secure and entrench the eternity of our people.

CHAPTER 12

## God

### I

THE FULL understanding of Jewish survival requires an insight into the ideas and ideals which are its propelling forces. Among these, none equals in importance the God idea. It is central to Judaism, nay, it is its very fount and foundation.

God has been differently interpreted by many generations of Jews. But then there are probably no two persons, unless they be shackled by dogma, who define God in identical terms. God concepts differ in accordance with mental horizons and emotional resources, creedal differences and cultural backgrounds, psychological needs and the hopes born of them. As a matter of fact, even an individual's interpretation of God is not static, but changes as he travels along the road of life. The primitive and tangible childhood image of God is gradually replaced by a God concept which, though inadequate, is yet more commensurable with the Divine than the child's simple fantasy. And as the individual gradually wends his way toward a maturer God idea, so groups of men, too, are forever advancing toward a better understanding of His being.

From biblical times to this day, Jewish teachers and thinkers have wrestled with the difficulty of defining God. It speaks in their favor that, one and all, they recognized the impossibility of understanding and grasping the infinite, perfect Being of God with the finite and imperfect tools of human intelligence. One and all they were mindful of the Pentateuchal warning: "Take ye therefore good heed unto yourselves; for ye saw no manner of form on the day that God spake unto you in Horeb out of the midst of fire."

The abiding and eternal Jewish contribution to the world is the discovery of the One, Unique and Incorporeal God. This collective contribution surpasses in significance the contributions of individual Jews to human progress. Through Christianity and Islam, the Jewish God idea, modified and adapted to the reach of those for whom the uncompromising monotheism of Judaism is too exacting, has completely reshaped and determined the civilization of the West.

Why was the Only God "discovered" by the Jews—and not by another people? This question has perennially troubled the "discoverers." They answered it, and their answer has been accepted by all generations of believers since, that the Only God *chose* to choose the Jews for the privilege of this discovery. Even the Church concedes this choice, although it adds the reservation that Israel's chosenness was suspended with the coming of the Christian savior and the Jews' refusal to accept him. Still, despite the calumnies and persecutions visited by the Church and its followers upon the "stubborn Jews," Christianity has never disputed God's revelation to Israel.

Biblical scholars and theologians have advanced numerous theories in attempting to explain why monotheism was born among the Jews, a mere pigmy nation in the ancient Near East, while its mighty neighbors walked in spiritual darkness.

From Ernest Renan's theory that the "barren desert," where Israel passed its youth, was conducive to the evolution of the "barren" creed of the Only God, in contradistinction to variegated polytheism, to the pan-Babylonian and pan-Egyptian theories of the origins of Hebrew monotheism, there is no satisfactory explanation of *why* the Only God was discovered by Israel. The genesis of Jewish monotheism is the most conclusive refutation of the type of historical materialism that would explain all cultural and religious achievements as corollaries of economic conditions. There is no "economic reason" why the ancient Hebrews should have become the God-seekers and God-finders of mankind.

The dismal failure of the savants to explain the "miracle" of the birth of monotheism, should make even skeptics and agnostics examine a bit closer the traditional Jewish doctrine of Divine choice, as interpreted on its highest intellectual plane.

The Jews emerged as Divinely "chosen" in the manner every genius reveals himself as "chosen" in a very special sense, namely, they were singled out, by self-dedication, for a roll all their own.

The nature of genius defies ordinary categories. It contains an element of spontaneity, of "choice," or of "special endowment," if you will, that cannot be explained with the terminology of psychological tests and measurements. It is this intangible, unmeasurable something with has sustained Israel and which—perhaps for lack of a better term—Jews call "chosenness." The revolutionary feat resulting from this "chosenness" was the uncompromising break with the cults of the many idols and the unswerving acceptance of the Only God. Judaism is not committed to a fixed, dogmatic definition of God. Many interpretations of the nature of God have been evolved by Jewish sages and thinkers. But there is one point on which all are agreed: the unique Oneness of God understood as qualitative and not merely quantitative singularity.

The emphasis on God's qualitative singularity is based on the insight that the "Oneness of God" must be implemented by "Uniqueness" if monotheism is to emerge in pristine and majestic purity and force. Mere quantitative Oneness logically permits of additions and accretions, to wit, Christian trinitarianism. Only the "Uniqueness of God" precludes any and every infringement upon the Oneness of the Creator. This is why Judaism insists that God is not only "the One" but "the Only One," that is to say, the Unique One.

Schopenhauer, notwithstanding his frequent outbursts against Judaism, yet deserves credit for appreciating the true nature of Jewish monotheism. "Judaism," he wrote, "cannot be denied the glory of being the only genuine monotheistic religion on earth: there is none beside it that possesses an objective God, the Creator of heaven and earth." The Uniqueness of God also precludes the belief in another creative force besides Him, or the deification of human beings. Judaism knows God as the Creator of light and of darkness—there is no realm exempt from His sway. Simultaneously, the emphasis on Divine Uniqueness has been the most powerful single force in Judaism to hold the human and the divine apart. Rather typical of the Sages' anxiety to keep man on earth, and God in His heaven, is the talmudic statement, with distinct polemical undertones, that "even the most perfect of human beings is only a mortal born of woman. Moses too was only mortal." In keeping with this anxiety to avert the debacle implicit in the deification of men, the Sages of the Talmud held that the Bible does not reveal the place where Moses was buried lest "the Israelites come to pray at Moses' grave: 'O Moses, intercede for us.'"

To the Jew, God is the only true Unity, the "only Reality," beside Whom none must be feared or worshipped. The extent to which this consistent monotheistic avowal was carried may be judged from a teaching of the *Gerer Rebbe,* a saint of our own period, who warned that "if a person fears anything besides God he is guilty of idolatry—as fear is a tribute related to worship, and only God should be worshipped."

It goes without saying that his type of spiritual punctiliousness made superstition virtualy impossible in the official realm of the synagogue. As to the superstitious beliefs and practices that were, and are, current among Jews, the explanation is that the masses find a greater measure of consolation in the tangible sphere of the myth than in the realm of the unique spirituality of Jewish belief. What matters is that authoritative Jewish thinkers, from biblical times to our own day, have decried superstition as detracting from pure monotheism. Although they knew that the full knowledge of the true Being of God would forever elude them—they would yet not compromise for a knowable God. They gloried in the enigma that is God, Who would not be God if He could be known. A voluminous and inspired portion of Hebrew literature treats of the gulf which separates the sphere of God from that of man. Its most characteristic and most touching expression, perhaps, is Solomon Ibn Gabirol's "Royal Crown," which addresses itself to God:

> Thou art One, the first of every number, and the foundation of every structure.
> Thou art One, and at the mystery of Thy Oneness the wise of heart are struck dumb,
> For they know not what it is.

> Thou art One, and Thy Oneness can neither be increased nor lessened,
> It lacketh naught, nor doth aught remain over.
> Thou art One, but not like a unit to be grasped or counted,
> For number and change cannot reach Thee.
> Thou art not to be envisaged, nor to be figured thus and thus ...
> Thou existest, but hearing of ear cannot reach Thee, nor vision of eye,
> Nor shall the How have sway over Thee, nor the Wherefore and Whence.
> Thou existest, and before Time began Thou wast,
> And without place Thou didst abide.
> Thou existest, and Thy secret is hidden and who shall attain to it?

Saadia Gaon and Maimonides, the rationalists, were not the first in the Jewish orbit to express the conviction that man's intellect is inadequate for fathoming the Being of God. Isaiah already had despaired of the possibility of knowing Him: "To whom will you liken Me, that I should be equal?", he hears the Lord thunder at man whose puny intellect would dare to unravel the secrets of His Being. God is "unknowable," for to know Him requires divine faculties. In the words of Yedaya Ha-Penini, "Could I ever know Him, I would be He."

The Sages of the Talmud, who were men of considerable psychological acumen and insight, perceived that the multitudes crave more substantial and satisfying fare than the avowal that God defies description in human terms. They gravitate to take literally the profusion of anthropomorphic descriptions of God in the Bible, which represents Him as being possessed of some of the physical and mental faculties which are man's equipment too. The Sages stressed that human traits are associated with God to enable men better to comprehend His

Being. The purpose of these anthropomorphisms, they pointed out, is "to bring the understanding of Him within the human mind's ken." The rabbinic sanction to interpret anthropomorphisms as methaphors and parables, made it possible for latter-day rationalists to philosophize and yet remain within the confines of traditional Judaism. Judaism simply has no dogma defining God, with the exception of the axiomatic affirmation of His Unique Oneness. As a result, many definitions of God have been propounded by faithful sons of the Synagogue.

It is mistaken to date the beginnings of Jewish philosophy in the time of Saadia Gaon (10th century). The Talmud and Midrash abound in philosophical soliloquies and dialogues on the Being of God and related metaphysical problems. Moreover, some of the early Rabbis were keenly alert to the finer shadings of the God idea, as may be seen from their profound and succinct observation that although "God is the place of the world, the world is not His place." Spinoza's conflict with Judaism arose primarily from his thesis of God's immanence in the world, which is irreconcilable with the authoritative Jewish doctrine of God's transcendence. No later philosopher succeeded in improving upon the talmudic differentiation between monotheistic transcendence and pantheistic immanence expressed in the dictum that "God is the place of the world, but the world is not His place." "We did not know," the Rabbis stated, "whether the Holy One, blessed be He, is the place of the world, or whether the world is His place— until Moses explained it as follows: 'Lord, Thou hast been our dwelling place...'" With striking simplicity, the opening verse of Psalm 90, which is traditionally ascribed to Moses, is taken as a proof text for the assertion of the world's immanence in God, which precludes a pantheistic solution of the God enigma.

## II

The rarified spirituality of the Jewish God idea is probably to be held accountable for Israel's frequent "backslidings" in biblical times, when they espoused the cults of their idolatrous neighbors. Only mature minds can find satisfaction in praying to an invisible and indefinable God. Christianity's sweeping success was largely made possible by its concessions to human frailty which desires a tangible God. To be sure, the intelligent Catholic knows that the figure to which he bows is not God but only a symbol. Yet there is a definite element of anthropomorphism about the cross.

Talmudic literature records some quaint stories about how the Rabbis convinced Gentiles of the logical necessity of God's invisible and indefinable ideality. When Rabbi Joshua ben Hanina, was commanded by Emperor Hadrian to *show* him the Jewish God, he replied: "This is impossible." When the Emperor persisted, the Rabbi bade him gaze at the summer sun, high in the zenith. "This is impossible," the Emperor declared. Whereupon the Rabbi explained: "You admit that you cannot gaze at the sun, which is only one of the servants of the Holy One, blessed be He. How, then, could you gaze at God Himself?" The many different versions of this story prove that the mystery of the Invisible God agitated some Gentiles—and probably many Jews too—in the talmudic era.

Judaism allows its followers considerable leeway in defining God, aware of the fact that such definitions do not affect the real being of God. The various philosophical theories on God's nature are regarded as experimental attempts of better approximating the understanding of the Divine. "You must not believe," the Rabbis caution, "that because you have different conceptions of God, there are many deities in heaven. Know ye that I am the Only God." The same view was expressed by a Hasidic Rabbi, some fifteen centuries later, who explained that the Lord is acclaimed as "God of gods" (Deuteronomy 10,17), to emphasize that He is above definition, that is to say, He is exalted above any idea which the human mind can conceive.

Among medieval Jewish philosophers, Maimonides, the staunch rationalist, was the most consistent foe of anthropomorphism. He denied the very possibility of arriving at positive knowledge about God, to wit, his theory of the negative Divine attributes. According to Maimonides, it is only possible to state what God is *not*. Thus, instead of describing God with positive terms, He defined Him by means of negative statements. Instead of saying God is active, he declared that He is not inactive, etc.

There is an unbroken continuity in Jewish tradition and creativeness. This does not mean that nothing new was added; it implies, however, that all accretions to the primeval legacy were of the same pattern and spirit. The medieval philosophers, too, did not introduce a revolutionary innovation by spiritualizing the God idea. They merely pursued and ramified the biblical trend, exemplified by the Deuteronomic exhortation: "Ye heard the voice of words, but ye saw no form; only a voice.... Take ye therefore good heed unto yourselves —for ye saw no manner of form on the day that the Lord spoke unto you in Horeb out of the midst of fire."

In submitting that he "who defines God as a corporeal being is an apostate," Maimonides only drew the logical inference from the sum total of biblical and talmudic teachings.

He paraphrased, as it were, the Pentateuchal passage which records that when Moses requested to see the Divine glory, he was told: "Thou shalt see My consequences (literally, My back), but my face shall not be seen." This text, and Isaiah's "To whom will ye liken Me, and make Me equal, and compare Me, that I may be like," have been the perennial watchword and motto of the Jewish quest for God.

## III

While Judaism is averse to regimentation, there is a remarkable latitude of freedom of expression within the clearly defined realm of the Law. There is much truth in the colloquialism that, with a biblical or talmudic passage, one can prove virtually everything and its opposite. That this is the case is due to the circumstance that Judaism respects the "minority opinion." It is characteristic of Jewish tolerance that even the teachings of an heretic like Elisha ben Abuya are recorded in the Talmud, whose editors did not hesitate to reserve for posterity this proverbial sinner's statements.

Thanks to this regard for the "minority opinion," the Bible and, especially, talmudic literature, abound in statements describing God in shockingly corporeal terms. Almost side by side with such statements as: "We describe Him in terms borrowed from his creatures, so that the ear may get it," and the assertion that in the future-to-come Divine spirituality will be such that even the many synonyms used for God will be replaced by One Name, there are biblical and talmudic descriptions of God which wholly reduce Him to the sphere of man.

He is depicted as visiting the sick, burying the dead, and consoling the mourner. Some Rabbis envisaged Him as complying with the commandments of the phylacteries and occupied with studying the Torah three hours a day.... As against the bulk of the spiritualizing attempts of defining God, however, the few anthropomorphic imaginings of naive souls do not really count. They are recorded because the Jewish genius is extremely sensitive in matters pertaining to freedom of expression.

The authoritative Jewish definition of God was epitomized by Maimonides, in his Thirteen Articles of Belief: "I believe with perfect faith that the Creator, blessed be His Name, has no bodily form, and that no form can represent Him." An integral part of the Jew's daily prayer, this definition is his unfailing guide in the quest for God. Whatever God may be, He is not corporeal and must not be represented in bodily form.

Monotheism is as much a protest against anthropomorphism as against idolatry. In the words of Rabbi Joseph Albo, "the belief in a corporeal God is altogether no God belief. For he who thinks that God has a body and acts by means of bodily strength, lacks the firm trust in God's existence."

On the whole Judaism has been rather averse to speculations about the nature of God. With keen psychological insight the early Sages and their successors perceived that man, shackled to the limitations of the human mind, must of necessity define God by means of mundane categories.

The reluctance to explore and venture into the secrets of the Divine did not, however, minimize the quest for ascertaining man's ethical obligations, incumbent upon him because, being created in the Divine imagine, he is infused with a spark of God's ethical perfection. God thus becomes the ethical impulse which stimulates the Jew to strive for holiness—because God is holy.

Despite its Messianic orientation, Judaism is thoroughly

this-wordly. It stresses that the good life must be achieved in this world, and that genuine piety is tested and found not wanting in human relations. Notwithstanding the importance it attaches to the ritual law, Judaism militates against wronging one's fellow men more severely than against ritual lapses. God is not in need of worship and prayer. He demands, however, that man "do justly, and love mercy, and walk humbly" with Him. The worship that pleases Him most is the unflagging effort of emulating His goodness and kindness. Thus viewed, the ethical attributes ascribed to God do not offend against the principle of Divine spirituality. For although they cannot convey an adequate idea of His being, they are useful in guiding men to greater ethical perfection. Thus when we say that God is good, merciful and just, we really mean to express the willingness to "emulate" His goodness, mercy and justice. In this manner, God becomes the ethical impulse of the Jew and His perfection the standard which he sets for himself.

The standard term for a perfectly righteous deed is *Kiddush Hashem*—"Sanctification of the Name of God." An unethical deed is designated *Hillul Hashem*—"Profanation of the Name of God." Throughout the ages Jewish spiritual leaders stressed that the conduct of those who confess God is the most conclusive proof of the "truth" of Judaism. This is why all Jewish codes stress that, when dealing with Gentiles, the Jew must adhere even more scrupulously to the highest standards of integrity than in his relations with Jews. "Defrauding a non-Jew is more reprehensible than defrauding a Jew because it entails the profanation of the Name of God."

Although Judaism is not actively missionary, in the manner of Christianity, it is animated by the hope of leading all of mankind to know the Only God. Averse to zealous missionarizing, Jews yet feel that their religious teachings and, especially, their conduct can be highly effective in raising the prestige of Judaism.

The God Whom Judaism "knows" loves the poor and downtrodden. He is concerned about the widow, the orphan and the stranger. This partiality to the "downtrodden," who walk in the darkness of misery, is the most revolutionary aspect of the Jewish God idea. The idols of ancient Israel's neighbors, as well as the gods of the Greeks and Romans, preferred the rich and powerful; they had no love to spare for the weak and lowly. As a result, the idolatrous ancients concluded that poverty and afflictions are signs of the sufferers' rejection by the gods.

Ethics cannot thrive in a civilization which regards success and physical well-being as evidence of divine favor, and poverty and sickness as signs of the gods' wrath. Judaism introduced new ethical standards by pointing to suffering as God's servant's badge of honor, thus proclaiming the eternal truth, reiterated by Christianity in due course, that suffering is the mark of distinction God bestows upon his beloved.

The novel Jewish intrepretation of suffering inevitably gave rise to a new ethics. Its code prohibited to exploit and abuse the poor in their helplessness and to oppress defenseless widows, orphans and "strangers." The discovery that God "loves" these underprivileged ones fired the Jew with zeal "to emulate God" by extending help to the sufferers.

The talmudic Sages and the medieval philosophers ramified and refined the idea that suffering is the hall-mark of God's elect. They argued that man's terrestial fortune and destiny are apportioned on the basis of the lesser part of his deed. But as even the perfect saint is not entirely free from sin, he is punished in this world so that his reward in the world-to-come may be all-glorious. The sinner, on the other hand, who is not without *some* pious merit, is rewarded in this world and punished in the world-to-come.

This interpretation removes the bitterness and sting from suffering and introduces a new prototype of the hero, favored and loved by God. The true "Servant of God," the hero glorified by Judaism, is not the handsome and happy youth of the Greek ideal, but the sufferer of Isaiah's vision—the "Servant of God," whose agony is *not* a sign of rejection, but the crown of Divine election. Isaiah's vision of "the suffering servant" has revolutionized the ethical outlook of mankind by holding aloft the torch of this new banner of goodness.

Sympathetic commiseration, that is to say, pity and the kindness born of it, can arise only when we regard the sufferers as "tested" rather than as "punished" by God. Hermann Cohen succinctly epitomized the Jewish interpretation of suffering by observing that "suffering is not punishment, or else poverty would be a penalty, while wealth would have to be regarded as the reward of virtue. On the contrary, poverty is the hallmark of piety."

As the result of such an interpretation of temporal adversity, Judaism could proclaim that God inclines with special love toward the poor. They are His people, as it were, and those who espouse their cause are fighting God's battle. God's special predilection for Israel is likewise due to His preference for the poor. Their "divine election" is synonymous with arduous and often painful service.

Judaism is intensely conscious of the unbridgeable gulf which separates the sphere of man from God's realm. At the same time, however, the Jew knows himself to be close to God, because of God's love for man—and man's love for God. The Torah commandment, "And thou shalt love the Lord thy God with all thy heart, and with all thy soul and with all thy might," also holds out the promise that God will fully return the love shown to Him.

## IV

Love is the medium of the correlation of God and man. The Prophets metaphorically pictured the covenant of God and Israel as a pact of betrothal and marriage. When Israel committed idolatry they chided it for the sin of "adultery."

"Thou has played the harlot with many lovers,
And wouldst thou yet return to me?
Saith the Lord."

Hosea chose God's love tryst with Israel and her faithlessness as his basic theme. In order better to understand God's sorrow, as it were, over Israel's betrayal, the Prophet, married a woman of ill repute who betrayed him. In his own personal tragedy and frustration Hosea found the key to the understanding of God's grief over "adulterous" and idolatrous Israel whom He had "betrothed" unto Himself in eternal love.

Hosea forgave his wife when she repented of her faithlessness. And so he anticipated the day when God, too, would be reconciled to Israel repentant—for the love that binds Him to her is the powerful attachment of youthful ardor.

The Sages of the Talmud and, especially, the medieval Kabbalists did not tire elaborating on and embellishing the biblical simile of the God-Israel love tryst. They declared that "The Song of Songs," aflame with passion and sensuousness, is a symbolism descriptive of God's love for Israel and her devotion to Him.

That the saintly Jewish teachers had no qualms to describe the God-Israel correlation in terms of sensuous love, goes far to prove the indigenous Jewish aversion to celibacy. The Jew is not embarrassed by physical love. As he sees it, the marital union is fraught with such holiness (*Kiddushin*—santification) that it is adequate even for serving as a parable of God's bond with His chosen one. This does not mean that Judaism invests the God-Israel correlation with gross physical sensuality, as the idolatrous cults did. On the contrary, Judaism sublimated and transfigured "sex" by stressing its inherent spirituality on the human level.

God's love for Israel is sensuous ardor as well as the tender emotion of parental love. And as all men are "God's children," Judaism conceives of the Creator as encompassing them all with His kind mercies. God's love goes out to all His creatures. Still, Israel holds a special niche in His affection, for when all of mankind were still worshipping idols, they acclaimed the Only God. Israel was the "first born" of the Lord, Who in turn assigns to him all the prerogatives of the birthright.

God, as the Jew knows Him, is the stern Judge of mankind as well as the loving and merciful Father of all. There is no contradiction between these two functions of God; the Sages held that God is just because He is merciful and that He is merciful because He is just. There is no justice without mercy and no mercy without justice. The Hebrew genius instinctively grasped this fact when it invested the word *zedakah* with two meanings: *justice* and *charity*. To Judaism provision for the needy and helpless is not something that may be left to the *subjective* emotion of love (caritas—love, from which charity is derived); it is an *objective* requirement of justice, complied with by means of *personal* devotion and loving-kindness.

Justice *and* mercy rule the universe, as the Jews sees it. He submits that when God set about creation, He said: "If

I create the world with mercy only, sins will abound. If I create it with justice only, how can the world exist? I will therefore create it with both so that it may endure." The Sages knew that with insistence on "strict justice the world cannot exist," and so they represented God, the Judge of the universe, as changing from His throne of justice to the throne of mercy upon realizing that according to justice the world deserves to be destroyed. The eminent Rab figuratively represented God as praying to Himself: "May My mercy conquer My justice, so that I may be gracious to My children..." In the same tenor the acute legalist Resh Lakish had it that God admits suffering loss when He "conquers" and to gaining when He is "conquered." For God recalls, as it were, that when he punished the generation of the Flood and the builders of the Tower of Babel and the people of Sodom and Gomorrah He really suffered a grievous loss. But when the Israelites made the Golden Calf and Moses would not let God punish them, He won all those multitudes. "Therefore," God said, "I pardon My children, so that I may not suffer loss."

Talmudic literature reciterates the basic Jewish conviction that God is merciful and kind. To be sure, He is pledged to uphold justice, but, as the Rabbis have it, His mercy invariably triumphs over His justice. They deduced from the wording of the second commandment that Divine mercy exceeds Divine justice five hundred fold and they pointed out that when the Bible makes mention of the greatness and majesty of God it also refers to His love and mercy. They were convinced that Divine mercy prevails over Divine justice in dealing with the sinners, for do not thirteen different synonyms for mercy occur in the Bible?

God "remembers mercy even when He is angry." He is "longsuffering toward the righteous and also toward the sinner." Even when He must inflict punishment, He is slow in doing so hoping for the regeneration of the sinners. Even when He punishes, He cannot help being saddened by the sufferings of the sinners. Nor does He only grieve because of the inevitable sufferings of Israel. No matter how grievously men may sin, they are and remain God's children. This is why a Hasidic Rabbi would utter this prayer: "Would that I loved the best of men as much as God loves the worst."

A standard rabbinic term for God is *Rachmana,* the Merciful. According to the Rabbis, the Merciful God accepts the testimony of one voice defending the sinner against nine hundred and ninety-nine accusing angels. A pithy *Midrash* has it that the Prophet Habakuk, angered at God's patience with the wicked, insisted that He explain His unwarranted mercy. The Divine answer was: "I am longsuffering so that they may return and repent . . ." God is loath to deal with the sinners according to the law. "I have no pleasure in the death of the wicked, but that the wicked turn from his way and live."

God's love for mankind is such that he actually suffers with the sinners. According to Rabbi Meir, the Divine Presence sighs with the afflicted sufferer: "How heavy is my head! How heavy is my arm!" and, moralized the great master of the Law, "if God suffers so much because of the blood of the wicked, how much more so for the blood of the righteous." The sufferer, therefore, has no right to complain. God suffers *with* him (not *for* him, as under the Christian dispensation), and "it is enough for the slave to be in the position of his master." So firm is the Jewish belief that God is with man in suffering and tribulation that a medieval pietist prayed: "O God, speedily bring about the redemption. I am not in the least thinking of what I may gain by it. I am willing to be condemned to all tortures in hell, if only the *Shechinah* will cease to suffer."

Judaism regards creation as the manifestation of Divine love. All of nature, animate and inanimate, man and beast are infused and quickened by the love of the Creator. The human being, however, is especially privileged and "beloved," for not only was man made in the image of God but, as a further mark of love, "it was revealed to him" that he was thus created. The Bible and talmudic literature abound in poetic and inspiring descriptions of and reflections on this manifestation of Divine love.

The Law, too, is to the Jew a symbol and sign of love. It is not a burden but a gift of Divine love. *Hesed zu Ha-Torah* —Love is a synonym for Torah, according to Jewish conviction. And so the Jew prays: "With great love Thou hast loved the house of Israel..." Again and again the Jewish prayers and benedictions stress that the commandments were given "in love." *Hasiduth,* denoting piety, is characteristically derived from *hesed*—love. The Jew is so thoroughly imbued with the conviction that all that comes from God is infused with love that he even goes to the extent of interpreting sufferings as a sign of love and as a means of cementing the bond between God and man. *Yissurim shel ahavah*—sufferings of love—help man in the ascent to the ethical heights that must be scaled, and so they too are a sign of the love and mercy of God Who desires to purge man of his sins.

Judaism makes the love for God an insistent commandment. "And thou shalt love the Lord thy God with all thy heart and with all thy soul and with all thy might." But how can mortal, finite man "love" the infinite and eternal God? The answer is: by acting in such a manner toward his fellow men that he loves God in them and thus is instrumental in making "the Name of God beloved by mankind." The commandment to love God is unconditional and all-embracing. One is to fulfill this commandment with one's every fiber—not only with the good inclination but also with the evil one for, according to an interesting talmudic exegis, the emphasis on loving God with "*all* thy heart" means that He must be worshipped and loved with the good *and* the evil desire. Similarly, the expression "with *all* thy soul" is explained to mean: "Even when He takes thy soul." "With *all* thy might" implies that God must be loved "for every measure; whether conditions are good or bad, you shall love God." A rather interesting interpretation of the three faculties with which God must be loved is offered by the 15th century philosopher Joseph Albo. He held that "*With all thy heart* signifies that all the ideas of the intellect must be concentrated upon loving God. *Thy soul* refers to the love of the animal instinct, while *thy might* refers to the love of the appetitive power."

The Prophets and Psalmists gloried in Divine worship motivated by love. "I love Thee, O Lord..." was their theme song, as it were. Their love for God was of an intensity sufficiently ardent to inspire the later generations, who held that the fear of God, although commanded, is unbefitting the true lover of God. "Let not a man say," warned Maimonides, "I will fulfill the commandments of the Torah, occupy myself with its wisdom, for the sake of obtaining all the blessings which are written therein and to merit the life of the world-to-come—and I will refrain from the transgressions against which the Torah utters a warning in order to escape the curses which are written therein, or in order not to be cut off from the life of the world-to-come. It is unbefitting to serve God in this manner; for he who serves God thus serves from fear, which is neither the manner of the Prophets nor of the Sages." Maimonides, the rationalist codifier of the Law, turned mystic when he dwelled on the theme of piety born of love. "When man loves God with genuine love," the great legalist taught, "he will perform all pious deeds because of the love of Him." If Jewish rationalists and mystics were divided on other points they were unanimous in emphasizing that true worship of God means to love Him. To Rabbi Abraham Abulafia, therefore, prophecy was identical with the love of God and so, quite consistently, he regarded the Kabbalists, who transubstantiate the fear of God into the love for God as the true disciples of the Prophets. The identification of the fear and love of God in the Kabbala is stirringly expressed by a 13th century Kabbalist who described the state of the soul filled with the love of God as follows: "The soul is filled with the love of God and bound to Him with ties of love, in joy and gladness of heart. He is not like one who serves his master unwillingly, but even when one tries to hinder him, the love of service burns in his heart, and he is glad to do the will of his Creator. . . . This lover aspires not to advantage in the world; he does not care about the pleasures of his wife or of his sons and daughters. All this is as nothing to him; all he craves is to do the will of his Creator, render good unto others, keep sanctified the Name of God."

Israel's love for God was not very constant in biblical times when they prospered. It turned into an all-consuming and abiding passion only when the Lord, long-suffering and patient, finally punished Israel and visited upon them all the dread penalties foretold by the Prophets. Yet the more God smote them, the more ardently they became devoted to Him. In exile, Israel abandoned the irresponsible ways of the spoiled son who takes his Father's love for granted. In the school of suffering, Israel learned that love and grace must be earned every day and every hour. Thanks to this insight, Israel could shoulder the burdens of exile and bear the agonies of persecution, proving to himself and to God that his love had become strong as tempered steel.

In exile Israel also discovered the true meaning of the commandment to "love the Lord." According to a pithy rabbinic interpretation, it means we should so conduct ourselves that, through us, the name of God will become beloved among men. On the anvil of suffering, Israel learned that man's love of God must be unmotivated and free from selfish desires and hopes. It must be a strong and fervent love, capable of being put to harsh tests.

The millions of Jewish martyrs, who "santified the Name of God" throughout the ages, exemplified this love in the sublimest manner. Medieval chronicles of Jewish woe record that those condemned to agonizing, slow death on the pyre mounted the stakes happily, "as one goes to the marriage canopy." Their love for God gave them courage and strength, so that no physical pain could shake their unwavering equanimity.

Essentially, the God-Israel correlation is profoundly tragic —and in this respect, too, it is symbolical of correlations among men. For when God showered upon Israel His lavish favor, they betrayed Him; and now that they are aflame with the passion for Him, He will not incline to them.

Yet Israel does not abandon hope. It cherishes the Divine promise that ultimately, when the measure of punishment will be full, God will forgive and redeem them. This hope, more than anything else, has sustained Jewish survival stamina. The confidence that "in His own good time God will redeem Israel," has been our people's beacon light.

The devotion to God may be said to be the meaning and purpose of Israel's career. The love of God inspired and fired the sages and saints, the poets and philosophers, even while it suffused with light and splendor the drab abodes of the children of the ghetto. It gave them a sense of worthwhileness, while easing the agony of their homelessness. Nor was it only "God-kissed" poets, like Yehudah Halevi, or "sweet nightingales," like Solomon Ibn Gabirol, who consummated their souls' longings and aspirations in rapturous songs glorifying the tryst of God and Israel. Matter-of-fact legalists and moralists, too, turned poets when dwelling on the theme of the love of God. Thus Rabbi Eleazer Ben Yehudah, the thirteenth-century Talmudist and author of the ethical treatise "Rokeach," describes the bliss of mind that is the portion of those who love God, as follows:

"When man is filled with the love of God, he cannot but serve His Maker faithfully, though his fellows attempt forcibly to make him abandon his devotion to God. He is filled with a consuming desire to mold his life according to God's will. Delight in God makes him forget all terrestial pleasures. . . . His life has but one purpose: to fulfill the Divine commands with unwavering loyalty, so that God's Name be hallowed. Men of this kind do not exalt themselves above others; they do not indulge in idle talk, nor do they long wretchedly for the love in woman's eyes. They are silent when blame is poured on them, for their thoughts are not where they themselves are—but always with Him whose praises are sung by their faithful lips."

The love of God, as Judaism knows it, spells lasting spiritual happiness for man. Is is not a jealous love requiring the renunciation of other joys and bonds. On the contrary, it bids the truly pious to enjoy their earthly portion, for "the Divine Presence dwells only with those who are joyful."

## V

How can the love of God be translated into terms of daily living? All authoritative Jewish voices, throughout the ages, have emphasized that man's love of God is synonymous with and tested in humane love—kindness, solicitude and unselfish devotion to follow men. One serves God most pleasingly when he alleviates human suffering. The Hasidic Rabbi who, in the "Ten Days of Repentance," chopped wood for the stove of a poor and ailing widow while "Penance Services" were in progress at the Synagogue, exemplifies Jewish worship of God at its best.

This should not lead one to assume that Judaism makes light of ritual and prayer. "The hour of prayer is the essence and the flower" of the Jew's day, to quote Yehudah Halevi. But this hour is meaningfully consummated only when the other hours are "pathways leading to this hour."

The last wills and testaments of medieval Jews allot little space to the disposition of their wordly goods, of which most possessed preciously little. Their wills were taken up with matters of the soul and the spirit. The love of God and its practice in life was a favorite theme of Jewish parents, who recommended and bequeathed this love to their children as the choicest legacy. "And when you recite the verse which commands, 'love the Lord thy God!' speak as one ready to deliver up life and substance for His sanctification, thus yourself fulfilling the words of the Psalmist: 'For thy sake are we killed every day . . .'" the eminent Rabbi Asher ben Yechiel admonished his children. "Have full confidence in Him, and believe in His special providence... Day and night let your lips make mention of Him. When you lie down rejoice in His love, and in your dream He will be with you. When you will awake you will delight in Him, and He will guide your paths. Do all your pious deeds in the spirit of humbly walking before Him.... This is the service which He has chosen, the service acceptable in His sight."

Judaism knows many paths of service leading to God. While the rationalists hold that knowledge and reasoning lead man to the Divine, the mystics acclaim intuition and love as the royal highway leading to "nearness to God." Both the rationalists and the mystics, however, are agreed—and in this they have been upheld by the rank and file of the people— that the love of God is tested in man's relations with his fellows.

Notwithstanding the emphasis Judaism places on the incorporeality and the strictly ideational character of God, He has yet always been a reality, living and near to Jews throughout the ages. To the praying Jew, the Lord is definitely a *personal* God, although He is never degraded to the level of a person. It is important to understand the distinction between a *personal* God and a *personified* God. The *personal* God "is exalted above His world. And yet, when a man enters a House of Prayer, standing behind a pillar and praying in a whisper, the Holy One, blessed be He, inclines to his prayers. For God is as near to His creatures as the mouth to the ear." The implicit trust in God's nearness is the theme of many prayers of the Synagogue and especially of the Psalms. They proclaim the nearness of the incorporeal God with a certainty that brooks no doubt.

The Only God revealed Himself to Israel because the Jews *searched* for Him. But the fact that God is in a very special sense, the "God of Israel," does not imply that He is Israel's God exclusively. He is the Lord of the Universe and the Father of *all* men. Jews respect the image of God even in their enemies. The Sages have it that "at the drowning of the Egyptians in the Red Sea, the Ministering Angels wanted to offer a song of triumph to God; but He restrained them, saying, 'The work of My hands is drowning in the sea, and you would offer Me a song!'"

The Universal Lord was not the discovery of the Sages. He is firmly anchored in the Bible. Isaiah envisioned the future restoration of Israel as part of a general restoration of the Mediterranean orbit—the restoration of Egypt and Assyria—the former the enslaver of his nation, and the latter the despoiler of the Kingdom of Israel.

Similarly, Amos represents God as being profoundly vexed and chagrined on account of the transgressions of Israel's neighbors. This universalizing tendency found its culmination in the Prophet Jonah, who was appointed to "proclaim against Nineveh," the capital of Assyria. That the Jewish genius could conceive of a Hebrew Prophet ministering to a foreign and hostile nation attests forcefully the universalistic orientation of Judaism and its hope that "the Lord shall be King over all the earth." It is for the sake of this hope that Jews pray thrice daily: "We therefore hope in Thee, O Lord our God, that we may speedily behold the glory of Thy might.... When the world will be perfected under the kingdom of the Almighty, and all the children of flesh will call upon Thy Name, when Thou wilt turn unto Thyself all the wicked of the earth..... Let them all accept the yoke of Thy Kingdom and do Thou reign speedily over them, forever and ever."

CHAPTER 13

## Fellow Man

### I

AMONG THE eternity-oriented Jewish ideals which have entrenched the Jewish survival potential, none has been more consequential than "fellow man." As Judaism sees it, man represents the highest value. By adhering to this conviction throughout the ages, Judaism has been considerably in advance of other civilizations, not excepted Western civilization, which only now, and perhaps too late, is discovering that the technological emphasis inevitably leads to ruin. Contemporary leaders of thought now are stressing the importance of "the worth of man" as the panacea for survival in the face of the atomic challenge. But it was Judaism which first propounded this truth, thus preparing the road for ethical progress.

The Hebrew genius discovered early that all men are created equal, irrespective of race, nation and religion. God is the father of all men and thus all men are brothers. The Fatherhood of God implies the Brotherhood of Mankind. Thus to wrong or degrade any member of the human family means to offend God. He is profoundly concerned about the manner in which His "children" conduct themselves with their "brothers," and He is pledged to reform, or punish, if necessary, those who fail to honor the obligations of brotherhood. The ancient Rabbis represented God as exhorting man: "The commandment 'Thou shalt love thy neighbor as thyself' was proclaimed with a strong warning. I created him—if you love him, I shall reward you generously; if, however, you don't love him, I shall sit in judgment over you and inflict punishment."

Every wrong committed against *any* man is, as Judaism sees it, aimed at God in Whose image he is created. "He that oppresses the poor blasphemes his Maker, but he that is gracious to the needy honors Him." The Jew conceives of God as the Omnipresent and Omiscient Father of all men, and so he who takes revenge really injures God. For he who says: "I was insulted, so let him who insulted me suffer likewise; I was cursed, he too should be cursed," is told: "Know whom you insult—him who was created in the image of God."

The "One World" utopia was anticipated more than three thousand years ago by the Hebrew genius in the proclamation of the "One Mankind" as the necessary corollary of the "One God." Malachi's words, "Have we not all one Father? Hath not One God created us? Why, then, do we deal treacherously every man against his brother?" sets forth the most cogent reason for the unity of mankind: the One and Only God.

The logical nexus of the axiomatic oneness of God and the unity of mankind implies that the Creator is honored when we respect His creatures. Rabbi Joshua the son of Levi, therefore taught: "When man proceeds on his way, angels precede him and proclaim: 'Make room for the image of the Holy One, blessed be He.'"

Thanks to this identification of human dignity with the honor of God, religious-ethical democracy gained an early ascendancy in Israel. Its principal tenet is that to wrong man is tantamount to wronging God, as there is a Divine spark in every human being. Biblical and rabbinic literature stress this conviction insistently: "One does not act treacherously toward one's fellow man, unless one first denies God." For he who sheds human blood diminishes the Likeness in which that man was created. Moreover, God sorrows, as it were, not only for the tribulations of the righteous. The Sages stressed that He also mourns when the wicked suffer, for they, too, are His children.

To the Jew human life is sacred above all else, for it is invested with the dignity and worth of God. The preservation of life is therefore a primary duty of piety. Even the Law *must* be ignored when its keeping might jeopardize the saving of an imperilled life. As the Jew sees it, to preserve life means to save the Divine spark embodied in it.

Each and every human being is important and indispensable as a child of God. Unlike the Greek philosophers, Judaism does not postulate an abstraction of man as the measure of all things, but singles out each and every individual for this distinction. It views the individual as a microcosm, which is a perfect replica of the macrocosm of mankind and reflects the Divine Glory. Every person represents both mankind and God—and so there can be no trifling with human life. The Sages expressed this basic truth as follows: "The plants and the animals were created in multitudes. Man, however, was created singly, so that he should know that he is a world by himself and represents the full value of life. And so every person may say: 'The whole world was created for my sake.' He who saves one human being maintains the whole world, and he who destroys a single life really destroys a whole world."

"Life," as the Jew sees it, is not private property; it belongs, first of all, to God and then to mankind. The preservation of one's health, therefore is more than self-interest. Jewish law rules that he who wantonly risks his life sins, for man does not merely belong to himself. He who says: "I am endangering my own life—why should others care, if I don't?" deserves to be punished. No one dare presume that his welfare is of no concern to his fellows. Every person is linked by destiny to mankind and his weal and woe have repercussions on the fate of all.

By aligning the unity of mankind with the Unity of God, Judaism also provides a rationale for ethics: the fact that he is created in the Divine image imposes upon man the obligation of striving toward the ethical perfection of God. Although Jewish teachers and thinkers have persistently stressed that the true nature of God cannot be fathomed by man's defective cognitive faculties, for practical purposes they ascribed the perfection of all desirable ethical qualities to God and then demanded that man emulate them. Man is commanded to "walk in the ways of God," that is to say, he is bidden to realize in his conduct a part of the ethical perfection of God. "As He is merciful, showing mercy even to the sinners, you shall be merciful." In this manner the biblical exhortation, "Thou shalt walk in His ways," was interpreted as the call to emulate God's mercy, lovingkindness, forebearance, justice and truth. The criterion for pleasing God is the extent to which one succeeds in giving help and joy to one's fellow men. In the words of Rabbi Hanina the son of Dosa: "He in whom the spirit of his fellow men delights, the spirit of the Omnipresent delights; and he in whom the spirit of his fellow men takes no delight, in him the spirit of the Omnipresent takes no delight either."

True piety does not consist in withdrawing from the world

and its needs but, on the contrary, in seeking and finding God in the world. Judaism disparages the would-be saint who ignores human needs and the obligations growing therefrom for the sake of Heaven. "He who occupies himself exclusively with the study of the Torah and does not practice deeds of lovingkindness resembles the godless." Ritual piety and study of the Torah cannot atone for the neglect of the duties of neighborly love. Although Judaism regards deeds of mercy as Divine service, it does not equate prayer and ritual piety with mercy and lovingkindness. The equation: human service= Divine service is not reversable.

Judaism, therefore, draws a line of distinction between ceremonial duties and ethical obligations, according the latter precedence over the former. While sincere repentance atones for ritual transgressions, it does not erase sins against fellow men. God will not grant forgiveness for such sins unless those who have been wronged are conciliated and amends are made.

As a result of Judaism's emphasis on the Law, the notion is prevalent that it is indifferent to mercy and lovingkindness. This is a false conclusion. Indeed, Judaism assigns to the Law great importance, at the same time, however, it stresses the place of love in religion. In point of fact—and by no means accidentally—the Hebrew term for piety, *hasiduth* is derived from *hesed,* meaning love. The Golden Rule, "You shall love your neighbor as yourself" was first enunciated in the Law of Moses, and, moreover, in the book of Leviticus which is almost exclusively devoted to the detailed exposition of the ritual law. God's love for Israel, poetically compared to the affection of a husband for his bride, was the favorite theme of the biblical authors. God, the Lawgiver and Judge, did not seem incompatible to them with the God of love and mercy.

"Love" and "justice" are not mutually exclusive, but complementary in the Jewish realm.

Judaism insistently stresses the importance of altruistic love in human relations, while insisting that love must be joined to justice to be benefically effective. Talmudic and rabbinic literature, although primarily concerned with Law, abound in inspiring lessons on how to make love a palpable reality "Love your fellow man" and "What is hateful to you, do not to your fellow man" are the two basic teachings governing the human relations of the Jew. The Rabbis held that "the beginning and the end of the Torah is the rendering of loving-kindness."

Some medieval mystics and ethical teachers carried the idea of the "One Mankind" to its loftiest heights by averring that the commandment "love your neighbor as yourself" really means "love him *for he is as yourself*." All men, through their One Creator and common descent, they argued, are inseparably linked, so that it is impossible to determine where the "I" ends and the "you" begins.

This self-identifying love implies that we must refrain from treating our fellow man in a manner we would not want him to act toward us. Hillel's formulation of the Golden Rule, "What is hateful to you, do not do unto your fellow man," must be the norm of conduct in all human relations.

According to Jewish law, it is a more grievous sin to insult a man than to wrong him in money matters, for, as Rabbi Samuel the son of Nahmani said, the damage sustained in money is calculable, while the injury of insult is inestimable. Talmudic and rabbinic literature therefore abounds in teachings and homilies aiming to implant gentle consideration for one's fellow man's sensibilities. Disgracing a man in public is placed on a par with shedding his blood, and he who so sins "has no share in the world-to-come." Even if one's fellow man's conduct calls for censure, one should reprove him "only in private, with moderation and tact, stressing that all this is done for his own good."

## II

The extent to which the Sages of the Talmud would go in sparing their fellow men humiliation may be judged from their comment on the biblical exemption from military service of "those that have built new houses and have not dedicated them; those that have planted vineyards and have not yet eaten their fruits; those that have betrothed wives and have not taken them; and those that are fearful and faint-hearted." That these four classes of men were asked to leave the armed ranks *together* was taken by the Rabbis as an indication of God's regard for human sensibilities. For when the faint-hearted returns home, his comrades, giving him the benefit of the doubt, will say, "Perhaps he has built a house, or planted a vineyard, or betrothed a woman," rather than suspecting him of cowardice.

The regard for fellow man's honor must be extended especially to those whose feelings are easily hurt. As a repentant sinner will be sensitive about his past, one must not remind him, "Remember what you used to do!" Similarly, one must not reproach a proselyte for the actions of his ancestors, nor tell one beset by severe calamities that God is just. The extent to which one must avoid any remark that could give hurt is indicated by the midrashic comment on the Pentateuchal text, "When an ox or sheep is born." — "Is it, then, born as an ox?" the Rabbis wondered. "Is it not a *calf* at birth? However, because the Israelites made the golden calf, Scriptures say 'ox' and no 'calf,' so as to spare humiliation to other calves..."

According to a talmudic opinion, the institution of the silent prayer was motivated by the desire to enable the sinners to confess their transgressions privately. Even in cases where physical punishment is mandatory, it must be administered without injury to the human dignity of the transgressor. The Pentateuch therefore limited the number of stripes to forty, which talmudic law, by ingenious exegesis, reduced to thirty-nine.

The concern for the honor of fellow man permeates all of Jewish social legislation. Over and over again it is emphasized that the poor must not be humiliated and that true charity consists in sparing the sensibilities of the needy. Thus he who gives charity in secret is compared to Moses, while he who give ostentatiously is severely disparaged. The Sages regarded it as preferable not to give at all rather than to humiliate the needy recipient of the charitable gift.

Midrashic literature abounds in stories about pietists who gave charity without putting the poor to the blush. There was, for instance, Abba, "the bleeder" and physician, who never asked a fee from his patients lest he embarrass the indigent. In front of his office there was a box for the fees to be deposited. Those who could afford it paid, while the poor were spared embarrassment. Yet Abba was none the worse off for placing his patients on an honor system. The Talmud records that he did so well that he was able to give his poor patients, in addition to free medical treatment, money for food.

Among a people who, like the Jews, consider scholarship the *sine qua non* of social standing, to be known as an ignoramus is degrading. "The Book of the Pious," therefore, warns the householder against engaging a stranger in scholarly discourses. "Perhaps he is uneducated, in which case you would put him to shame." The same volume cautions that one should not praise one author in the presence of another author and generally to refrain from paying tribute to persons who are engaged in the same calling in the presence of their colleagues.

The Sages knew how trying it is to a man's self-respect to be reminded of favors received. According to the Talmud, Nehemiah's book was not named for him (being reckoned as part of the book of Ezra) because he wrote, "Remember unto me, O God, for good, all that I have done for this people." To gloat over one's good deeds is regarded as a sign of poor taste. Moreover, it offends the sensibilities of those who benefited by those favors. The rule of the pious therefore should be: "Act in keeping with your words, but let not your words betray your actions."

When Rabbi Nehumya's disciples asked their master to what he ascribed his longevity, he replied: "I never sought honor by disgracing my fellow men and I never retired with a curse against any one." The effect of this conduct on physical vigor is not very insistently stressed. But that it is the road to the good life is emphasized by all Jewish teachers. Judaism categorically demands that we guard our fellow man's honor. In the same tenor, it is commanded that his property "be as dear to you as your own." This outlaws any impropriety through which another person might suffer loss. Integrity and honesty in business are part of the commandment to love one's neighbor as oneself. According to the Rabbis, honesty in business is so important that, in the world-to-come, the first question directed to the soul will be: "Have you dealt honestly and faithfully with your fellow men?", and not, as one might expect, whether the ritual commandments were properly observed.

## III

Talmudic law has devised a remarkable system of protecting the poor against unscrupulous overreaching by fixing ceiling prices, providing adequate consumers' protection and by prohibiting the export of vital goods. As war usually precipitates inflation, Jewish law empowers the authorities to set price ceilings and to protect them by keeping profiteers from depreciating the quality of the merchandise.

Biblical law summarily prohibits the traffic in money for profit. Later, when an expanding economy made the availability of credit necessary, the law was implemented to permit the charging of interest on business loans. Nevertheless, representative Jewish teachers continued to decry trading in money as contrary to the spirit of the Law, although its letter can be reconciled with it.

While biblical law unconditionally prohibits interest on loans to Jews, it permits the charging of interest on loans to non-Jews. Since hoary antiquity this provision has been gloated over by Jew-haters. In truth, however, this law attests Jewish tolerance. For since non-Jews may charge interest, it would be unfair to keep them from dealing with Jews by subjecting them to the Jewish business code. The law therefore obliges the Jew to pay interest to the Gentile, although he is forbidden to pay interest to a Jew—quite naturally, however, this also entitles him to interest when lending money to a Gentile. This does not prove that Jews do not regard Gentiles as "fellow men." On the contrary, it attests the broadmindedness of Judaism which does not expect the non-Jew to conform with Jewish law.

The commandment of neighborly love implies the duty of succoring the needy. Judaism, however, demands more than provision for the physical needs of the poor; it calls for compassion and self-identification with the sufferers, for only the awareness that the afflicted are part of us, as it were, can bring out the best in social solicitude and effort. The unequivocal condemnation of complacency in the face of suffering—even the suffering of a dumb creature—is characteristically stressed by the talmudic tale of Rabbi Judah the Prince, who was severely punished for having hardened his heart to an animal's plea for compassion. Once, as the Rabbi was teaching, a calf about to be slaughtered, ran to him, lowing plaintively, as if pleading, "Save me!"

"What can I do?" the Rabbi said. "For this purpose you were created!"

As punishment for his lack of sympathy, the great Rabbi and editor of the Mishnah was afflicted with a toothache which plagued him for thirteen years, until he showed kindness to another animal—a weasel. "Because he had pity, pity was shown to him," it was said in Heaven when he saved the life of that lowly creature.

Compassion is the tribute we owe to our suffering fellow men. No one must be denied sympathy—not even the enemy. "Take heed not to deprive *anyone* of your commiseration." For he who does not commiserate with his stricken fellow men is as the idolater. Indeed, lavish support should not be showered upon the undeserving, as this might confirm them in their evil ways. However, also those who do not merit kindness should not be totally forsaken. They, too, are our brothers. "Be charitable toward everybody, whether he deserves it or not. For although he may not merit your kindness, you are obliged to extend it to him."

Despite their insistence on the letter of the Law, the Sages —the legalists *par excellence*—were keenly aware of the inadequacy of the Law in alleviating human suffering. They demanded that, in human relations, the Law be implemented with kindness, extending beyond the letter of the Law (*lifnim mishurat haddin*).

What the Sages meant by going "beyond the letter of the law" may be seen from the account of the law suit Rabbi Bar Bar Hunah's workers brought against their master. The men carelessly broke a cask of wine. To indemnify himself for the loss, the Rabbi confiscated their coats. When the workers brought suit against the Rabbi, the court did not only sentence him to return the coats but also to pay the men their wages, although they had accomplished little more than causing their employer a monetary loss. When the Rabbi protested, "Is this the law?" His colleagues replied, "Yes, for it is written, 'And keep the path of the righteous!'" Although the letter of the law may not require the master to pay the wages of laborers through whose carelessness he has suffered loss, righteousness and neighborly love impose this obligation, even if there is no legal claim. Neighborly love, however, is not only proved by deeds, but also by sharing our fellow men's mental anguish. "To love means to know what hurts and may hurt our fellow men," a Hasidic Rabbi taught.

## IV

Judaism early recognized that the love of the like for the like is natural and easy. What is difficult is the cultivation of love for the unlike. Most men are possessed of the primitive instinct of fearing and disliking the *un*like. National, religious, racial and class hatreds are largely motivated and fed by the instinctive aversion to the unlike. Suspicions and clashing interests and backgrounds render the recognition of fellow man in the "stranger" difficult. The history of mankind proves that, throughout the ages, "strangers" have been oppressed, persecuted and discriminated against even under the most progressive governments. Our own contemporary "minority" problems are, in the final analysis, but the result of the inability, or the unwillingness, of the majority to recognize in the person with a different complexion, nationality or religion a brother and fellow man.

Perhaps it was their close familiarity with the harsh lot of the stranger, acquired during their servitude in Egypt, that made the Jews so singularly and keenly aware of the ethical challenge represented by minorities. The Pentateuch bases the commandment to love the stranger on the fact that "Ye were strangers in the land of Egypt." Since you know what it feels like to be a stranger—to be hated, oppressed and persecuted—you shall not subject to this fate those who will be strangers in your midst.

Ever realistic, Judaism knows that it is difficult to love the stranger. But God loves Him—and we are commanded "to walk in His ways"—so what else is there to do? Precisely because the temptation to insult and wrong the stranger is so powerful, the Bible inveighs against it in thirty-six places, while the Sages declared that denying justice to the stranger is tantamount to the spoliation of God.

Jewish law places the stranger in all respects on a par with the Jew, except where ritual obligations are concerned. If he is poor, he is to benefit from all the special provisions the Law makes for the needy of Israel. In biblical times the indigent resident alien shared with the poor Israelites the produce of the corners of the fields and the spontaneous harvest of the Sabbatical year. Talmudic law obliges the Jewish community to provide for the poor Gentiles—to feed them, clothe them, visit them in sickness, bury their dead and comfort their mourners. Likewise, they must not be overreached or exploited. Their possessions are to be protected in the same manner as Jewish property is safeguarded. Moreover, if a Jew knows that another Jew wrongs or cheats a Gentile, he must protect the Gentile and oppose his fellow-Jew.

This humane and progressive legislation is based on the conviction that all men are, first of all, members of the human family, and only secondarily members of a particular nation or religion. This broad and tolerant philosophy triumphs in the pronouncement that a Gentile need not be converted to share in the world-to-come. He can qualify by espousing righteousness, for the "righteous Gentiles share in the future world." The narrow view that the acceptance of doctrine is the key to salvation is alien to Judaism, which regards national and religious differences as insignificant in comparison with the common possessions of mankind. As a result of these teachings, Jews gravitate rather naturally toward movements emphasizing the brotherhood of men.

Judaism enacted a protective legislation for minorities more than three thousand years ago, in a world where the stranger was unprotected. Even in Greece and Rome, where hospitality was held sacred, the stranger had no rights and protection unless he procured them through the mediation of a citizen by means of a complicated procedure. The idea of human equality and brotherhood is not the legacy of Athens, but the gift of Jerusalem where it was taught that *every* human being is a fellow man in whom the Divine image is reflected.

Under the Jewish dispensation, "the other man" is always a "fellow man." Even if he wrongs us, we must honor in him the spark of the Divine. To be sure, we must fight evil by punishing the evil-doers who undermine the ethical foundations of human society. We dare not, however, let hatred guide our actions. No matter how dastardly the cruelty of the enemy and how perverted his crimes, the retribution and punishment must be dictated not by the spirit of vengeance, but by eagerness to uproot evil while reforming the evil-doers. Punishment should never be revenge. The Jewish attitude to the complex problem of punishment is that, regardless of the sternness of the sentence, it must be free from hatrd. For "he who hates a human being is as if he hates God."

The Torah, however, does not merely interdict hatred manifest in words or action. It also commands: "Thou shalt not hate thy brother in thy heart." Hatred is a natural reaction to hurt suffered. But man must curb his primitive instincts. It is difficult not to crave or wreak vengeance and so biblical and talmudic law detail at length what constitutes forbidden acts of revenge. As the Hebrew conscience sees it, vengeance is expressed not only in deeds, but also in passively looking on the misfortune of the enemy. We dare not stand by idly when our enemy is in distress. He, too, is a fellow man. And so the Pentateuch commands: "If thou meet thine enemy's ox or his ass going astray, thou shalt surely bring it back to him again. If thou seest the ass of him that hateth thee lying under its burden, thou shalt forbear to pass by him; thou shalt surely release it with him." In the same vein "Proverbs" admonishes: "Rejoice not when thine enemy falleth, and let not thy heart be glad when he stumbleth." For "if thine enemy be hungry, give him bread to eat, and if he be thirsty, give him water to drink..." The Rabbis commented on this exhortion: "Even if you suspect him of scheming evil against you, give him to eat and drink when he comes hungry to your house."

With all that, however, Jewish ethics is thoroughly realistic.

It never loses sight of the fact that the desire for revenge is a natural, instinctive reaction to hurt suffered. But though revenge is sweet, it is forbidden, for "through the practice of the commandments one is to subdue the evil inclination. And so one should be even readier to assist one's enemy than one's friend." The only retaliation that is permitted, if retaliation it may be termed, is the refining of one's own character to the extent that the evil-doer cannot but be smitten with remorse for having fallen short of the ethical ideal which was in his reach as well. A strange sort of "revenge," indeed!

The proper attitude toward those who offend one is not to take offense while being extremely careful not to give hurt. "If others speak ill of you, let the worst they say seem small to you. But if you speak ill of others, let a small thing seem big to you." We must cultivate the art of forgetting insults, for "mankind can only exist if one forgets the insults one has been made to suffer." Obviously, this is easier said than done, what with the "evil instinct" ever on the alert to lure men to retaliation. The Jew, therefore, petitions for Divine assistance in the fight against the temptation of revenge. Thrice daily, he prays: "Oh, my God! Guard my tongue from evil, and my lips from speaking guile; and to such as curse me, may my soul be silent."

A pithy rabbinical word has it that the true hero is he who turns an enemy into a friend. The extent to which Jews strive for this crown of valor is illuminated by some pertinent admonitions of medieval last wills and testaments, in which parents bequeathed to their children the accumulated wisdom of a life time. Thus one father counseled his children: "Refrain from all hatred, be it silent envy in your heart because of your neighbor's good fortune, or because of weakness of character, or because of business competition. If your neighbor has caused you harm, which the Lord may prevent, forgive him forthwith, for you should love your neighbor with all your heart.... If your neighbor has suffered loss in his property, pray to the Lord that He may compensate him for such losses, do so even from your own money; for you should love your neighbor with all your heart.... Be always anxious to cause your fellow man joy or some favor and do not be anxious to have others do such favors to you..."

Modern psychologists warn against nursing hatred and grudge as they are double-edged swords. Medieval Jews, too, knew that hatred is a deadly boomerang. And so the anonymous author of a "Testament," spuriously attributed to Maimonides, warns:

"Glory in forbearance, for that is real strength and true victory. If you seek revenge, perchance you will not attain it, and your heart will be sick with hope deferred. And you may add shame to your disgrace, like the one who rolls a stone which returns unto himself. And if you do attain the desired revenge, behold, you have sinned against the Lord. For realize what the results must be to yourselves. Hatred, a vindictive heart, confusion of mind, sleeplessness, interruption of your work, the exposure of your faults and failings, degeneration in looks and speech, destruction of the soul, a devouring jealousy, disturbance of family peace and, in the end, remorse."

The sort of neighborly love which should be shown to those against whom causes for grudge exist is touchingly set forth in the will of Joel the son of Abraham Shemariah (18th cent.):

"It was often my way at assemblies to raise my eyes and regard those present from end to end, to see whether I really loved everyone among them, whether my acceptance of the duty to love my fellow men was genuine. With God's help

I found that indeed I loved all present. Even if I noticed one who had treated me improperly, then without a thought of hesitation, without a moment's delay, I pardoned him. Forthwith I resolved to love him. If my heart forced me to refuse my love, I addressed him with words of friendship, until my heart became attuned to my words. So, whenever I met one to whom my heart did not incline, I forced myself to speak to him kindly, so as to make my heart feel affection for him. What if he were a sinner? Even then I would not quarrel with him, for I wonder whether there exists in this age one who is able to reprove another. On the other hand, if I saw that he would listen to advice, I drew near to him, turning towards him a cheerful countenance. If, however, I fancied that he would resent my advance, I did not intrude on him. As there is a duty to speak, so is there a duty to be silent."

To what extent Judaism wants its followers to go in suppressing the desire for revenge is forcefully demonstrated by the example of Rabbi Josi the Galilean. The Rabbi was married to a shrew "who embittered his days." Finally he divorced her. She remarried. Before long, however, her second husband became impoverished and stricken with blindness. Eventually, he was compelled to go begging, with his wife leading him about. When Rabbi Josi learned of his former wife's misery and that her husband mistreated her, "he gave them one of his houses and provided for them all the days of their lives."

## V

Their insight into human nature and the conviction that a spark of the Divine Image dwells in even the most corrupt, has made Jews poor haters. In many contexts Jewish literature emphasizes that the enemy is, first and last, a human being—and therefore entitled to humane consideration. As a result, Jewish law also abounds in precepts for humane conduct in war. It is remarkable that these laws date back to a time when the most unspeakable cruelties were perpetrated in war. To be sure, there were Jewish warlords, like Samson and Gideon, who fell short of the ideal. But these exceptions only prove the rule that Jews were exceptionally merciful toward defeated enemies. The Bible records a rather remarkable instance of mercy shown to the Arameans by King Ahab of Israel, who was anything but a model of piety. When Ben Hadad of Aram and his armies were defeated by Ahab and in flight, "Ben Hadad's servants said: 'Behold now, we have heard that the kings of the house of Israel are merciful kings; let us, pray thee, put sackcloth on our loins, and ropes upon our heads, and go out to the king of Israel; peradventure he will save thy life?' So they thereupon put on mourner's attire and went to Ahab pleading: Thy servant Ben-Hadad saith, 'I pray thee, let me live,' And he said: 'Is he yet alive? He is my brother.' And he let him go and made a covenant with him."

Among the sins for which the Prophets castigated Israel, cruelty was conspicuously absent. As the Prophets were stern and unbiased judges, it may be assumed that, since they did not upbraid Judah and Israel for cruelty perpetrated upon enemies, this sin was non-existant.

The Jewish attitude to the enemy is evident especially from the manner in which the memory of the Egyptian bondage has been kept alive. The sufferings endured in Egypt are cited as compelling ground for—showing love and kindness to the stranger! Moreover, Jewish literature expresses profound sympathy for the punishment visited upon the sinful Egyptians. Indeed, the penalty was inevitable. This, however, does not exempt one from pitying the sinners. According to the Rabbis, God Himself sorrowed when the Egyptians were drowned in the sea. The Passover ritual emphasizes the sorrow over the death of the Egyptians, side by side with the exultation in the redemption. The joyous "Hallel" prayer is not as often recited on Passover as on the Feast of Tabernacles, because the Egyptians died on Passover and it is commanded, "Do not rejoice when thine enemy falleth." For the same reason, the Jew flings drops of wine from his cup at the *Seder* recitation of the ten plagues, a symbolic tribute of sorrow to the Egyptians. They were punished in keeping with justice, but they are not denied the commiseration that is the sufferer's due. The God of Israel is not pleased at the destruction of the sinners. They, too, are his creatures—"and what artisan wants to see destroyed what he fashioned?"

The ability to forgive while not forgetting has had a beneficial influence upon Jewish survival. For a people that pities even its worst task-masters and enslavers could not become bitter and pessimistic as the reult of persecution.

Jewish law knows of no case that could set aside the sacrosanct commandment, "Thou shalt love thy neighbor as thyself." No matter how low our fellow man may sink and how atrocious his actions may be—he is and remains our fellow man and brother. Justice must and will take its course. The criminal must be punished. But the penalty must be inflicted humanely and the accused must be tried fairly and without undue humiliation. For although "he is a sinner, he is still your brother."

Until he is found guilty by a duly constituted court, the defendant is regarded as innocent. The utmost consideration must be shown to him and no one must lay hands on him. Ancient Israel, too, faced the problem of mob justice. Unlike the American South, however, the ancient Jews controlled the disgrace of mob justice by placing those who participated in a lynching under a murder charge. As a result, this shameful disgrace was stamped out completely.

Because the criminal, too, is "a brother," Jewish law prohibits any kind of torture for procuring a confession. Most countries abolished painful and degrading physical tortures only in the last century; even the Church saw no incongruity in reconciling "Christian love" with the horrible torture chambers of the Inquisition, where suspects were subjected to the kind of excruciating tortures which induced some of the bravest to sign "confessions of guilt."

Jewish law provides that mercy be not denied to *any* criminal. Even in the criminal condemned for a capital crime, the image of God must still be loved and respected. Lest the glory of God be degraded in His image, the court must choose an easy form of death for the criminal condemned to die. He must be executed on the very day sentence is pronounced, to spare him the fear of death which is worse than death itself. Lest there be a miscarriage of justice, Jewish law does not admit circumstantial evidence in capital cases and, moreover, requires the testimony of *two* eye witnesses whose integrity and honesty must be above suspicion. As all cases were tried before the supreme court of the Sanhedrin, the law which required the execution of the condemned on the day he was sentenced did not deprive him of a possible revision of the sentence, but only spared him anguish and suffering. Moreover, the judges remained in session until the execution to consider any last minute favorable evidence. Also, they fasted on the day a capital punishment was passed, as an expression of the sorrow that filled their hearts because of the necessity of returning a death verdict.

Proposals of sparing those sentenced to die the agony of walking "the last mile" have been greeted by veritable storms of protest in modern civilized countries. The advocates of euthanasia for criminals are decried as unworldly sentimentalists, the prevailing opinion being to let the murderer feel the full brunt of the penalty. Jewish public opinion, more than two thousand years ago, decided differently. Since Judaism conceived of punishment not as retribution but as reconciliation of violated justice and a protective measure of safety for society, it could well afford to let the sinner die painlessly. In Israel, where executions were extremely rare, it was the custom to give the criminal about to be executed a drink of wine with narcotic spices to stupefy and dull his senses. This last service of love to the condemned criminal was regarded as so sacred that "the pious women" vied for the privilege of mixing the cup of mercy.

Death penalties were not easily and readily passed by Jewish courts. In fact, some of the foremost Rabbis openly declared themselves opposed to capital punishment. Still, as long as Jewish courts had to judge capital cases, the death penalty remained the mandatory punishment for murder. Yet, a court that passed one death sentence in seven years was decried as "murderous." And Rabbi Eleazar the son of Azaryah did not hesitate to stigmatize thus a court that passed only one death sentence in seventy years.

There is no conceivable aspect of human relations which has not been ennobled, refined and spiritualized by the Jewish interpretation of fellow man. Now, more than ever, the world is in need of this concept of man as the only infinite and absolute value in the universe, next to and beside God.

CHAPTER 14

## *The Family*

### I

THE FAMILY as the Western world knows it is the creation of the Jews, who laid the foundations of family living—reciprocal love and respect between husband and wife and parents and children—in the remote past. While government agencies and church groups began to focus attention upon the family only recently, Judaism has always emphasized it as the basis of civilization and a powerful prop of Jewish survival.

Jewish ceremonial practice is inseparably bound up with the home and the family. The Sabbath and Jewish festivals are essentially family holidays. The *kiddush,* on the Sabbath and the holidays, the *zemiroth,* which grace the Sabbath meal with charm and festiveness, the *seder,* the *sukkah* and the Purim *seudah,* and many more ceremonies and rites require the setting of the traditional Jewish home, which thus becomes invested with sanctity and dignity.

The religious importance of the home has contributed much to developing and strengthening the family instinct of the Jew. To be sure, the pressure from the outside contributed to it as well. But the Jewish family instinct is more than a mere defense mechanism; it is, first and last, the proud fruit of the importance and value Judaism assigns to the family.

While other civilizations, not excepting our modern Western civilization, tended to deprecate the hum-drum routine and labor that go into the making of a home, Judaism has invariably exalted them. Even the men folk of the traditional Jewish community of yesterday considered it a privilege to assume some household chores in preparation for the Sabbath. The Talmud records that some Sages would stay away from the academy on Friday in order to busy themselves about the house and the kitchen. They would get the fires going, chop wood, take a turn at cooking the Sabbath dainties and make themselves generally useful about the house.

Medieval Jewish husbands, too, did certain household chores in honor of Sabbath, the bride. They would go marketing for the Sabbath delicacies, especially the Sabbath fish, and assist their wives in getting the house spic-and-span for the reception of Princess Sabbath.

The traditional Jewish home is altogether different from the typically modern home, a combination refueling station and dormitory. It fills not merely the physical wants of those under its roof, but also their religious, spiritual, intellectual, esthetic and emotional needs. The Benedictions before and after the meals, the study of the weekly Pentateuchal and Prophetic Portions in the family circle, the discussion of worth while themes at the table (according to a talmudic dictum, the table at which matters of the Torah are not discussed resembles an idolatrous altar), and the efforts of the parents to stimulate their children intellectually and guide them ethically and religiously, make the traditional Jewish home a shrine of sacred devotion and high spirituality.

"Modernism" and the prevalent discarding of traditional

patterns have also had a deleterious effect upon the Jewish family. Still, it has weathered the storm more successfully than the Christian family. "Friday night" remains even in families that have drifted from Jewish traditions and religious observances an "occasion."

The home has always been the sanctuary where the Jew found rest and succor from the harshness of a hostile world. Despised and shunted about in the street, his human dignity was restored to him when he crossed the threshold of his home. The affection the family circle has been a very important ingredient of the magic potion which has strengthened the Jew to survive.

All monotheistic faiths define the correlation of God and man in terms of the symbolism of the father-child relationship, under the influence of the Hebrew Bible which compares the God-Israel correlation to the mutual love of father and children, or to the love and affection of husband and wife. The fact that the Jewish genius conceived of the God-man relationship in these terms attests the unique dignity with which the family was invested.

Jewish literature proves this even more compellingly. Of special interest in this connection are the last wills and testaments of Medieval Jews who invariably devoted considerable space to impressing their heirs with the importance of family loyalty. Rather typical is the will of Rabbi Elijah De Veali (18th century), who admonished his children as follows:

"Be eager to honor your mother, in heart, in speech and in deed ... Furthermore, I ask of you to live together in love, brotherliness and friendship. For it is goodly and lovely when you live together as one, with peace within your walls, and prosperity within your houses ... And as for you, O husbands, I say to you: Honor your wives; and let the wives do full honor to their husbands... Be faithful shepherds of your flocks, watching your offspring, regarding their doings, wisely leading them to graze in the garden of the Lord... And as for you, your conduct should be a light to their paths."

In a similar vein the Gaon Elijah of Vilna wrote:

"I beg my wife to honor my mother in accordance with the precept of the Torah, especially as she is a widow... And I beg my mother to live peacefully with my wife, each bringing happiness to the other by kindliness, for this is a great commandment and incumbent on all mankind. And man is asked in the hour of judgment: 'Were you kind towards your fellow men?' The Torah, in large measure, strives to make man happy. Let there be no dissension of any kind among the members of my family, men and women, but let love and brotherliness reign. In case of offense, forgive each other, and live for God's sake in peace. I also ask my mother that she teach my sons and daughters in gentle terms, so that they may accept them."

## II

The importance and dignity with which Judaism invests the home had a favorable effect upon the status of woman, the home-maker.

The comparative study of the legal and social position of woman in the ancient Near East and in ancient Israel shows that the Hebrew woman enjoyed the highest legal and social advantages, while her sisters elsewhere were oppressed, exploited and degraded. Although Judaism assigns to woman a sphere different from man's—in keeping with the biological and psychological differences of the sexes—authoritative Jewish voices have invariably stressed that in the scales of human values woman is not found to be inferior to man. Indeed, there are some quips at the expense of woman in talmudic and rabbinic literature. On the whole, however, the Rabbis professed respect and veneration for womanhood.

Jewish literature contains no such devastating and unqualified condemnations of woman as Greek literature, or such crude deprecations of her human dignity as Schopenhauer uttered. To Jews woman has always seemed to be God's good gift to man (complaints about the obnoxious traits of the shrew are not missing!). She is the crown of Adam, as it were, for without her he was sadly incomplete.

In many respects Judaism is considerably kinder to woman than Western civilization. Unlike the French, who would burden woman with the responsibility for all troubles, (*cherchez la femme*) the Jews emphasize woman's beneficent influence. "All depends upon the woman" (*ha-kol min ha-ishah*), that is to say, woman's formative influence determines her husband's conduct; a sinner is metamorphosed into a righteous man, thanks to a pious wife—on the other hand, a pious man may easily be misled by an impious women.

Jews regard marriage both as a spiritual and a physical union, an attitude which flows from the respect for woman's *human* worth. Although Jewish law discriminates against women in some legal matters, it gives them absolute equality in the human sphere. If the Rabbis exempted women from the religious duties which must be observed at definite times, it was not discrimination but rather a tribute of respect to their family obligations. Because the duties of the mother cannot be synchronized with the religious obligation to attend services at definite times, woman's exemption from this, and other religious duties to be discharged punctually at a definite time, is a concession to her primary obligations as wife and mother.

Although Judaism exempts woman from the duty of *inten-*

*sive* Torah study, i.e., the study of the Oral Law in all its multifarious talmudic and rabbinic ramifications, it expects women to be conversant with the Bible and the popular realms of Jewish knowledge. Girls should be instructed in all Jewish disciplines which bear on life and popular culture. The Jewish educational program for women was rather aptly summed up by the "Book of the Pious" (13th cent.): "They must be instructed in the teachings of our faith and be taught what goes into pious conduct." While the schooling of the boys was geared to developing the logical and reasoning faculties, the training of the girls aimed at molding the character in accordance with Jewish ethical ideals.

The Sages held that man excels by his reasoning powers, while woman is endowed with keener native intelligence and intuition. "The Holy One, blessed be He, gave to woman more understanding than to man," and "a woman is quicker than a man in recognizing the character of guests," are two talmudic statements which prove that the early Rabbis were far from making light of feminine qualities.

Nor were the Sages blind to woman's foibles. They good-naturedly ribbed some females' loquaciousness and curiosity and viewed somewhat bewildered woman's love of cosmetics and jewelry (yet they made it obligatory for husbands to supply their wives with them). A few Rabbis even judged women as "flighty-minded".... By and large, however, Jewish literature reflects respect and veneration of woman.

Jewish women scholars were rare in the traditional Jewish community, although its women were far from illiterate. The fact that the complex dietary laws are entrusted to the women necessitates that they be sufficiently well informed to observe them properly. Moreover, the place of honor the mother holds in the Jewish family makes it imperative that she be well versed in the religious and ethical teachings of Judaism.

Traditional Jews regard Torah study as the choicest and most meritorious endeavor. As a result, sons have always seemed a greater blessing to Jewish parents than daughters. Economic considerations, too, may have influenced this predilection, to say nothing of the imponderables that make even some progressive moderns wish for male children. The Sages were divided in their opinions on the blessing of daughters. While some held that it was better to have only sons, others thought that a family is incomplete without a daughter. Most parents, however, preferred sons, the prevailing opinion being that boys were less of a worry than girls. "A daughter," the Sages quoted Ben Sirah, "is a vain treasure to her father. Worry on her account gives him sleepless nights. When she is small he worries lest she be seduced; when she is a young girl lest she conduct herself in an unbefitting manner; later, lest she remain unmarried; when she is married, lest she be barren, and when she grows old, lest she become addicted to witchcraft." Others held "a boy is born with a loaf of bread while a girl arrives empty-handed," meaning that a man can look after himself better than a woman. The prevailing opinion was that, while women are as indispensible as men, "happy is he who has sons and woe to him who has daughters."

The preference for male children is not least due to the desire to leave behind a son to carry on the family name and to recite *kaddish* for the parents. This does not mean, however, that Jews are not fond of their daughters. With the ancient Greeks and Romans it was a common practice to abandon unwanted children, especially girls. Such instances of cruelty were unknown among Jews. Jewish parents may pray for a son, but when the newborn is a girl, she is showered with the same love and affection that would have been given to a boy.

Even cultured Greeks held that "Zeus who thunders on high made women to be an evil to mortal men, with a nature to do evil." This opinion was the logical result of the negative Greek attitude to marriage. The Greeks regarded wedlock as little more than a necessary evil for the propagation of the race. Love, affection and friendship they sought not at the side of their wives and children but in the company of the heterae and their drinking companions. Hesiod therefore saw the only purpose of marriage in providing for one's old age, for "whoever avoids marriage and the sorrows that women cause and will not wed, reaches deadly old age without anyone to tend his years."

In contradistinction, Jewish literature sings the praises of marriage. The greatest blessing of man is a loving, virtuous wife of the type of the "Woman of Valor" glorified in Proverbs. "Her value is far above rubies. . . . Her children rise up and call her blessed; her husband also and he praises her: 'Many daughters have done valiantly, but you have excelled them all.'" A people that pays such tribute to the wife obviously cannot despise women. If, especially among Eastern European Jewry, there was a certain disdain for women abroad, it was not the result of Jewish teachings but the fruit of assimilation to alien standards.

According to a rabbinic opinion, neither man alone nor woman alone is a "human being," for only when they are joined in marriage do incomplete man and incomplete woman add up to a "human being." This statement perfectly sums up Judaism's high esteem for marriage. "It is not good for man to live alone." He needs a companion to share his joys and sorrows and "therefore shall a man leave his father and his mother and shall cleave unto his wife, and they shall be one flesh."

## III

To the Jew marriage is, first and last, a sacred union. The Hebrew term for marriage *Kiddushin* (literally, "sanctification") well expresses what Judaism intends the marital union to be: sacred self-fulfillment. Only in marriage can man and woman fully realize themselves. "The unmarried lives without joy, without blessing and without goodness." The Sages knew that "a woman finds peace of mind only in her husband's house" and that "even more than the man wants to marry, the woman desires to be taken to wife."

Judaism acclaims marriage joyously. It is far from the ascetic pessimism exemplified by the New Testament, which considers marriage as a concession to the weakness of the flesh.

Judaism accepts "the physical Adam" with glad optimism. It sees nothing disgraceful in the physical union of man and woman. On the contrary, it recognizes its ethical and esthetic possibilities—besides its procreative potential. The fact that the Rabbis interpreted "Song of Songs" as a symbolism of the mutual attachment of Israel and God attests their profound esteem of sensuous love. The Sages symbolically conceived of God's love for Israel as the intoxication of a youth with the charms of his beloved, and of Israel's attachment to God as the passionate longing of the betrothed for her promised one. The ancient Rabbis were not embarrassed by "sex," otherwise they could not have employed its reality as a symbolism for the God-Israel relationship. Here, too, the Sages were on thoroughly established ground, for the Prophets already defined the bond uniting God and Israel as "betrothal" and "marriage."

The medieval Kabbalists further embellished this symbolism. Yet, their almost shockingly sensuous descriptions of Israel's love for God, elevated the physical love relationship, from whose realities these symbolisms were derived, rather than degrading the idea concretized by the images.

Judaism, with common sense realism, advocates early marriage. Eighteen is considered the right age for a man to assume family obligations; a girl should be married upon reaching maturity. As these maxims originated in the East, where maturity is attained considerably earlier than in the temperate zone, the Rabbis did not really advocate "child marriages." To be sure, there were a few zealous supporters of very early marriage, as Rabbi Hisda, for instance, who ascribed his intellectual proficiency to the fact that he was married at sixteen. By and large, however, the rule of "at eighteen to the *Huppah*" was followed.

The Rabbis of the Talmud and traditional Jews of yesterday looked askance at those who hesitated too long before getting married. Rabbi Huna held that he who was not married at twenty would be sinful all his life. When a famous young scholar, Rabbi Hamamuna, called on him, he dismissed him angrily upon learning that he was unmarried, saying: "Don't visit me again until you have taken a wife." Bachelors were regarded with misgivings and constituted an almost unknown species. Among the Sages of the Talmud only one seems to have been an avowed bachelor and this because he feared lest family obligations interfere with his studies.

The bachelor had no social standing in the traditional Jewish community. He was barred from all synagogue honors and offices and was "discriminated" against to the extent that, as late as the middle of the 18th century, Rabbi Jonathan Eibeschutz refused the full ordination as a rabbi to the then still unmarried Moses Mendelssohn as "it is against the prevalent custom to confer the title of *Morenu* (our teacher) upon a bachelor."

So as to enable young people to get married, the Jewish community of yesterday boasted numerous societies for dowering poor brides. Young and indigent couples were provided with furniture, linen, pots, and pans—besides cash to give them a start. Jews never regarded poverty as a reason for staying single, nor was it considered humiliating to accept a communal marriage subsidy when one's own family was poor. The prevalent custom of early marriage made it imperative for parents, or for the community, to contribute to the young couples' support during the first years of marriage, while the husband was trying to get established.

The Jews of yesterday did not approve of postponing marriage because of financial reasons. They also were averse to older men marrying young girls. The Jewish teachers disapproved of marked differences in the ages of husband and wife. Some did not hesitate to denounce unions of unlike partners as "harlotry," and lest young girls be deceived as to the age of their suitors, they declared that "it is highly objectionable when older men dye their gray hair black to deceive young girls as to their years."

Although Judaism regards the marriage bond as inviolably sacred, it does not prohibit divorce; nor does it place insurmountable obstacles in the path of those who are unhappily married. To be sure, "God's altar sheds tears when a man divorces the wife of his youth," still, divorce is a *necessary* evil. Alert to the inevitability of divorce in certain cases, the Rabbis assigned a whole section of the Talmud to the legal and religious problems of the dissolution of unhappy marriages.

While most modern countries do not recognize incompatibility as a ground for divorce, Jewish law accepts it unflinchingly. This does not imply, however, that rabbinical courts issue divorces readily and lightly. While there is no legal hindrance to divorce when both husband and wife wish to dissolve the union, the Rabbi will endeavor to effect a reconciliation.

Jewish law carefully protects the wife's interests if the husband seeks a divorce for selfish reasons of his own. The Rabbis knew that divorce is preferable to marital discord and therefore counselled," if you hate her, divorce her." This, however, does not change the fact that he who divorces his wife is "hated." Judaism does not countenance irresponsible divorce, although it places no insurmountable obstacles in the path of couples desiring to be free.

The medieval Responsa, the legal writs and opinions of eminent Rabbis, also contain numerous case histories of divorces. Although the Rabbinical judges and the witnesses were men, the women got a remarkably fair deal. Male solidarity did not prejudice the Rabbis sitting on divorce cases. If anything, they favored the women, sympathizing with their plight. As an example we might quote an opinion handed down by the illustrious Rashi, who gave a wayward husband this calling down:

"That man is conducting himself unbefittingly and has shown that he is not acting like one of our father Abraham's children whose nature it is to be kind to his fellow man, and particularly so to his own flesh with whom he has entered the covenant of marriage. If that husband had set his mind on keeping his wife as much as he concentrated on getting rid of her, her charm would have grown on him. Behold our Rabbis have said, 'Every spot has a charm for those who live in it,' even though it may be cursed with bad water and barren land.

Similar is the charm exerted by a woman on her husband, and happy the man who has been fortunate enough to get such a wife and to acquire through her a share in life eternal. Even among those who deny God we find many who do not reject their wives and whose wives in turn act in like manner toward them, for they believe that the good they do serves as an expiatory sacrifice for the sins they have committed. But this fellow, though a member of the household of our Father in heaven, has acted cruelly toward the wife of his youth, as God himself can testify.

"According to the law of right it is incumbent upon him to treat her as custom prescribes for all Jewish women; and if he does not care to receive her back in kindness and in respect, then he must divorce her and pay the entire amount stipulated in her marriage contract."

Adultery was rarely appealed to as a ground for divorce in the Jewish community of yesterday. According to Saadia Gaon, "reason cannot permit sexual promiscuity which reduces man to the animal level." Thanks to this conviction, Judaism does not countenance a double standard of sexual morality. Chastity is expected of the man no less than of the woman. The flirtatious male "who counts money into a woman's hand to gaze at her" will not escape Gehinom, according to the Rabbis, for an adulterer is not only he who sins with his body, but also he who sins with his eyes.

Although Jewish law did not proscribe polygamy until the 10th century, monogamy was the norm already in biblical days. Although polygamy was legally permissible, the Sages held that one wife is man's allotted portion—otherwise God would have created more than one Eve for Adam.

Except for royalty, polygamy was considered proper only as a solution to a vexing problem. Thus when a wife was barren, it was considered preferable, at least in biblical times, to permit the husband to take a second wife, in addition to the childless woman, rather than divorcing her. The same solution was applied in cases where the wife had become permanently incapacitated or incompetent. On the other hand, however, talmudic law provides for the dissolution of marriages which have remained without issue after ten years.

The negative Jewish attitude to polygamy, a thousand years before it was legally abolished, is illustrated by the talmudic story of Rabbi Judah Hanasi's son's marriage. After his wedding, the young man left home to study in various academies. Upon his return, after an absence of twelve years, his wife had become barren. Said Rabbi Judah: "What shall we do? If you divorce her, people will say, 'This poor woman's faithfulness was futile.' If you will take another wife, in addition to her, people will say, 'This one is his wife and that one his harlot.' " The solution was prayer on behalf of the barren wife with the desired results. This story attests that, already in the second century (C.E.), monogamy was taken for granted.

## IV

The Sages, keen students of life as well as of the *Torah*, had a wholesome outlook on human relations. They knew what goes into the making of a happy marriage. While latter day Jews tended to minimize the element of love in favor of security, the Sages emphasized that love is the primary requisite for marital happiness. The Sages disapproved of marriages of convenience and threatened that "he who marries a woman for her money will have disreputable children."

The manner in which many Jews of yesterday married off their children in their early teens, and not infrequently without the young husband and his child bride having met before the wedding, was contrary to the spirit of Judaism. Indeed, there were good reasons why Jewish parents were anxious to see their children married, such as the all-pervading sense of Jewish insecurity resulting from incessant pogroms and expulsions. Then there was the influence of the mystical teachings of the Kabbala. It was believed that the Messiah could only appear after all souls destined to come to life had been born. And so, to speed the advent of the Messiah and the redemption, Jewish parents saw to it that their children married young.

Modern students of marriage who stress the importance of the sex factor only echo identical opinions of the Rabbis of yore. With perfect frankness and candid delicacy the Sages discussed the most intimate aspects of marriage. They emphasized the importance of the love play and admonished the husband to woo his wife. In the summary of Maimonides: "The sexual union should be consummated only out of desire and as the result of the joy of the husband and wife." In another context Maimonides writes, "He must not approach her when he thinks of another woman—and certainly not when he is under the influence of alcohol or while they are quarrelling and hatred divides them. He must not approach her against her will, or force her to submit to him out of fear."

Psychologists and physicians know that many marriages suffer ship-wreck as the result of inauspicious beginnings. Blundering young husbands and timid, fearful brides not seldom create situations where the first union is rape rather than joyful fulfillment. The Sages, aware of this pitfall, interpreted the words of "Song of Songs, "*Let my beloved come into his garden* as a lesson teaching the bridegroom patient gentleness;

he should not enter the marriage chamber until the bride consents.

As a happy marriage is the achievement of both partners, there are not lacking either admonitions addressed to the wife. Rather characteristic is the exhortation which the 17th century author of the ethical guide *Lev Tov* ( A Good Heart), addressed to the women of Israel:

"My dear daughter, when your husband is cross, don't you be jolly; and when he is jolly, don't you be cross. When he is angry, smile at him and answer him with kind, soft words and speak pleasantly to him.... Find out what he likes to eat.... Try to have his meals ready on time, for hunger does nobody any good. When he comes home and doesn't find his meal ready on time, he'll get angry.... When he sleeps, guard his sleep lest he be disturbed, for if he doesn't get a good night's rest he may become very angry.... Don't be anxious to know his secrets.... Find out whom he likes and like that person, too, and him whom he dislikes, you dislike too. Don't like his enemies, and don't hate his friends.... Don't oppose him. Do everything he tells you.... Don't expect of him anything that he considers difficult. He may take a dislike to you because you expect something of him which he believes is too hard.... Heed the requests which he may make of you, expecting that he will love you if you do so, and will be your slave and will serve you with joy.... If you treat him like a king then he will treat you like a queen."

The husband is expected to contribute an equal share to marital happiness. He is commanded to honor, love and respect his wife "for whatever blessing enters the house is due to the wife." He must be careful not to hurt her feelings, for woman is sensitive and "her tears flow easily." He should make allowances for her shortcomings and, of course, he must liberally provide for her.

Throughout the ages the Jewish wife has enjoyed a position of singular honor and respect. Even in the "dark ages" the savage practice of wife-beating was unknown among Jews. As Rabbi Meir of Rothenberg (13th cent.) put it: "Jews do not beat their wives, as it is the prevalent custom of our time." If Jewish moralists dispensed advice to women on how to please their husbands, they did no less impress upon "the lords of creation" what was expected of them. Thus the famous scholar, Rabbi Judah Ibn Tibbon, bequeathed this "will" to his son, Samuel: "I command you to honor your wife to your utmost capability ... treat her with consideration and respect. To act otherwise is the way of the contemptible."

Jews are proverbially fond and loving parents because they look upon children as the crown and fulfilment of life's purpose. "He who has no son is dead and cut-off," but "he who leaves a son after him studying the Torah is as if he had never died." As Judaism sees it, the purpose of life is, first of all, procreation, for if there are no children to assume the heritage, "on whom shall the Divine Presence rest, perchance on the trees, or on the stones?" And so God Himself "hates" those who die without issue.

Judaism extols propagation as a sacred religious duty, for "he who does not beget children diminishes the Divine likeness" in which man is created. While some Rabbis held that at least two children, a boy and a girl, are required to fulfill the commandment "be fruitful," others maintained that the minimum is two boys and two girls.

Rabbinic literature anticipated modern psychology by some two millennia in the discovery that babies are human beings and entitled to respectful ministration to all their needs, even as "a kings, high priests, and scholars are." The Sages also were thoroughly modern in stressing that education end environment are of greater importance than heredity. And they also knew the pathos implicit in the fact that "a father's love goes out to his children, and his children's love to their children." This natural displacement, however, is no exemption from the duty of honoring parents. The Talmud extols the great Sages who in honoring their parents went beyond the letter of the law. Rabbi Tarphon, for instance, who would serve as a footstool for his mother, and who, on one occasion when her shoe had slipped off her foot on the Sabbath in the courtyard, spread his hands under her feet. Yet, when his mother related these examples of filial devotion to her son's colleagues, they remarked: "Even if he had done a thousand times more, he would still not have fulfilled half of the commandment to honor one's parents." There are few complaints about ingrate children in Jewish literature.

The humane civilization of Judaism, which demands not merely "charity" but love and sacrifice for the downtrodden and the poor, leaves no room for disrespect toward parents. In ancient Greece and Rome unwanted newborn children and aged parents frequently shared the identical fate: they were abandoned to perish. The record of Judaism is clean in this respect, too.

It is no accident that the idea of fellow man originated and flowered in Israel. It is the natural concomitant of the Jewish family ideal. At first, this ideal encompassed blood relatives only. Then, however, the circle was enlarged to take in all those created in the image of God.

Jewish family life and ideals have cemented Jewish survival on the physical and the spiritual plane. The high standards of Jewish sexual morality, marital fidelity and child care have sustained our physical vigor and survival power, while the idealism nurtured in the family was carried over, first, to the national sphere and, then, to the realm of humanity at large.

Jewish family life underwent many changes in the era of emancipation and assimilation. Unfortunately, they have not been advantageous. The loosening of family ties and loyalties, in approximation to "modern standards," have immeasurably contributed to undermining Jewish survival strength. A return to traditional Jewish patterns of family life would greatly contribute to secure the Jewish future, for physical and spiritual Jewish survival stamina is anchored in the home.

CHAPTER 15

*The Paths of Piety*

I

THE DUTY of uncompromising and unwavering truthfulness is to the Jew the logical conclusion of the belief in the Only God of Truth. Jewish ethics is, first and last, *imitato dei*—the effort of emulating the ethical perfection of the God of Truth, Who hates any form of untruth and deceit.

Jewish law commands truthfulness with stern insistence. "Keep thee far from a false matter," for only those may dwell on God's holy mountain who "walk uprightly, and work righteousness, and speak the truth." God hates "a lying tongue" and will not brook the perversion of untruth. Although He is the Creator of everything in existence, He has not created lies. "Men have invented them out of their own hearts." God will have no traffic with liars, for untruth and deceit add up to denial of the Divine. The Sages feared the lie more than actual deception and fraud. They held, that "sinning with words is more reprehensible than sinning in money matters," because a lie corrupts the soul even more than a dishonest deed, as it affects the very core of the personality. Moreover, for damages resulting from fraud amends are possible; but there can be no reparations for the harm a man does to himself and to his fellows by lying.

The psychological acumen that made the Sages declare that lying is worse than fraudulent actions also enabled them to recognize that "the sinful thought is worse than the sin." Impure thoughts despoil man's choicest faculty, the ability of attaching himself to the eternal verities by means of his intellect. The extension of the imperative of integrity to the sphere of the "unsaid" attests the keenness of Jewish ethical perception.

The practical ethics of Judaism is intensely concerned with inculcating love of truth and hatred of untruth. The early and latter day Rabbis and teachers delighted in homilies about pietists whose integrity soared high. A delightful talmudic tale glorifies Rabbi Safra's honesty. This Sage once had an article for sale and it so happened that a buyer presented himself as he was reciting the *Shema*. As it is forbidden to interrupt one's prayer for the sake of business, Rabbi Safra did not reply when the prospective buyer offered him a price for his goods. The man, interpreting the Rabbi's silence as a refusal to sell at the offered price, raised his bid. When the Rabbi was done with his prayers, he turned to the buyer. "You may have it at the price you first offered, as this is what I intended to sell it for."

This kind of integrity was the fruit of the teaching that justice, truth and peace are the foundations of the world. As the Rabbis, saw it, the three are really one because they are interdependent, for "where truth reigns, peace is established—and where justice is done, peace and truth are practiced." Truth is the foundation, the core and the ultimate purpose of the world. The Rabbis deduced this from the Hebrew word for truth—*emeth*—whose three letters are the first, the middle and the last letters, respectively, of the Hebrew alphabet. Truth, however is more than an ethical imperative; it is also a requirement of logic. According to Saadia Gaon, "reason obligates us to speak the truth and abstain from lying."

Judaism is meticulously scrupulous in defining what constitutes a deviation from integrity. Even the slightest semblance of untruth is outlawed. Here belongs, first of all, what is termed "the stealing of the mind," by which the Rabbis meant attempts of creating impressions not warranted by the facts. Thus, for instance, "stealing of the mind" is committed when one quotes "a good interpretation or a word of wisdom" without acknowledging its source, for thus one leads people to believe that this wisdom is one's own. Other cases of "stealing of the mind" are the extension of invitations, which, one knows, will not be accepted, making one's guest believe that special efforts are made in his honor, when they are, in fact, part of the usual household routine. Although the truth may hurt, it is preferable to "stealing of the mind." Thus, if one is asked for a loan one does not wish to grant, one should state the truth rather than resort to an excuse.

The rigid standards of truthfulness may be relaxed in only one instance: to preserve and promote peace, especially between husband and wife. As the Bible represents God as withholding from Abraham Sarah's rather unflattering references to his senility, the Sages concluded that man, too, may gloss over an unpleasant truth. Thus while the Shammaites felt misgivings concerning exclaiming the traditional praise of the bride, "O, beautiful and pious bride!" when a girl's homeliness belied that tribute, the Hillelites asserted charitably that all brides are beautiful and that, at any rate, it would disturb the peace of the family were the acclamation of bridal loveliness be withheld from a homely bride. It redounds to the credit of the

Rabbis' humane chivalry that the Hillelites won in this controversy.

In certain exceptional cases the true facts may be glossed over for the sake of the happiness and peace of others. One must not, however, do so for one's own benefit. This unique "double standard" is rather quaintly stressed in the talmudic account of the famous Rab's marital troubles. The eminent Sage was married to a shrew who invariably would act contrary to his requests. If he wanted lentils, she cooked peas, and if he asked for peas she served him lentils. When their son reached the age of discretion, matters changed for the better and Rab would find the table set as requested. Delighted, he told his son: "Your mother is certainly improving." To which the boy replied with his tongue in the cheek: "Not at all—I always reverse your requests when giving mother your messages." Rab's first impulse was sheer delight, and he exclaimed: "That is what people mean by saying that your son will teach you wisdom!" On second thought, however, he asked his son to abandon this strategy as it implied "teaching one's tongue to speak lies."

According to Jewish conviction, half-truths and "white lies" are to be shunned no less than patent untruths. For while the brazen lie is readily detected, half-truths may easily pass undiscovered. The hyprocrite, whose mouth does not speak what is in his heart, is decried with special vehemence in Jewish ethical literature. To the Rabbis the hyprocrite is "the chieftain of the thieves" and they compared him to the pig, ritual uncleanliness incarnate. For when the pig lies down, it stretches out its feet (the pig is cloven-footed, which is one mark of the ritually clean animal), as if to say, "Look, I am of the clean animals," thus trying to hide its marks of ritual uncleanliness. The hyprocrite acts likewise when putting his best foot forward. The Sages therefore demanded: "Act at home as in public." Also, "let your mouth speak what is in your heart," for God hates him whose words do not harmonize with his thoughts.

Flattery was one form of hypocrisy which Jewish teachers attacked relentlessly. They held that the Divine Presence shuns the flatterers no less than the liars, for as the result of flattery "the judgments became crooked and men's actions corrupted." A community that abets flattery "will ultimately be exiled." Rabbi Eleazar held that the sycophant "brings wrath upon the world and his prayer is not heard.... Even the unborn in their mothers' wombs curse the insincere flatterer." The Jewish aversion to obsequious blandishment is also strongly motivated by fear lest flattery obstruct justice by procuring undeserved favors and advantages for the sycophant.

The acute ethical sensibility which made the Rabbis brand the lie as more dangerous than the sinful deed, also induced them to denounce slander more determinedly than more tangible offenses. The Torah outlaws slander unequivocally: "Thou shalt not go up and down among your people as a talebearer." And the Psalmist threatens, "Whoso slandereth his neighbor in secret, him will I destroy."

The Rabbis likened the habitual slanderers to those who deny God, and who are therefore shunned by the Divine Presence. The Sages had nothing but contempt for the slanderer. "He deserves to be stoned," they declared. "He should be thrown to the dogs—he has no share in the world-to-come." Some Sages held that the sin of slander equals the sum total of the heinous crimes of idolatry, incest and murder. Other representative rabbinic opinions are that the Israelites' transgressions in the wilderness went unpunished, except for the sin of slander which is "the source of all afflictions." Even

Divine mercy does not avail against calumny. "I can save you from all afflictions," God is said to address Himself to men, "except from calumny. Guard yourself, therefore, and you will not come to harm."

Jewish teachers insistently stressed that slander is a triple-edged sword; it injures the slanderer, the one who listens to him and the defamed person. Calumny not infrequently proves more fatal than the mailed first. "The hand does kill and so does the tongue." If anything, the evil tongue is more dangerous. A popular talmudic adage has it that "slander uttered in Rome will slay in Syria." Jewish folklore likens the slanderer to the serpent that kills for sport and not because of hunger. When the serpent is asked why it bites when it does not devour its kill, it replies: "And what profit has the slanderer from his calumny?" As keen realists the Sages knew that for many people there is no more tempting enjoyment than gossiping about all and sundry. Jewish ethics therefore demands that one abstain from discussing personalities. One should not even praise one's friend "lest from talking about his qualities one be led to mention his faults," which is but one step short of calumny.

## II

The malevolent fiction that Jews do not respect the sanctity of the oath precipitated the institution of the degrading "Jew Oath," which was administered in most countries well into the 19th century, despite the fact that Jewish tradition surrounds the oath with an aura of inviolability. The third commandment, "Thou shalt not take the name of the Lord thy God in vain" has been universally respected by Jews throughout the ages, who regarded perjury as a "desecration of God's

Name and the perjurer in the same class with the idol worshipper."

The regard for the sacredness of the oath makes traditional Jews most reluctant to swear, in keeping with the Sages' admonition that "taking the name of the Lord thy God in vain does not only refer to perjury but also to the unnecessary oath." Jewish courts refrain from making witnesses swear, for unless life is at stake, "it is improper to swear, even to affirm the truth." The Shulchan Aruch therefore ordains: "One should abstain from swearing, even for the truth." He who swears lightly is like the perjurer and classed with the idolater. The respect for truth must be such that yes or no is an oath.

As far as the oath of the witness is concerned, it is fraught with speical sacredness, for perjury in court involves the violation of two of the Ten commandments.

Although everyone is obliged to serve as a witness, regardless of whether his testimony is favorable or not, Jewish law disqualifies from giving testimony those who do not lead exemplary lives. Thus gamblers and money lenders cannot qualify as witnesses. Also, "he who is suspected of dishonesty in money matters is to be suspected of being ready to commit perjury."

As the Jew sees it, any violation of the principles of ethics implies religious sacrilege—*Hillul Ha-Shem,* Profanation of the Divine Name. Perjury is an especially obnoxious form of *Hillul Ha-Shem,* for, "if you bear false witness against your neighbor, I (God) regard it as if you deny that I created the world."

The Day of Atonement, the most sacred day of the Jewish year, is ushered in with the chanting of the *Kol Nidre* prayer, which petitions for Divine absolution for hasty and rash vows in the religious sphere. Although *Kol Nidre* refers only to vows of a strictly personal religious nature, this prayer has been denounced as a stratagem of unscrupulousness. The text of this prayer, however, as well as the general Jewish attitude to oaths and promises, prove that this charge is unwarranted. The relevant texts insistently stress that repentance and prayer on the Day of Atonement cannot procure forgiveness for sins against fellow men but only for ritual lapses. Ethical transgressions are only forgiven if the offender conciliates and indemnifies those he has wronged. The vows for which remission is asked in the *Kol Nidre* prayer are such "important vows" as the following which are listed in the Talmud: "He who says I shall rise early and study this chapter of that section, has uttered an important vow. If he fails to rise as early as he pledged, he may ask for Divine forgiveness in the hope of being heard, as this vow does not affect another human being. If, however, he vowed to donate a certain sum to charity, or to assist a friend in a certain matter, there is no Divine forgiveness for his failure to keep his promise, except by indemnifying those he injured by not fulfilling his vow."

A promise or a vow in the human sphere is binding, regardless of whether it is pledged to a Jew or a non-Jew, or even to a minor. "A promise given to a child or a non-Jew cannot be broken, except with the consent of the one to whom it was given." The Jewish regard for truth is such that the Rabbis even warned against giving "idle promises to children, lest one accustom them to untruth."

The sacredness of the promisory pledge is in the same class with the sanctity of the oath. As a result, Jews are reluctant to make definite commitments lest "the habit of vowing leads to disrespect for the sacredness of the oath." Jews are in the habit of adding the words *belee neder*—"this does not imply a vow"—to a promise, not to detract from its obligation, but to stress that if for any reason beyond one's control, sickness for instance, one would be unable to keep it, the omission should not be counted as a violation of the vow.

This type of high integrity is also binding for the Jew in all business dealings. The Bible commands: "If thou sell aught unto thy neighbor, or buy of thy neighbor's hand, ye shall not wrong one another." Further, "Thou shalt not have in thy bag diverse weights, a great and a small. Thou shalt not have in thy house diverse measures, a great and a small. A perfect and just weight shalt thou have; a perfect and just measure shalt thou have..."

Talmudic law implemented these biblical precepts. Thus the Sages ordained that a grain merchant must wipe his measures at least once a month, lest, unwittingly, he give a false measure. Such scrupulousness is absolutely necessary, as the penalty for cheating on weight or measure is severer than the punishment for unchastity. Integrity is of supreme import: "In the hour when man must render account for his life on earth, he is asked: 'Were you honest in your business dealings?'"

The Sages considered cheating on measure and weight a more heinous sin than stealing. They argued: "Restitution is possible for theft but not for losses due to false weights or measures... It is impossible to ascertain who has been defrauded and the total amount involved."

As Judaism sees it, cheating is a capital crime. According to Rabbi Yohanan, "he who defrauds his fellow of a penny's worth is as if he had taken his life." Moreover, dishonesty on the part of a Jew implies his denial of Israel's peoplehood. For he who is honest when measuring and weighing "accepts the fact of the Exodus, while he who is dishonest denies it."

Judaism has invariably insisted that ritual piety does not

atone for lapses of integrity. "Cheating a human being is a graver sin than defrauding the Sanctuary." The Jewish definition of fraud is exceedingly exacting. Even an attempt of making one's merchandise more attractive than its quality warrants is classed as deception. Thus it is prohibited to revamp used goods and sell them as new. It is forbidden to mix or adulterate foods and merchandise and sell them under a false label. Judaism early enacted pure food laws and regulations of fair business practice and its has insisted on these high standards throughout the ages.

Integrity in business is the acid test of ritual piety, as Judaism sees it. "Piety is proved by honesty in money matters," declared a 17th century moralist. "He who is truly pious does not lust after ill-gotten gain, nor does he act deceitfully." Judaism demands this type of integrity both in relations with Jews and non-Jews. Moreover, defrauding a non-Jew is regarded as even more reprehensible than cheating a Jew, as if reflects unfavorably on the honor of Judaism. Jews know of no double standard in business. The anti-Semitic canard that Judaism sanctions the betrayal of non-Jews is a malicious lie. All Jewish authorities, ancient, medieval and modern, stress that when dealing with non-Jews the Jew must, if anything, be more scrupulous than when doing business with Jews, as only thus the Gentiles can be brought to respect Judaism. "Take heed to be as sincere with non-Jews as with Jews," the "Book of the Pious" admonishes. "It is better to live on charity than to abscond with money that is not yours, to the disgrace of the Jewish faith and name. If a non-Jew seeks your advice, tell him where he will find a reliable man and not one who will deceive him in the place whither he journeys. If you see a stranger of another religion about to commit a sin, prevent it if you can, and let the Prophet Jonah be your model. If a murderer seeks sanctuary with you, do not shield him even though he be a Jew; if one weighed down by a heavy burden meets you on a narrow and difficult path, make way for him, even though he be a non-Jew."

The Jewish categorical imperative of integrity also extends to the civic realm. Taxes must be scrupulously calculated and promptly paid, for, according to Maimonides, "cheating the government of taxes is robbery." The Talmud places tax-fraud in the same class with murder, idolatry, unchastity and the violation of the Sabbath.

The Jew's conduct must be exemplary in every respect. The "Book of the Pious" demands: "Deceive no one, be he Jew or non-Jew. Do not argue and quarrel with people, regardless of what religion they confess. Be honest in business. Do not say that a certain price has been offered for your merchandise when it is not so, and do not pretend to be unwilling to sell when you are. Such conduct is unbefitting a Jew.... If a contract is concluded between Jews and non-Jews, mutually binding, the former must live up to it even if the latter do not.... No one must be wronged, whether he belong to our religion or to another."

The "Book of the Pious" also warns against repaying evil with evil and cheating the swindler out of his ill-gotten gain. "Trust in God," Rabbi Judah the Pious counsels. "He will protect you. If some one has cheated you by false weights, robbed you, or testified falsely against you, be not so misguided as to exact revenge in kind."

CHAPTER 16

## *The Future to Come*

### I

THE QUEST for life eternal may not be man's dominating drive, but it is certainly his most agonizing hope; for the fear of death is his most painful anguish. This is why primitive men practiced witchcraft and magic while, on higher levels of culture, men evolved theories of immortality in order to face more composedly the dread prospect of the valley of death.

Judaism, too, had to come to grips with the challenge of death by reconciling its followers to the idea of "crossing the bar" when the time was up. As a people of considerable intellectual acumen and vast religious resources, activated and animated by an indigenous dynamism, it was natural that, in the course of their long history, the Jews should progressively modify and qualify their doctrines of the future-to-come. As the centuries grew into millennia, some of the early hopes were implemented and reinterpreted, until a well-rounded eschatology emerged. Into the making of this eschatology three separate, yet interdependent, strands are woven: The

Messianic hope, the trust in the immortality of the soul, and the belief in the resurrection of the body.

Contrary to the normal curve of evolution Jewish eschatology did not progress from the primitive belief in physical resurrection to the maturer faith in the immortality of the soul and, thence, to Messianism. As in many other respects here, too, Judaism was "contrary" by evolving first the mature Messianic doctrine to which the more primitive beliefs in immortality and resurrection were added considerably later.

In the delineation of Jewish eschatology, due allowance must be made for the fact that Judaism, in different periods, espoused diverse interpretations of the meaning of the future-to-come. The Bible, the Talmud, early and late Rabbinic literature, the medieval philosophical tracts, the commentaries and codes, and the authoritative utterances of normative Judaism of more recent date bespeak widely dissimilar beliefs in the realm of eschatology held by your people through roughly three millennia.

In biblical days the future-to-come was generally identified with a period of great national prosperity, the reward for Israel's faithfulness to God and His Torah. To the Prophets the "End of the Days" was first, though not exclusively, the time of Israel's national salvation and triumph, contingent upon its return to God. This hope was thoroughly this-worldly. It yearned for national, collective security on earth, without concern for individual immortality and resurrection.

Judaism is basically this-worldly. Although he is anything but disdainful of the metaphysical realms, the Jew is yet primarily concerned with transforming this mundane sphere into a better place for the largest possible number. Save for the mystics, Jewish teachers never disparaged this world in favor of the future world. As a matter of record, the realism of the *young* Jewish nation in biblical times was such that, to the acute discomfort of present-day theologians, there has not been discovered even one unequivocal **early Hebrew confession** of belief in resurrection.

As a result, it has become a foregone conclusion with many that Jewish eschatology is the late fruit of extraneous stimuli and influences. This theory, however, has little to recommend it. Although some external features associated with the Jewish belief in immortality and resurrection may have been shaped by foreign precedents, a people endowed with so unique and creative a religious genius as the Jews certainly had no need to turn to inferior heathen cults for the essentials of its eschatology.

Nor is the absence of early Hebrew attestations of the belief in resurrection and other-worldly reward and punishment an indication of a want of spirituality, as some critics conclude. It proves, however, that the ancient Hebrews' quest for life eternal was centered and consummated in the collective effort of projecting heaven onto earth. To these men **individual immortality** was synonymous with the eternity of their people. This is why the Hebrew Bible expresses no concern over the fate of the individual, being wholly absorbed in securing the eternity of the nation. The individual's fate beyond the grave held no interest for the Hebrew Prophets; they were, first and last, concerned with the survival of the nation of which the individual was part. Being normal and warm-blooded men, the early Hebrews did not relish the melancholy prospect of death and decay. They were eager to postpone entering the valley of death.... Yet death did not blight their joy and zest of living. The biblical Jew did not waste his life in speculations about death; he acquiesced in the inevitable.

The complete disregard of the selfish, though natural, desire for individual survival is one of the crowning glories of biblical ethics, which sublimated the petty fears, the egotistical aspirations and the grossly sensuous representations of the after-life which occupied the minds of the neighbors of ancient Israel. In this manner the individual's fear of death was transmuted into the collective aversion to injustice and moral corruption.

The obligations imposed by the exalted ideals of justice and righteousness espoused by Israel are so staggering that the Jew, who is fully and wholly in the service of this national program for building a better future for his people and all of mankind, has neither time nor strength to spare for worrying and speculating about the transcendental fate of his own person. Fully and inseparably integrated into his people and mankind, the Jews is too absorbed in national and universal problems to worry about his individual immortality which, he knows, is secure and safely bound up in the "bundle of life" of his people.

As a result, the energy spent among Israel's neighbors on evolving a rationale of individual immortality was transmuted by the ancient Hebrews into the quest of securing life eternal for their nation. The Bible does not refer the hope for a better world to the transcendental spheres of heaven; it proclaims that "heaven" must be realized on earth. There is neither need nor justification, therefore, to deprecate life in the flesh—its joys, sorrows, and temptations—in order to qualify for eternal bliss in the world-to-come.

The reward of the pious is life and happiness in *this* world. And the punishment of the wicked is misery on earth and premature death. This realistic approach is best expressed perhaps in Moses' parting message to the children of Israel: "I call heaven and earth to witness against you this day, that I have set before thee life and death, the blessing and curse. Therefore choose life, that you may live, you and your seed;

to love the Lord your God, to hearken to His voice, and to cleave unto Him; for that is your life, and the length of your days; that you may dwell in the land which the Lord swore to give to your fathers, to Abraham, Isaac and to Jacob."

Life in the community of his people and on the soil of his land—and not the bliss of Paradise—was the reward the biblical Jew desired. The references to reward and punishment, which are profuse in the Hebrew Bible, clearly refer to *this* world. There is no evidence that the early Hebrew Prophets and teachers considered, to say nothing of acquiesced in, the possibility of assigning the reward of the pious and the punishment of the wicked to a transcendental future. It remained for later generations of Jewish teachers, tried and taught by the sufferings of exile, to console their fellow-sufferers with the hope of another-worldly future, where the righteous would bask in everlasting bliss and the sinners be consumed in eternal shame. The Jew of biblical times, however, would not consider happiness on-high a fair compensation for misery endured on earth. He was committed to making the earth, which was given to the children of man, a better place. He wanted to turn the earth into heaven, and not to flee to heaven from the realities of the earth. Sharing fully in the life of his free nation, cultivating its soil and shaping its political destiny, gave the biblical Jew a sense of security, belonging and self-fulfillment which reduced the after-life to unimportance. The prosperity of his people inspired the early Hebrew with confidence that he would live on in his nation, even after death would have claimed him. The biblical metaphor "to be gathered unto his people," used as a synonym for "to die," proves rather conclusively what kind of after-life the ancient Hebrews desired. The melancholy prospect of "the realm of the shadows" lost much of its depressing gloom thanks to the Jew's confident belief that the life of which he was a part and to which he gave his best would go on, and that in this "bundle of life" his contribution would be preserved and endure. To the biblical Jew the promise of the eternity of his nation and its mission spelled complete satisfaction beyond which he craved no other personal reward. This is most strikingly demonstrated perhaps in the answer the woman of Shunem gave to Elisha. When he asked her, through Gehazi his factotum, what recompense she desired for her liberal hospitality, she proudly replied: "I dwell among mine own people." Dwelling among one's own people, in life and death, in joy and sorrow, in periods of national prosperity and in the long night of exile, is the quintessence of the Jewish Messianic ideal.

Obviously, the average biblical Jew did not theorize in such a fashion, but he stanchly believed that the Kingdom of God is being established on earth through justice and righteousness. And he also knew that only the living can praise the Lord. This conviction is boldly, almost impudently, proclaimed in King Hezekiah's prayer upon his recovery from a mortal sickness: "For the nether-world cannot praise Thee, death cannot celebrate Thee; they that go down into the pit cannot hope for the truth. The living, the living—he shall praise Thee."

The same conviction speaks from such passages as: "What profit is there in my blood, when I go down to the pit? Shall the dust praise Thee? Shall it declare Thy truth?" "The dead praise not the Lord, neither any that go down into silence." "Wilt Thou work wonders for the dead? Or shall the shades arise and give Thee thanks? Shall Thy mercy be declared in the grave, or Thy faithfulness in destruction? Shall Thy wonders be known in the dark, and Thy righteousness in the land of forgetfulness?"

Ecclesiastes therefore counseled: "Whatsoever thy hand

attaineth to do by thy strength, that do; for there is no work, nor device, nor knowledge, nor wisdom in the grave whither thou goest."

In a similar vein, Job mused: "As the cloud is consumed and vanishes away, so he that goeth down to the grave shall come up no more."

The biblical Jew's zeal to prolong life, a quest which was no less pronounced in post-biblical days, was the natural result of a doctrine of the grave, which was unrelieved by any definite promise of future bliss and resurrection. Life on earth is all you have! This was the inevitable conclusion the biblical Jew was compelled to face. Still, this could be no legitimate cause for regrets. For was this short and evanescent span not fraught with limitless opportunities for bringing heaven down to earth? Provided only one was granted the allotted three-score-and-ten, there was much to be thankful for. Was not the future, nay, eternity itself in the palm of him who hitched his own brief span to the Messianic promise of the eternity of goodness, justice and righteousness?

## II

The Messianic ideal presents a happy synthesis of national and universal elements. It looks to Jewish national redemption, so that the knowledge of the Only God and the practice of His commandments may redeem a world lost in error and sin. There was no special need to elaborate on the role of the individual Jew in the Messianic setting; he was a member of the Jewish nation and so his personal salvation was contingent upon the redemption of his people. The Prophets, with superior disdain, completely ignored the problems of individual salvation, or rather it did not exist for them, for the biblical Jew was so indissolubly bound to his people that for him there could be no other salvation except the collective one.

The perfect blending of the national and universalistic elements in Jewish Messianism was eventually reduced to the formula that Israel was to acquire the right knowledge of God and establish the good life *in order* to guide mankind to the same perfection. The Prophets would not rest satisfied with merely envisioning "The mountain of the Lord's house as the top of the mountains." This narrow, national supremacy was meaningless—unless "all the nations will flow unto it . . . and say: 'Come ye and let us go up to the mountain of the Lord, to the house of the God of Jacob; and He will teach us of His ways, and we will walk in His paths."

Thus interpreted, the Messianic ideal is neither circumscribed nor static. For it does not rest satisfied with the law established *in* Zion and the word of the Lord abiding *in* Jerusalem; it has higher aspirations: "For *out of* Zion shall *go forth* the law, and the word of the Lord *from* Jerusalem."

The ethical perfection of Israel is only a partial fulfillment of the Messianic ideal which limns a time when all of mankind will practice the tenets of prophetic ethics. *The earth must be full of the knowledge of the Lord,* for the Jewish utopia of justice, peace and brotherhood can be realized only when all peoples will acknowledge the One and Only God. It was such motives, and not narrow chauvinism, which impelled the Prophets to pray for the day when all nations would worship the Lord and when in Jerusalem would be "the house of prayer for all nations." It was not for the sake of imperialistic goals, but in the hope that the espousal of monotheism would lead to the practice of the eternal commandments of the Only God that the Prophets prayed for the day when all men would acknowledge the God Israel knew.

A fair appraisal of Messianism necessitates the appreciation of its dynamic and universalistic orientation. Messianism does not strive for stagnant perfection but for unbounded progress and advance. Ease and complacency are irreconcilable with the Jewish Messianic ideal; there are no limits to the knowledge of the Lord and so there are no bounds to ethical progress. In this mundane sphere, where Messianism must be realized, the complacent relaxation of ethical effort would be tantamount to inert retrogression.

In contradistinction to virtually all other nations and religions, the Jews did not model the ideal future on a "Paradise Lost," or a vanished "Golden Age." They were alone in advancing the revolutionary idea that the present is *always* better than the past and that the future is bound to excel the present. Judaism is progressive and consequently committed to the future. It has no patience with men and creeds who would revert to the past to by-pass and escape the challenges of the present. The only escape permitted by Judaism is the flight of the ethical imagination into the future. Thus, while all nations of antiquity consumed their best creative resources in giving expression to the yearning for a vanished Golden Age, the Jewish religious genius steered clear of the mythological and mystical lures of the past, without, however, minimizing the importance of tradition. This consistent slanting of all phases of Jewish life in keeping with the requirements of the ideal future has immeasurably contributed to fortifying the will to Jewish survival. Had Judaism been geared to and centered in the past, or hedonistically sought fulfillment in the present, it could not have stood the wear and tear of the millennia.

The Jew has always lived for the sake of the future: the Messianic ideal of enthroning the Kingdom of God—justice, righteousness and brotherhood—on earth. By hitching its star to this eternal task, Israel has become the eternal people.

If Israel did not die when it had nothing to live for in the present, it was solely because of the Messianic obligation which this people, stiff-necked in more than one respect, would not forsake and which compelled it to suffer in the present and forego the nostalgic immersion into the past for the sake of the future—its own and the future of mankind.

The Prophets and Sages emphasized that the national restoration of Israel is imperative for ushering in the Messianic age. Unless Israel's national independence is restored, the better world, governed by justice, and the new mankind, led by righteousness, cannot be born. The Prophets were far from being narrow nationalists solely occupied with the welfare of their own people. But they were also far from being hazy, unrealistic universalists worried over the fate of all peoples, except their own blood and flesh. With the Prophets "charity began at home." However, and this is important, it did not end there, but extended to all mankind. Jewish Messianism is healthy, organic and *logical*. It synthesizes national and international aims and, being logical, is not abashed to insist that Israel's physical restoration must precede the moral regeneration of mankind. Israel must be restored to healthy national normalcy, for only then can it muster the strength required for executing its "mission."

The early proponents of Reform Judaism, who endorsed the universalistic elements of Messianism while denying the national character of Judaism and stamping as "obsolete" the hope for the return to Zion, completely failed to understand the tenor of Jewish Messianism. Without the solid basis of the hope for national restoration, Messianism is suspended in the air, as it were. The essence of the Messianic message is that nationally restored and ethically regenerated Israel will help enthrone the universal supremacy of ethics and humaneness.

The millennia of national degradation, persecution and homelessness intensified the Jewish national hopes bound up with Messianism to such an extent that the trust in national restoration became virtually invulnerable. The agonies and tribulations of exile failed to break Israel's national will. On the contrary, the persecutions and sufferings were taken as proof of the certainty of the ultimate fulfillment of the Messianic promise, for had not Isaiah taught that the Lord's servant, meaning the Jewish people, is "despised and forsaken of men, a man of pains, and acquainted with disease, and as one from whom men hide their face?" Israel, the "suffering servant" bore his chastisements patiently, trusting that they would be instrumental in speeding the promised salvation.

In this manner, the many afflictions visited upon the nation lost their sting and became desirable "sufferings of love," inflicted by God because of His Love of Israel; for does not a loving father chastise his son? Thanks to Isaiah's chapter of the "Suffering Servant of the Lord" and its Rabbinic interpretations, the Jews were patient and proud in their sufferings, comforted by their perennial philosophy that "those merit to see the full splendor of God's glory who accept humiliation but do not humiliate others; who bear insult but do not insult others, and who endure a life of martyrdom in pure love of God." The oppressed and persecuted Jew suffers proudly, for does not "the Torah select for the sacrifices of the altar only the animals which belong to the pursued, but not the pursuers. . . . So also God chose Israel, the lamb, from among the seventy nations—the seventy wolves, that it should bring His Law to Mankind."

Although Israel bore its sufferings manfully, it was inevitable that questions were asked as to the duration of these seemingly eternal "birthpangs" of the Messianic era. The Galuth sufferings intensified the desire for the early dawn of the Redemption. Although the leading talmudic Sages disparaged and interdicted calculations aiming at determining the date of the Messiah's advent, such speculations occupied some of the best Jewish minds. Even a Sage of the intellectual acumen of Rabbi Akiba was so steeped in Messianic dreams that he acclaimed Bar Kochba, the leader of the Jewish revolt against Roman oppression, as the "King Messiah." Not all Sages, however, were so eager to confer the crown of Messiahship. An interesting talmudic passage records that when Rabbi Akiba endorsed Bar Kochba, his colleague, Rabbi Yohanan the son of Torta, sternly reproved him: "Akiba, grass will grow in your cheeks, and still the son of David will not have come."

In general, there was anything but unanimity among the Rabbis of the Talmud concerning the interpretation of the Messianic promises. While the rationalistically inclined Sages were loath to engage in or permit speculations on the realia of the Messianic world, the masters of the Aggadic interpretation immersed themselves with glee in comforting and compensating dreams about the delights of the Messianic era. While there was considerable disagreement on the date of the Messiah's advent and on the manner of his revelation and reign, all the talmudic Rabbis, however, thought of the Messianic era in this-worldly terms.

In the Middle Ages, the this-worldly character of the Messianic order was strongly emphasized by Maimonides who, on the strength of biblical and talmudic authorities, declared: "Let it not enter your mind that in the days of the Messiah anything in the world's order will cease to exist, or anything new will be introduced into the scheme of the universe. The world will follow its natural course. The statement of Isaiah, 'The wolf shall dwell with the lamb, and the leopard shall lie down with the kid' is a metaphor signifying that Israel will dwell in safety among the wicked of the heathens who are likened to wolves and leopards. They will be converted to the true religion and will no more plunder and destroy, but will live honestly and quietly like Israel."

Elsewhere Maimonides elaborated on the national and ethical implications of the Messianic era: "The Sages and Prophets did not yearn for the days of the Messiah in order to dominate all the world, nor to rule over the heathens, or for the sake of being exalted by the peoples, or for eating, drinking and rejoicing. They wanted to be free and to devote themselves to the Torah and its wisdom, without oppression and interference.... In that era, there will be neither famine nor war, and no jealousy and strife. Prosperity will be universal and there will be an abundance of good things with all men striving to know the Lord."

Although "the world will follow its natural course" in the Messianic era, there will be one important change: "Israel will possess the kingdom." That is to say, the Jewish people will be relieved of the curse of homelessness and return to its own soil. Still, the national restoration under the aegis of the Messiah is not "desired as an end in itself," as Nahmanides emphasized.

As to the person of the Messiah, Maimonides summarized the traditional conviction that he would be a mortal and not constrained to prove his legitimacy by miracles. "Let it not enter your mind that the King Messiah must necessarily perform signs and miracles, establish some new thing in the world, revive the dead, or do something similar." The acid test of Messiahship is not the faculty of performing miracles, but the realization of nature's higher purposes in ethics. The Messiah, according to authoritative Jewish belief, is "a king of the house of David, who will turn his spirit toward the Torah, and like his forefather, David, will practice both the written and the oral Law. And if he shall cause all Israel to live according to the Law and strengthen it; and if his labor prospers, and if he conquers the surrounding peoples, rebuilds the Temple and reassembles the scattered remnants of Israel, then there will be no doubt; he is the true Messiah."

## III

Such was the Messianic doctrine on its authoritative plane—but there were also many popular superstitions abroad. The harsh bitterness of exile stimulated the escape into wishful dreaming about the Messiah. To be sure, most of these dreams and mystical speculations lacked the ethical note and emphasis that were so powerfully stressed by the Rabbis of a more rationalistic trend of mind. Yet, the spurious pretenders to the Messianic crown, who intermittently disturbed the peace of the medieval Jewish community, were greeted by the masses with enthusiastic abandon. The insecurity of their lives had brought medieval Jewry to the point where they were ready to follow anyone who promised relief. The leaders of Jewish thought, however, stanchly upheld the traditional interpretation of the national-ethical meaning of Messianism. Their unflinching trust in the ultimate victory of right over might and of light over darkness—a victory which necessarily would spell the righting of the wrongs visited upon the Jewish sufferers, is perhaps most sublimely and touchingly expressed in the prayer: "Now, therefore, O Lord our God, impose Thine awe upon all Thy works and Thy dread upon all that Thou hast created. That all Thy works may fear Thee, and all creatures prostrate themselves before Thee; that they may form a single bond to do Thy will with a perfect heart, even as we know, O Lord our God, that domination is Thine, strength is in Thy hand, and might in Thy right hand and that Thy name is to be feared above all that Thou hast created. Give glory, O Lord, unto Thy people, praise to them that fear Thee, hope to them that seek Thee, and free speech to them that wait for Thee, joy to the land, gladness to the city, a flourishing horn to David Thy servant, and a clear, shining light unto the son of Jesse, Thine anointed, speedily in our days. Then shall the just also see and be glad, and the upright shall exult, and the pious triumphantly rejoice, while iniquity shall close her mouth, and all wickedness be wholly consumed by smoke, when Thou makest the dominion of arrogance to pass away from the earth."

While Messianism represents the Jew's quest for eternity on the highest plane of ethics and spirituality, it would be erroneous to think that the entire nation always adhered to such a mature philosophy. There are numerous biblical passages which show that the masses held to current superstitions concerning the shadowy existence of the dead in the nether-world. Ancestor-worship, widespread among idolatrous peoples, had gained ground also in Israel, otherwise the Pentateuchal injunctions against consulting ghosts and the spirits of the dead would have been superfluous. Later, Samuel purged the land from the objectionable worship of the dead and the consulting of the spirits of the departed. Yet, this did not keep Saul, who in the early years of his reign had supported the fight against these superstitions, from calling on the witch of En-Dor with the request to bring up for him the spirit of Samuel, so that he might consult him on the outcome of the impending battle. Even Isaiah still found it necessary to taunt those who consulted the dead, instead of trusting in God.

The determined opposition to ancestor-worship on the part of Israel's spiritual elite was motivated by socio-economic considerations no less than by the zeal for monotheism. The idolatrous nations invariably worshipped the dead by inflicting hardships upon the living. In Egypt the entire nation labored under staggering taxes and forced labor levies to make possible the building of sumptuous Pyramids, the burial vaults of the Pharaohs and the aristocracy. In ancient Sumeria it was customary for the royal household to accompany their ruler into the grave. At the death of a king or queen, the royal servants were slain and buried with their masters, as the Sumerians believed that royalty must be served also in the nether-world.

The Prophets of Israel were too vitally concerned with the sufferings of the living to give thought to the destiny of the dead. They wanted *all* men to know the truth of the Only God and to abide by His ethics; they wanted peace and social justice to be established and happiness and plenty provided for all created in the likeness of God. The Prophets opposed magic motivated by fear of the inexorability of fate, for in the ethical climate of Jewish monotheism, predicated on freedom of the will, there is no room for predestination or fate. To the Prophets and the Psalmist the dead were the symbol of utter impotence and weakness. Thus Isaiah, when sketching an imaginary picture of the nether-world ready to welcome the slain king of Babylonia, depicted the departed kings of that nation as addressing the new arrival, "Art thou also become as weak as we? . . . The maggot is spread under thee, and the worms cover thee."

Save for a few poetic allegories, the Bible is silent on the nature of the grave. This, together with the absence of even one clear statement on the fate of the departed soul, seems to prove that the moulders of biblical thought did not venture beyond asserting the individual's collective immortality in the nation. They rested satisfied in the assurance and hope that "the dust returneth to the earth as it was and the spirit returneth unto God who gave it."

There is no doubting that the Messianic hopes and promises took the edge off death's sting. Still, the desire for personally sharing in these blessings could not be entirely absent. To be sure, the desire for personal survival remained suppressed; yet it was sufficiently potent to erupt in Isaiah's vision "thy dead shall live, my dead bodies arise," and in Daniel's pledge that "many of them that sleep in the dust of the earth shall awake, some to everlasting life, and some to reproaches and everlasting abhorrence." As both passages are of late origin, however, there is no need to assign to them great significance for early Hebrew eschatology. Had resurrection been a generally held tenet of biblical belief, this hope, or the threat of eternal perdition, would surely have been referred to by the Torah and the Prophets. Yet neither the Torah nor the Prophets ever demanded pious conformance for the sake of a reward beyond the grave, nor did their threats delineate the horrors of other-worldly punishment. Both held out only this-wordly rewards and penalties, which raises the question whether Isaiah's and Daniel's references to resurrection are more than chance flashes.

## IV

Messianism is centered in the Jewish nation, through whose perfection the prophetic ideals of justice and peace are to be achieved for all mankind. Messianism presupposes a potent Jewish nation. With the collapse of the Jewish state it was inevitable that Messianism should lose much of its power to console the individual Jew over the inevitability of death "whch devours for all eternity." So long as the Jewish nation prospered in its own land, the Jew's quest for life eternal was consummated in national Messianism. When however the Jewish state collapsed, the national Messianic promises were no longer adequate to satisty the quest for life eternal. It was at this juncture, when the outlook for national survival was precarious, that the Jews first began to clamor for individual salvation. Until then the collective salvation vouched for by Messianism had sufficed to allay the fear of the grave. When, however, the average Jew could not but doubt the possibility of sharing himself in the national salvation, it was inevitable that he should seek solace in other realms. Thus the doctrine of the "future world," as a transcendental sphere, was born.

The fall of the Jewish state and the destruction of the Temple alerted the Sages to the inexorable instability of temporal power and institutions. As a result, they defined the Messianic era as a transition period, although the Prophets had unequivocally proclaimed it as the final and eternal state of perfection. The Rabbis, distrustful of this-worldly endurance, introduced the distinction between the Messianic era, a transition period, and the world-to-come, the world of definitive and lasting fulfillment and consummation. The views on the duration of the Messianic era differed widely. While Rabbi Akiba thought it would last forty years, Rabbi Eliezer the son of Josi assigned to it a century; Rabbi Judah the Prince ventured the guess that the Messianic era would last four hundred years, while other Sages suggested that it would endure for six hundred, a thousand, two thousand and seven thousand years, respectively, when the future world would supplant the present.

However, even when under the tragic impact of homelessness the this-worldly orientation of Judaism was implemented by the promise of immortality and resurrection, the conviction remained firm that piety must be proved in the terrestial sphere. The Sages, who envisioned the future reward as the Academy-on-High where the pious will eternally relish the bliss of studying the Torah, were sufficiently realistic to counsel: "A man should always occupy himself with the Torah and the commandments before he dies." As their predecessors, who had declared that only "the living can praise the Lord," these latter day realists, too, knew that death rings down the curtain. For "the dead is exempt from the Torah commandments, and the Holy One, blessed be He, can get no praise from him." The same view was expressed and eloquently qualified by medieval and more recent teachers. "This world is the only place where the commandments can be practiced," declared the 18th century moralist Moses Hayim Luzzatto, notwithstanding his Kabbalistic predilections. The pristine realism of the Bible was still sufficiently palpable in the 18th century Kabbalist to make him endorse Ecclesiastes' conviction that "there is no work, nor device, nor knowledge, nor wisdom in the grave."

In commenting on this passage, Luzzatto observed: "What a man does not achieve when in the possession of freedom of the will, bestowed upon him by his Creator, and which is for the length of his life rendering him both free and responsible, he can attain neither in the grave nor in the nether-world, where he is without this power. He who fails to do profuse good in life cannot, in death, compensate for this omission. He who fails to take stock of his actions in this world will not be able to do so in the next world. He who does not acquire wisdom in this world will not become wise in the grave." The belief in personal immortality and resurrection became articulate and a binding article of Jewish belief only in post-biblical days, when this implementation of Messianism became indispensable for strengthening the will for Jewish survival. Although there is no clear-cut, definitive statement concerning the after-life in the Torah, the Sages of the Talmud decided that "there is no section of the Torah which does not imply the doctrine of resurrection."

One method of adducing biblical proof for the resurrection was to interpret passages referring to events of the past, but couched in the future tense, as evidence of the future resurrection. Thus Rabbi Meir explained the passage. "*Az yasheer Moshe uveney Yisrael . . .*" which in keeping with its meaning, though contrary to its grammatical form, is rendered: "Then *sang* Moses . . ." as follows: "It is not said *sang* but *will sing;* which shows that the resurrection is attested by the Torah." Another Sage, Rabbi Joshua the son of Levi, by the same method explained the Psalmist's passage "Blessed are they that dwell in Thy house, they are ever praising Thee" (*od yehalalucha*) as referring to the world-to-come.

The Sages resorted to strenuous exegetical efforts to prove that "there is no Torah commandment coupled with a reward which does not refer to the future life." In this manner they deduced from the Pentateuchal repetition of the promise of long life and prosperity for those honoring their fathers and mothers and showing mercy to the mother bird, that only half of the reward is given in this world, while the other half will be apportioned in "the world of endless days." Similarly, the axiom "all Israel have a share in the world-to-come," was deduced from a biblical text, namely Isaiah's promise, "Thy people also shall be all righteous, they shall inherit the land forever." The land to be inherited became to some Rabbis, far removed from the this-worldly nationalism of the Prophets, "the future world."

The keen psychological insight which led Rabbi Yohanan Ben Zakkai to build the Yeshiva in Jabneh as a substitute for the doomed Temple, caused his colleagues to make other concessions to the national emergency. They gave the stamp of authority to an eschatology vouchsafing individual immortality and resurrection and thus compensated the people for the bleakness of the Galuth. It was not least for the sake of the survival of their nation that the Rabbis declared emphatically that "he who says that the belief in the resurrection is not founded on the Torah shall have no share in the world-to-come." Although Jewish ethics is self-sufficient and not in need of the prop of other-worldly reward and punishment, the morale of the masses of persecuted Jewry depended upon this belief for allaying despair. It would seem that the promises of transcendental rewards were aiming at entrenching Jewish survival strength rather than at stimulating piety. For notwithstanding the promises of other-worldly rewards, the Sages insistently demanded that piety be espoused for its own sake. The doctrines of the future world and of reward and punishment did not basically affect the cardinal principle of Jewish ethics that the reward of the pious action is its performance and that the punishment of sin the commission of the sin.

The national motives of the rabbinic doctrine of the hereafter are interestingly endorsed in Maimonides' Responsum on "Religious Martyrdom." According to Maimonides, martyrdom opens wide the doors of the hereafter. Even a sinner, "whose sins equal those of Jeroboam son of Nebat and his associates" will enter eternity as a reward for his martyrdom. Contrary to a rabbinic opinion to the effect that "those who are ignorant of the Torah will not be resurrected," Maimonides held that ignoramuses will enter eternal bliss provided they "Sanctified the Name of God" as martyrs, for in the words of the Talmud, "nobody can equal the perfection of those slain by an idolatrous government."

## V

It is significant that the doctrine of resurrection met with considerable opposition at its inception. It was determinedly rejected by the Sadducees, recruited largely from the aristocracy conversant with Hellenistic literature, who denied the legitimacy of adducing support for the doctrine of resurrection from the Torah. The Sadducees, as their later counterparts, the Karaites, opposed the re-interpretation of biblical texts in a manner doing violence to the literal meaning. The Pharisees on the other hand held that the literal sense is but the corridor to the real meaning, which must be established if Israel is to survive. The Pharisees therefore did not shrink from daring interpretations in order to prove the Scriptural origin of the doctrine of resurrection, which they regarded as indispensable for Jewish survival.

Talmudic and medieval rabbinic literature are replete with contradictory statements on the how and when of the world-to-come. Profound philosophical and inspiring ethical interpretations are found side by side with speculations on the fare which will be served to the pious in the world-to-come. As a matter of fact, this disparity is not restricted to the theme of the future world but extends to all matters discussed in the Talmud, whose makers were anything but regimented minds. With admirable fairness the Talmud also quotes the opinions of those opposing the majority decisions embodied in law. The editors of the Talmud did not hesitate to include in their imposing compendium, crystallizing Jewish thought and legal endeavor of almost a millennium, popular superstitions and philosophical heresies. To be sure, the makers of the Talmud determinedly opposed trends they thought detrimental to Jewish survival. Their intellectual integrity, however, would not let them strike their opponents off the record.

As a result, we find in the Talmud not only the views of its authoritative makers but also the opinions of the "opposition." The Sages were men of integrity and therefore did not attempt to conceal that not all of their contemporaries shared the views of the ruling majority of the Pharisees.

Thanks to this broadmindedness, talmudic literature records ethical-philosophical interpretations of the hereafter side by side with detailed descriptions of its physical splendors and and the culinary delights reserved for the banquet on-high. Representative of the spiritual interpretation of the world-to-come is Rab's dictum that "the world-to-come is not like this world." For in the future world "there will be neither eating nor drinking; no procreation and no business transactions; no envy, no hatred, and no rivalry. The righteous will sit enthroned and with crowns on their heads, enjoying the splendor of the Divine Presence." Maimonides, the most articulate proponent of the pristine spirituality of the doctrine of the world-to-come, commented on this passage as follows: "Those souls will reap bliss from their comprehension of the Creator.... Consequently, felicity and the final goal consist in joining this exalted company and attaining to this high state. The soul is eternal, like the Creator.... This is the great happiness with which none is comparable and to which no joy can be likened." An even bolder denial of a physical hereafter is Rabbi Simon Ben Lakish's assertion that "there is neither hell nor paradise. God merely sends out the sun in its full strength; the wicked are consumed by its heat, while the pious find delight and healing in its rays." He thus underscored the traditional conviction that piety is piety's reward and sin is the penalty of sin for "the wicked are called dead even during their lives, while the righteous are called living even after death."

Almost without exception, the leading Sages were reluctant

to describe the world-on-high. This hesitation is strikingly affirmed by the *Midrash* which records that when the Israelites pleaded with Moses: "Moses, our master, tell us what goodness the Holy One, blessed be He, will give us in the world-to-come," Moses replied, "I don't know, but you are happy on account of what is prepared for you." Like "the days of the Messiah" the future world was to the best Jewish minds of the past not so much a state of perfection as of perfectibility. Accordingly, we have such a remarkable statement as: "The disciples of the wise (*talmidei hahamin*) have rest neither in this world nor in the world-to-come, for, as it is said, 'they go from strength to strength, every one of them that appeareth before God in Zion.'" The world-to-come, even as this world, offers the boon of progress. The highest good is not perfection but progress—going from strength to strength on the road leading to the ultimate truth. Luzzatto therefore envisioned the world-to-come as the place where man will "realize to what extent he has failed of the perfection which he could have attained."

Maimonides, in underscoring the spiritual nature of the Jewish hopes of immortality and resurrection, emphasized that none of "the accidents" to which bodies are subject in this world, such as sitting, standing, sleeping, death, pain, laughter, etc., are extant in the future world. Lest the spiritual delights be not properly appreciated, Maimonides cautioned: "Perhaps this happiness will be lightly esteemed by you, and you will prefer that the reward for complying with the commandments and for walking in the paths of truth shall be the enjoyment of good food and drink, beautiful women, fine linen and embroidered garments, houses of ivory, and vessels of silver and gold, or similar luxuries.... Wise and intelligent men, however, know that all these things are vanity, and quite futile. We, in this world, consider them desirable because all these things are desired and required by the body. But the disembodied soul neither wants nor desires them." In the same context Maimonides denied, again in keeping with talmudic precedent, the possibility of ascertaining the nature of the future world. There is no possibility of comprehending it in this world; because here we are only concerned with the welfare of the body. The bliss of the world-to-come is exceedingly great and it cannot be compared to the happiness of this world, except figuratively speaking. It is therefore mistaken to liken the soul's bliss in the world-to-come to the happiness the body derives from eating and drinking in this world. The celestial bliss is unlimited and nothing can be compared or likened to it."

Although Judaism is far from being ascetic, it yet holds fast to the conviction that the joys of the spirit are superior to bodily delights. In keeping with tradition, Maimonides does not advocate denying the body is due. On the contrary, the legitimate wants of the body should be satisfied. But persons who hope for bodily delights in the hereafter are compared by Maimonides to "a king of sovereign power willing to give up his imperial realm in order to return to his boyhood games." Still, Maimonides realized that most people "place the delights of the body above those of the soul." However, "when you will examine the nature of these two pleasures, you will discover the cheapness of the one and the great value of the other."

Maimonides' intellectual utopia, however, was not palatable to the masses of Jewish believers—and for that matter not to all scholars either. The common man, tried in the crucible of sufferings, found greater solace in the type of promises exemplified by this *Midrash*: "The Holy One, blessed be He, will prepare a banquet for the righteous in Paradise. And there will be no need to provide balsam or perfumes, for the north and the south wind will stir the aromatic plants of Paradise, so that they will yield their fragrance." At this heavenly banquet, the righteous will feast on the meat of the legendary sea monster, Leviathan, whose skin will be fashioned into a sumptuous *Sukkah*. They will slake their thirst on delicious old wine stored for them since the six days of creation.

Although many Jewish teachers held that, as far as the masses are concerned, reward and punishment are indispensable for entrenching morality, others entertained serious misgivings concerning the doctrine of retribution. They held with Ben Azzai that genuine piety is not in need of stimuli. They warned against serving God for the sake of a reward and pointed out that the Psalmist's tribute to the God-fearing "Happy is the man that feareth the Lord, that delighteth greatly in His commandments," emphasizes that one should rejoice in the commandments proper, and not observe them out of fear, or for the sake of a reward.

Maimonides, while avowing the belief in the future reward and punishment, yet interpreted retribution, in keeping with certain talmudic statements, as the delight and joy bound up with righteousness, respectively as the remorse which will assail even the most confirmed sinner. In a touching and profound exposition of the true meaning of immortality, Maimonides, epitomizing the best of Jewish eschatological thought up to his time, stated: "When the Rabbis speak of Paradise and Hell, describing vividly the delights of the former and the torments of the latter, they merely resort to metaphors for depicting the agony which is part of sin and the happiness which is bound up with virtue. True piety serves God neither from fear of punishment nor from desire for reward, as servants obey their master, but from pure love of God and truth.... Only children need bribes and threats to be trained to morality." Although this emphasis of the pure spirituality of the future life drew upon Maimonides a flood of protests from more rigid believers, who refused to accept Paradise and Hell as states of ethical satisfaction or dissatisfaction, the credo of the man, of whom it is said that "from Moses till Moses there arose none like Moses," represents Jewish traditional belief on its sublimest plane.

It is not infrequently argued that Maimonides' philosophy of the spiritual nature of the hereafter cannot be reconciled with his articles of Belief: "I believe with perfect faith that the Creator rewards those who observe his commandments, and punishes those who transgress them." And "I believe with perfect faith that there will be a resurrection of the dead at the time when it will please the Creator." But there is no discrepancy between the two. The belief in reward and punishment does not compel us to interpret them in terms of physical reality, nor does the doctrine of resurrection imply a future life patterned along the lines of this-worldly existence.

Pertaining to eschatology there have always been two schools of Jewish thought: one presenting the future world as a glorified and improved edition of this world; the other avowing that the future world will in no way be like the terrestial sphere. These two schools of thought were distinctly articulate already in talmudic times. In the Middle Ages, the philosophers and thinkers of the Spanish school became the heirs of the Rabbis who had insisted on the purely spiritual nature of the hereafter, while the Kabbalists spun further the Midrashic fantasies of the physical delights of the world-to-come.

# INDEX

Abba, Rabbi, 36, 326
Abbasides, 43
Abraham, 23, 24, 117, 154, 232, 233, 353, 375
Abtalyon, 234
Abu-Isa, 43
Abulafia, Rabbi Abraham, 44, 313
Abuya, Elisha ben, 252, 303
Acco, 36
Adam, 13, 25, 224, 225, 346, 350, 354
Adams, John, 12
Africa, 191
Age of Reason, 94
Aggadah, 105, 145, 240, 243, 383
Aggression, 17
Ahab, King of Israel, 337
Ahasver, 153
Akiba, Rabbi, 43, 120, 204, 234, 267, 383, 389
Al-Charizi, 130
Aleichem, Sholem, 227
Alfasi, 73, 269
Alkabetz, Solomon, 84
Alshach, Moses, 38, 82
Amos, 120, 121, 227-229, 318
Amonites, 234
Amsterdam, 128
Anti-Semitism, 194, 195, 213
Apion, 256
Apocrypha, 68, 143
Apollo, 137
Arabic, 49, 54, 178
Aramaic, 49, 54, 249
Arameans, 228, 229, 337
Aristotle, 10, 192, 220, 235, 269
Armenian, 128
Art, 103, 104, 111, 115, 124, 127-129
Aryan, 223, 224, 236
Asher, Rabbi Judah, 271
Asia, 191
Assimilation, 220
Askari, Eliezer, 84
Assyria, 70, 165, 228, 318
Atomic Bomb, 5-26, 125
Avicebron, (Gabirol), 78
Azzai, Ben, 397
Bag Bag, Ben, 258

Balaam, 216
Baal Shem-Tov, Rabbi Israel, 73, 83, 210
Babylonia, 63, 68, 70-72, 88, 90, 91, 107, 387
Babylonian captivity, 224, 233
Babylonian Gaonim, 88
Babylonian Talmud, 45, 73, 87, 90
Basle Program, 41
Bar-Kochba, 43, 383
Benediction, 205, 236, 343
Bene-Israel, 262
Benjamin, 36, 257
"Beowulf", 180
Berdichevsky, 58
Berdyaev, Nikolai, 18
Bergen-Belsen, 203
Bernstein, Leonard, 140
Berokya, Rabbi, 39
Bethar, 43
Bezalel, 121
Bialik, 73, 80, 98, 134-137, 141, 143, 278-280, 290, 291
Bible 14, 29, 30, 32, 34, 48, 50, 98, 106-108, 121, 122, 139, 143, 146, 150, 156-158, 205, 211, 220, 228, 240, 259, 269, 296, 297, 309, 318, 326, 369, 373-375, 390
Birnbaum, Nathan, 58
"Book of the Pious, The", 268, 272-274, 326, 347, 370, 371
Books, honor of, 270
Boraisha, Menachem, 137-141, 143, 277
Brandeis, Justice, 60, 61
Bratzlaver, Rabbi Nahman, 84
Breasted, James H., 112, 113
Breuer, Isaac 58, 280
Britain, 241
Browne, Lewis, 262
Byron, 277
Caesar, 93
Cain, 153
Cairo, 274
Canaanites, 224, 228, 229
Canossa, 93
"Canterbury Tales", 180
Caphtor, 227

Catholic Church, 94, 95
"Century of the Child, The" (Key), 256
Chagall, 140
Children, 348
Chilion, 36
"Chosen People, The", 193, 194, 222-244
Christianity, 11, 12, 18, 25, 79, 101, 145-147, 166, 168
Cohen, Hermann, 220, 279, 306
Columbus, 270
Commandment, Second, 15, 103, 104, 125
Commandments, 40, 206, 207, 230, 236, 398
"Commentary on the Mishnah" (Maimonides), 54
"Confessions" (Heine), 114
Crescas, 149
Crusades, 163, 186, 205, 211
Cousins, Norman, 25
Dachau, 203
Daniel, Book of, 41, 45, 388
David, King, 101, 234, 250, 383, 384
Day of Atonement, 98, 367, 368
"Decline of the West" (Spengler), 5, 6
Diaspora, 21-23, 55-57, 59-62, 64, 65, 67-70, 72-76, 80, 82, 84-86, 149, 185, 187, 212, 213, 286; Survivalism, 182-201
Dietary laws, 19, 92, 100, 172, 174
Dignity of man, 9, 19
Divine Presence, 27, 35, 82, 365
Divorce, 353, 354
Draft Constitution of Israel, 19
Dubnow, 41
Dura-Europos, 129, 130
Ecclesiastes, 251, 390
Egypt, 32, 47, 68, 106, 107, 112, 114, 227, 228f., 232, 233, 291, 318, 331, 338, 387
Eibeschutz Rabbi Jonathan, 351
Einstein, Albert, 140, 236
Elijah, Gaon of Vilna, 38, 256, 345
Elimelech, 36
Eliot, Charles W., 158
Eleazar, Rabbi Simeon ben, 175, 266, 286, 365
Eliezer, Rabbi (son of Josi), 389

Eliezer, Rabbi (son of Pedath), 39
Emden, Jacob, 39
En-Dor, 386
England, 55, 111, 186
Enlightenment, Age of, 46
"Epistle to the Jews of Yemen" (Maimondies), 46
Epstein, Jacob, 140
Eretz Israel, 27, 32-41, 47, 56, 57, 59, 60, 62, 66, 57, 70, 73, 74, 82, 84, 85, 87-90, 102, 199, 213, 279
Esau, 226, 227, 229
Esther, 251
Ethical man, 9
Ethical reason, 17
"Ethics" (Aristotle), 269
"Ethics of the Fathers", 142
"Ethik der Reinen Vernunft" (Kant), 220
Ethrog, 33
Euclid, 269
Expulsion from Spain, 162, 176
Exodus, 117, 369
Ezekiel, 270
Ezra, 41, 56, 224, 279, 327
Family, 342-360
Feast of Tabernacles, 338
Fellow man ideal, 319-341
Fiscus Judaicus, 64
Flewelling, Ralph T., 10
"Fountain of Life, The" (Gabirol), 78
Friedman, Elisha M., 183
Frank, Jacob, 44
French, 81, 346; Constitution, 19; Revolution, 94
Gabirol, Solomon Ibn, 73, 78, 136, 137, 149, 297, 315
Galuth, 34-37, 39, 40, 73, 75, 82-85, 102, 281, 392
Gama, Vasco Da, 270
Gamaliel, Rabbi Simeon ben, 129
Gaon of Vilna, 73, 83
Gaon, Saadia, 29, 45, 51, 68, 70, 88, 101, 235, 276, 298, 299, 354, 363
Gehazi, 377
Gehinom, 354
Genesis, 23
German, 48, 54, 81
Germany, 52, 55
Gideon, 337

# INDEX

*Gleichschaltung*, 30
Golah, 57-63, 67-69, 87-91
"Golden Age", 380
Golden Age of Hebrew Literature, 49, 68, 70, 161, 163
Golden Calf, 309
Golden rule, 323, 324
Golem, 7, 125
Gomorrah, 309
Graetz, H., 40, 52, 78, 79, 159, 183, 202
Greco-Roman, 61
Greece, 10, 15, 16, 18, 145, 180, 332, 359
Greek, 12, 14, 54, 115, 122, 129, 160, 235, 346, 349
Greeks, 15, 16, 114, 120, 159, 180, 191, 236, 348, 365
Greek philosophy, 77
"Guide for the Perplexed" (Maimonides), 54, 178
Gutmacher, Solomon, 46
Ha'Am, Ahad, 36, 53, 58, 62, 73, 74, 82, 83, 92, 103, 142, 158, 250
Habakuk, 310
Haganah, 22
Haggadah, 291
Haggai, 278
Hadrianic persecutions, 43, 186, 204, 300
*Halacha*, 89f.
Halevi, Yehudah, 25, 35, 37, 57, 65, 72, 73, 84, 130-137, 141, 160, 178, 210, 315, 316
Half-shekel (tax), 63
"Hallel" prayer, 338
Halutzim, 84
"Hands of Esau", 107
Ha-Naggid, Shemuel, 136
Hanasi, Rabbi Judah, 355
Ha-Penini, Yedaya, 298
Hasidism, 37, 79, 83, 210
Hayyim, Rabbi (of Wolozin), 83
Hebrew, 12, 36, 49-55, 74, 81; Alphabet, 363; Bible, 68; **Language, 28, 48;** Language Board, 49; Literature, 106
Heine, 114, 207, 208
Hell, 397, 398
Hellenes, 235
Hellenism, 54, 61, 86, 114, 129, 393

Hess, Moses, 46
Herzl, Theodore, 46, 82, 86, 102
Hesiod, 349
Hezekiah, King, 260, 377
*Hiddur mitzvah*, 126, 127
Hillel, 24, 116, 220, 234, 246, 324
Hillel II, 88
Hindu, 262
Hiram, 108
Hiroshima, 5
Hitler, 176
Hittite, 104
Holy City, pilgrimages to, 65
Holy Land, 37-39, 65, 66, 84f.
Homer, 180
Horeb, 301
Horton, Dr. W. M., 9
Hosea, 130; Book of, 136
Humboldt, Alexander Von, 121, 122
Humanism, 25, 26
Hunah, Rabbi Bar Bar, 330
Hurwitz, Rabbi Isaiah (Shela), 84, 85
"Immortale Dei" (Pope Leo XIII), 95
"In Front of the Book-Case" (Bialik), 135
Inquisition, 44, 339
Isaac, 175, 233, 376
Isaiah, 8, 82, 121, 150, 156, 209, 226, 228, 229, 233, 241, 278, 302, 306, 318, 382, 383, 386-388, 391
Islam, 25, 44, 163, 166, 294
Israel, 13, 14, 16, 17, 19, 20, 22, 23, 26, 27, 31, 34, 36-38, 42, 46, 67, 71, 77, 80, 82, 85, 92, 97, 99, 106, 107, 113, 114, 121, 137, 153-157, 159-161, 171, 177, 180, 181, 185, 192, 203, 204, 206, 207, 209, 211, 222-231, 234, 237, 239-241, 243, 244, 249, 254, 260, 262, 270, 284, 285, 295, 305-308, 311, 313, 317, 318, 320, 337, 351, 357, 369, 373, 375, 379-382, 385, 387, 391, 393;
Israeli, Isaac, 70
Israelites, 47, 325
Israels, Joseph, 127
Italian, 81
Italy, 180
Jabneh, 169; Sages of, 234

Jacob, 31, 120, 148, 225-227, 233, 247, 376
Jechiel, Rabbi Asher Ben, 316
Jerusalem, 11, 24, 27, 31, 34, 37, 45, 61, 62, 65, 66, 77, 82, 84, 87, 98, 148, 165, 169, 209, 240, 379
Jeroboam (son of Nebat), 392
Jesus, 12, 101
Jethro, 232
Jewish art, 103, 127, 129
Jewish Commonwealth, Second, 51, 56, 59
Jewish Day Schools, 74
Jewish education, 76
Jewish ethics, 29
Jewish folklore, 105
Jewish law, 276-292
Jewish Mission, 22-24
Jewish nationalism, 28
Jewish religion, 28
Jewish State, 22, 56, 61, 74, 75, 86, 91, 97, 98, 100-102, 151, 161
"Jewish Survival or Extinction?" (Friedman), 183
Job, 70, 378
Josephus, 54, 256
Joy, 209
*"Juedische Selbsthass, Der"* (Lessing), 71
Kabbala, 44, 79, 82, 84, 356, 390
Kabbalists, 39, 307, 313, 351, 398
Kalisher Hirsch, 46
Kant, 150, 220
Karaites, 393
Karo, Joseph, 84
Kaspi, Joseph Ibn, 269
Key, Ellen, 256
*Kiddush,* 126, 342
Kishineff, 135
Klatzkin, Jacob, 58
Koestler, Arthur, 140
*Kol Nidre,* 367, 368
Krochmal, Nahman, 158
*"Kuzari"* (Halevi), 25, 178, 210
Lamentations, 251
"Law and Legend" (Bialik), 278
Lessing, Theodor, 71
Leviathan, 105, 397
Liebermann, Max, 127, 140
Literature, 130-139

Luria, Isaac, 84
Luther, Martin, 94, 149
Luzzatto, Moses Hayim, 46, 73, 84, 390
Lyra Nicholas, 78, 149
MacLeish, Archibald, 9, 25
Mahlon, 36
Maimonides, 25, 42, 45, 46, 51, 54, 
Mann, Thomas, 128
Marriage, 349, 350, 355-357
Martyrs, Ten, 204
Marx, Karl, 151
Materialism, 192
Meat inspection, public, 172, 173
Mediterranean, 43
Meir, Rabbi, 225, 234, 252, 286, 310, 391
Meir, Rabbi (of Rothenberg), 358
Mendelssohn, Moses, 44, 48, 69, 70, 179, 352
Mesopotamia, 180
Messiah, 19, 39, 41, 42, 45, 67, 191f., 222, 260, 356, 384, 385, 388f., 395
Messianism, 145, 192, 193, 373, 379, 380, 382, 386, 388
Micah, 109
Middle Ages, 33, 48, 50, 52, 94, 125, 172, 206, 277, 383, 398
Mishnah, 64, 69, 90, 178, 267, 269, 329
Midrash, 27, 32, 105, 108, 163, 166, 225, 238, 240, 257, 299, 310, 395, 396
Minyan, 99
Mithnaged, 38
*Mitzvoth,* 213
Moab, 228
Moabites, 234
Modern art, 115
Modernism, 343
Mohammedan, 54, 77, 268; Persecution, 205

Molko, Solomon, 44
Monotheism, 386
Morroco, 68
Moses, 29, 108, 111, 114, 227, 233, 254, 296, 299, 302, 309, 323, 326, 375, 391, 395, 398;
of Coucy, 269;
of the Isle of Crete, 43

# INDEX

Moslem, 98
Mount Seir, 229
Mount Sinai, 231, 240
Mourning customs, 89
Mumford, Lewis, 104
Nahman, Rabbi of Bratzlav, 38
Nahmanides, 35, 37, 65, 72, 84, 384
Nathan, Prophet, 101
Nationalism, 17, 29, 31
Nazis, 93, 185, 186, 188, 200, 203, 222, 224, 236
Nazi death camps, 204
Nehemiah, 41, 56, 63, 224, 327
Noahidic laws, 7, 92, 230
Nordau, Max, 261
Nuremberg 224; laws, 162, 236
Obadiah, 232
Omri, 36
"On the Threshold of the Bet Ha-Midrash" (Bialik), 135
One World Ideal, 23, 24
Oswiencim, 203
Palestine, 21, 43, 59, 61, 62, 67, 107, 110, 129, 171, 267
Paradise, 397
"Paradise Lost", 380
Passover, 92, 98; ritual, 338
Pentateuch, 37, 63, 146, 150, 209, 218, 225, 229, 237, 249, 282, 326, 331, 333
Pentateuchal, 106, 251, 302, 325, 343, 386; law, 247
"People of the Book", 106, 178
Persia, 55
Persians, 181
Pharaohs, 106, 387
Pharisees, 393, 394
Phidias, 16, 110, 111, 119, 123
Philo, 54, 61, 62, 68
Philistines, 227-229
Phoenician, 104, 108
Piety, 361-371
Pinsker, Leo, 46
Pius XI, 96
Plato, 10, 111, 192, 235, 236
Poetry, 132-139
Poland, 55, 203
Pope Leo XIII, 95
Portion of the Week, 251
Portugal, 186, 205
Prayers, 207, 231

Preamble (to Israeli Constitution), 20
Primitive art, 124
Promised Land, 32, 42
Protestant, 94
Psalms, 70, 104, 107, 121, 142, 317
Psalmist, 111, 148, 238, 273, 312, 365, 391, 397
Pseudo-Messiahs, 42-44, 46, 79, 82
Purim, 66, 342
Pyramids, 106-108, 114
Pyrenees, 163
Rab, 284, 309, 364, 394
Raba, 250
Rahab, 232
Rashi, 49, 68, 73, 78, 98, 149, 158, 163, 205, 353
Red Sea, 318
Redemption, 82, 383
Reform Judaism, 23, 28f., 286, 289, 381
Reform movements, 281
Reform Temples, 288
Reformation, 94, 149
Religious martyrdom, 392
Rembrandt, 128, 214
Renaissance, 93
Restoration, 62
Reubeni, David, 44
Renan, Ernest, 295
Ringelblum, Emanuel, 204
Rome, 10, 11, 15, 18, 70, 93, 94, 145, 146, 148, 332, 359, 366
Romans, 15, 16, 180, 191, 236, 348
"Rule Britannia", 241
Russia, 53
Russian, 28, 48, 81
Ruth, 37, 234, 251
Sabbath, 33, 40, 92, 100, 105, 175-6, 198, 207-8, 210, 251, 286, 342, 371
Samaria, 36, 118, 120, 165
Samson, 337
Samuel, 87, 157, 272, 386
Sanhedrin, 90, 257
Sanherib, 234
Sarah, 363
Saul, 386
Schechter, Solomon, 107, 227, 274, 288
Schneiour, S., 134
Schopenhauer, 296, 346

Scriptures, 325
Scrolls, five, 251
*Seder,* 290, 291, 338, 342
*Sefer Torah,* 271
Septuagint, 68
Shakespeare, 277
Shammaites, 363
Shaw, G. B., 223, 237
*Shechina,* 35, 36, 82, 83, 86, 310
Shekel (tax), 63, 64, 69
Shemaya, 234
Shulchan Aruch, 100, 271, 367
Sinaitic Revelation, 227
Sirah, Ben, 348
Sisera, 234
Slave, 10
Socrates, 236
Sodom, 309
Solomon, King, 108, 230
Song of Songs, 70, 120, 121, 130, 133, 156, 251, 350, 356
Sorokin, Pitirim, 24, 25, 125
Spain, 54, 55, 68, 70, 161, 186, 205
Spanish, 54, 81
Spaniards, 122
Spengler, Oswald, 5
Spinoza, 149, 299
State, separation of Church and, 94-102
Struck, Herman, 127
Steinschneider 52, 183
Sumeria, 387
Synagogue, 28, 29
Syria, 129, 366
Talmud, 13, 14, 32, 34-36, 39, 41-43, 47, 50, 52, 69, 75, 89, 90, 105, 366, 368, 369, 371, 373, 383, 391-394, 397
Tannaitic, 149
Targumim, 68
Tarphon, Rabbi, 359
Tchernichovsky, S., 73, 134, 137
Tel Aviv, 50, 88
Temple, the, 63, 97, 108, 121, 165, 170, 196, 385;
  Second, 56, 63, 65, 267
"Ten Days of Repentance", 316
Terman, Lewis M., 261
Teutons, 223
Teutonic tribes, 147
"Three Crowns, The", 247

Theory of Relativity, 109
Thirty Years' War, 44
"Thirteen Articles of Belief" (Maimonides), **303**
Tiberias, 39, 91
Tibbon, Rabbi Judah Ibn, 271, 358
Torah, 14, 24, 29-32, 35, 40, 65, 69, 72, 77, 82, 91, 101, 102, **106**, 116, 133, 142, 145, **149**, 166, 169, 170,
Tower of Babel, 309
Tradyon, Rabbi Haninah ben, 52, **106**, **204**
Treitschke, 16, 110, 119
Tribes, ten, 165, 257
Truth, 361
Twain, Mark, 181
"Uganda Congress", 86
Ukba, Mar, 91
United States, 79, 96, 172, 177, **261**
Universalism, 17
Van Gogh, 214
Vatican, 44, 94, 95
"Voice of Jacob", 107
"Wandering Jew, The", 153, 154, 181
"Wasteland" (Sinclair), 290
Wells, H. G., 223, 237
Werfel, Franz, 109, 128
Wissenschaft des Judentums, 52, 78
"Woman of Valor", 349
World War, 48, 52, 112
Yabneh, 200
Yehudah, Eliezer Ben, 49f.
Yeshiva of Sura, 90
Yiddish, 48
Yishuv, 56-62, 64-69, 86-88, 90, **91**
Yom Kippur, 277
Zakkai, Rabbi Johanan ben, 170, 200, 391
Zalman, Rabbi Shneiour of Ladi, 38
Zangwill, Israel, 171, 228, **239**
Zebi, Sabbatai, 44
Zechariah, 144, 278
Zerubabel, 41, 56
Zion, 24, 27, 31-35, 37-39, 41, 66, 77, 98, 131, 132, **134**, 379, 381, 395
Zionism, 41, 46, 56, 60, 61, 80, 82, 86, 168; cultural, 62
Zohar, 35
Zunz, Leopold, 51, 52, 73, 183